CASES IN MARKETING

CASES IN MARKETING

RICHARD R. STILL
Florida International University, Tamiami Campus

THOMAS H. STEVENSON
The University of North Carolina at Charlotte

PRENTICE-HALL, INC., *Englewood Cliffs, NJ   07632*

Library of Congress Cataloging in Publication Data

STILL, RICHARD RALPH (date)
  Cases in marketing.

  1. Marketing—Case studies. I. Stevenson, Thomas H.,
(date). II. Title.
HF5415.S838 1985   658.8   84-26549
ISBN 0-13-118985-9

Editorial/production supervision and interior design: Maureen Wilson
Cover design: Lundgren Graphics, Ltd.
Manufacturing buyer: Ed O'Dougherty

Printed in the United States of America

10 9 8 7 6 5 4 3 2 1

ISBN 0-13-118985-9   01

PRENTICE-HALL INTERNATIONAL, INC., *London*
PRENTICE-HALL OF AUSTRALIA PTY. LIMITED, *Sydney*
EDITORA PRENTICE-HALL DO BRASIL, LTDA., *Rio de Janeiro*
PRENTICE-HALL CANADA INC., *Toronto*
PRENTICE-HALL HISPANOAMERICANA, S.A., *Mexico*
PRENTICE-HALL OF INDIA PRIVATE LIMITED, *New Delhi*
PRENTICE-HALL OF JAPAN, INC., *Tokyo*
PRENTICE-HALL OF SOUTHEAST ASIA PTE. LTD., *Singapore*
WHITEHALL BOOKS LIMITED, *Wellington, New Zealand*

Contents

PART THREE · *MARKETING RESEARCH*

PART FOUR · *PRODUCT MANAGEMENT*

PART FIVE · *DISTRIBUTION*

PART SIX · *PROMOTION*

PART SEVEN · *PRICING*

PART EIGHT · *MARKET SEGMENTATION*

PART ELEVEN · NOT-FOR-PROFIT MARKETING

PREFACE

Increasing sophistication in marketing instruction sharpens the need for materials capable of bridging the gap between generalized textual explanations and specific problems facing today's business executives. Basic marketing concepts change slowly—some hardly at all—but marketing situations requiring analyses and decisions in the "real world" reflect endless change, even though underlying fundamental problems persist. The case method is an effective way to tie theory to practice, forcing students to apply what they have learned to practical problem-solving situations. Many years ago, Professor Charles I. Gragg of the Harvard Business School described what might happen to business students without experience in analyzing cases in this limerick:

> A student of business with tact
> Absorbed many answers he lacked.
>   But acquiring a job,
>   He said with a sob,
> "How *does* one fit answer to fact?"[1]

Of the fifty cases in this collection, twenty-eight have not previously been published and the other twenty-two have been updated and, in some instances, extensively rewritten. All fifty cases have been classroom-tested at California Polytechnic State University, at the University of Georgia, or at the University of North Carolina at Charlotte. The major features of this collection are:

[1]See "Because Wisdom Can't Be Told," in M. P. McNair, ed., *The Case Method at the Harvard Business School* (New York: McGraw-Hill Book Company, Inc., 1954), p. 11.

1. The eleven sections into which the cases have been organized represent the main areas of marketing, as implied by the coverage of most marketing texts.
2. The collection consists of 22 consumer marketing cases and 28 industrial marketing cases. U.S. cases predominate but eight cases involve international marketing and marketing strategy by non-U.S. firms.
3. For the most part the cases are concise and clear-cut, emphasizing some particular class of marketing decision and providing springboards for discussion of related issues. One section, "Marketing Strategies and Programs," features six more complex cases requiring students to analyze considerably more involved situations.
4. Several cases relate to the "newer" areas of marketing concern—marketing to minority market segments, marketing to stimulate supply, marketing and the corporate image, strategy in a mature market, to name a few.
5. Each case provides students with opportunities to apply what they have learned—or are learning—to a "real world" situation.

Many people made important contributions to this book. We greatly appreciate the cooperation and help of the executives who provided raw materials for these cases. We thank our graduate students at the University of Georgia, the University of North Carolina at Charlotte, and California Polytechnic State University, who helped us collect and write these cases. Particular acknowledgment goes to Dr. Clyde E. Harris, Jr., of the University of Georgia, who helped in the development of the cases that have been previously published.

Among the many Prentice-Hall personnel who provided help, encouragement, and advice were: Elizabeth Classon, Marketing Editor, and Maureen Wilson of the College Book Editorial-Production Department. Our families provided sympathetic understanding and encouragement. For all this assistance—both that acknowledged here, as well as that received from other colleagues, past and present students, and friends—we express our sincere thanks.

RICHARD R. STILL
THOMAS H. STEVENSON

CASES IN MARKETING

1–1

STAR MANUFACTURING COMPANY

Transition to marketing orientation

Last July Star Manufacturing Company's board of directors reviewed the company's progress following changes made several years earlier after recommendations by a management consulting firm. Many improvements had occurred, but some unforeseen problems had arisen. Although the consultants worked only in the marketing area, the changes resulting from their recommendations had a sweeping effect on the entire company.

Founded in 1879, Star was a product-oriented textile manufacturer, largely owner managed until recently. It produced a broad line of finished and unfinished textiles in twenty-five mills in South Carolina; with eighty-five hundred workers, it was the state's third largest employer. Its mills represented fixed assets of $105 million and, with sales of $150 million, the company ranked nineteenth in the textile industry. It manufactured high-quality products and gave excellent delivery and service.

When the consultants arrived at Star they had found the company using outdated marketing and management methods. Most executives had read or had heard of the "marketing concept," but its implementation proved difficult and slow, as older managers concerned themselves primarily with manufacturing and accounting. One manager, referring to notes taken at a national management conference, came upon a "model (see Exhibit 1) and definition" of this concept:

"The marketing concept is defined as a managerial philosophy concerned with the mobilization, utilization, and control of total corporate effort for the purpose of helping consumers solve selected problems in ways compatible with planned enhancement of the profit position of the firm.

At the time the consultants arrived, the company had just started

2

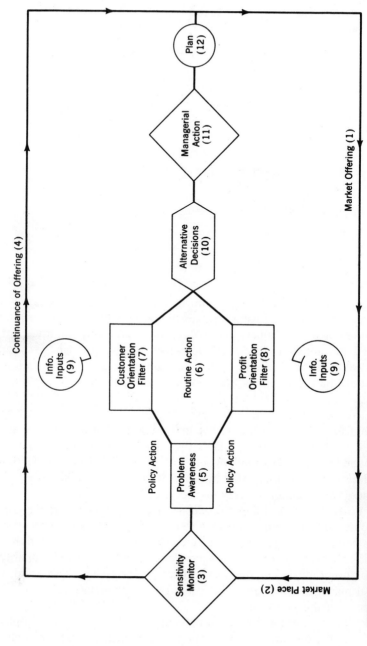

EXHIBIT 1 · Model of the Marketing Concept

production of synthetic fabrics; its main emphasis was on producing cotton and wool products. Management gave the consulting firm free rein in the marketing area but the manufacturing, finance, and accounting areas were reserved for later study.

The company had been organized into three departments: finance-accounting, production, and sales. Each department head was a substantial stockholder and had been with the company for years. The sales department received customers' orders and forwarded them to the production department, while finance-accounting took care of billing and collections. Market analysis was meager, product planning uncoordinated, promotion inadequate, and interdepartmental communication ineffective.

At the conclusion of their study, the consultants made seven recommendations:

1. The vice president of sales should be given an early retirement.
2. The sales department should be replaced with a sales and marketing department composed of four divisions: sales, technical services, marketing planning, and product management.
3. Marketing planning should survey the market constantly, recommend innovations, and coordinate long-range planning.
4. Technical services should coordinate market innovation with production and render technical sales advice.
5. Product managers should monitor their products, looking for new uses for old products, looking for new products, and recommending deletions from the product line.
6. The sales department should concentrate on enlarging sales in present markets while coordinating with the other three divisions.
7. The flow of communications should be increased among departments with emphasis on sales and product analysis.

Star implemented most of these recommendations in the following four years, and sales increases reflected improvements in technical service and market-product planning.

Minimal change took place in the sales organization; Star maintained six sales offices—four geographical and two located near large industrial customers. Thirty salespersons worked out of these offices, one-half of them calling upon specific customers. Star considered its salespersons among the best in the textile industry. Salespersons received annual salaries ranging from $18,000 to $35,000 and had liberal expense accounts. The sales job consisted of securing orders, servicing accounts, and proving Star's reliability and concern for the customer.

Before the consultants arrived, Star sold exclusively to a small number of large retailers and manufacturers. Forty-five percent of its sales were to such retailing giants as Sears, Macy, Belk, Penney, and Montgomery Ward. Most of the remaining 55 percent was to large manufacturers, such as Goodyear and Firestone, with only a small amount going to the federal government. Company sales nearly doubled in the next eight years as new products were put on the market. However, orders came in faster than anticipated, production lagged, and interdepartmental coordination proved inadequate. Marketing channels remained unchanged, but the sales mixture changed drastically with additions of new product lines (see Exhibit 2).

Eight years earlier the product line had consisted of cordage and twine, semifinished cloth and fabric, sheets, pillowcases, and blankets. Little attention was paid to buyers' needs; products *per se* were emphasized. The product-manager concept recommended by the consulting firm resulted in the setting up of five basic product areas: (1) floor covering, (2) rubber industry, (3) yarn, cordage, and twine, (4) cloth and fabric, and (5) consumer products. Overlapping of product lines and customers still existed and showed up in terms of ineffective coordination between the product managers and the sales force. While the product planning division had contributed significantly to the company's recent prosperity, other divisions of the sales and marketing department had difficulty keeping up with changing requirements.

EXHIBIT 2 · Product Lines

PERCENTAGE OF SALES	33%	27%
	HOME FURNISHINGS	INDUSTRIAL GOODS
	Finished carpet yarn	Tire cord
	Finished scatter rug yarn	Fabric for:
	Unfinished rug yarn	Belting
	Fabric for:	Auto upholstery
	Bedspreads	Auto convertible tops
	Upholstery	Shoe lining
	Drapery	Furniture
	Tablecloths	Waterproof shoes
	Trimming yarn	Sandbags
	Mop yarn	Cordage and twine for:
		Fishing line and nets
		Tobacco processing
		Post office wrapping
		Fire hose
PERCENTAGE OF SALES	13%	27%
	APPAREL	CONSUMER PRODUCTS
	Fabric for:	Sheets
	Women's skirting	Pillowcases
	Industrial uniforms	Blankets
	Nomex–space program	Bedspreads
	and airlines	Carpets
	fireproof fabric	Scatter rugs
	Wool and synthetic fabric	
	for double knit clothing	
	Knitting yarn	

Star management had never emphasized promotion in the company's marketing mix. In fact, Star's most recent advertising budget of $450,000, three-tenths of 1 percent of sales, was the largest in its history. Most of the budget was spent on advertising in textile trade magazines directed toward retailers' and manufacturers' purchasing departments. Trade advertising themes emphasized dependability, quality, and service. A small amount of institutional advertising appeared in area newspapers.

Most orders were negotiated with purchasers as reorders and price was not a key sales factor for most Star products until fairly recently. At that time the federal government lifted foreign quotas and reduced import tariffs, and American textile manufacturers met stiffer price competition. Star cut some of its prices; however, so long as its prices remained within reasonable range of similar competing products, old customers continued to reorder. Rising domestic cotton prices hurt the sale of consumer items relative to their foreign competitors, but sales of synthetics helped to offset this. The price cuts, along with rising costs, were reflected in declining profit margins, but Star's swift pricing reaction to import competition and its continuing emphasis upon rapid delivery and good service were instrumental in keeping customers.

In some instances, rather than turn down an order from a good customer, Star filled rush orders by purchasing from other producers. Many times the company accepted small orders from steady customers rather than have them go elsewhere. These practices irritated production executives who preferred scheduling production in large quantities so as to minimize average unit costs. Accumulated inventory on hand at the close of the previous year had mounted to $30 million at cost. The sales and marketing vice president was considering using jobbers to "job out" the excess inventory at drastically reduced prices.

The board of directors believed that the company had successfully implemented the consultants' recommendations; however, the current situation indicated the need for further adjustments. Top executives believed further changes were needed in the product management division, marketing channels, and promotional effort, as well as in the finance-accounting and production departments.

Questions

1. What kind of an organization did Star have at the time the consultants were called in? Why did it develop?
2. Could Star have implemented the marketing concept earlier? How?
3. Evaluate each of the seven recommendations made by the consultants.
4. What were Star's most pressing current problems?

1–2

NORMAL HARDWARE COMPANY

Proposed changes in retail strategy

Mr. John Ross, president and manager of the Normal Hardware Company, located in a midwestern town of 50,000 population, was reevaluating the company's operations. Changes in the town's retail marketing structure, including the rapid growth of shopping centers and the opening of a second large discount store within one mile of his store's location, made Mr. Ross wonder if changes in marketing strategy were needed.

COMPANY HISTORY

After returning from army service in World War II, Mr. Ross entered the construction business with his father. Building materials accounted for such a large percentage of construction expenses that Mr. Ross spent a large amount of time seeking ways to procure quality building materials at economical prices. Storage space was acquired to take advantage of quantity purchase prices and a few other builders began to purchase supplies from Mr. Ross. Demand grew steadily and in time the building material business evolved into the Normal Hardware Company, a store formally opened in 1950. In 1958 the company was incorporated, with family members holding all stock. Current sales volume was now $600,000 annually, and sales were growing at an annual rate of 4 percent.

PRODUCT LINES

Product inventory included a wide selection of hardware items, a moderate variety of housewares, and selected building materials. Approximately 7,000

6

inventory line items were stocked, including many "low-turnover" items which were carried as a service to customers and to enhance the image of "always having what the customer needs." (For instance, rubber gaskets and other spare parts for pressure cookers were carried, items demanded less frequently with increasing use of microwave ovens.) A line of paint with the store's label was carried, as were one national brand and a high-prestige brand of craftsman paint for which Normal was the exclusive dealer in the area. Building materials changed more rapidly than did other items stocked—for example, bricks were no longer handled because brick manufacturers had begun to sell direct to builders. Mr. Ross was not concerned about this development since the smaller number of building supply customers made it easier to determine and react to customer needs.

Periodic reviews, by department, were made to determine which inventory items to drop. The primary consideration, other than for profitability, was the overall effect of dropping the item: Is it a customer service item? Do our customers expect us to stock it?

Several specialized trade and market journals, along with publications from wholesalers and manufacturers, were studied in planning the items to add to stock. Sales representatives of wholesalers and manufacturers also gave advice and assistance on product lines. Overall inventory turnover averaged 3.1 turns per year.

PERSONNEL

Besides Mr. Ross, there were eight full-time and a varying number of part-time employees. A secretary/bookkeeper was the main administrative assistant. Four department managers (building supplies, hardware, paint, and housewares) were responsible for the ordering, pricing, stocking, and overall management of their respective departments. Above-average salaries were paid to attract quality personnel and to keep personnel turnover in check. Every effort was made to assign employees specific responsibilities and to make each employee feel like a useful member of the organization. The company's recruiting policy was to seek new employees with practical experience and enough knowledge of the hardware business to advise customers on products and techniques.

COMPETITION

There were three other local hardware stores. Two, although maintaining retail outlets, were predominantly wholesalers with established routes throughout the state. Their retail sales volume was lower than Normal's. The third had a sales volume approximately equal to Normal's. All three competitors were "old established businesses" with well established clienteles. More recent competition in housewares and hardware items had come from Sears, Zayres, and K-Mart (to be opened soon). Lowe's, Wickes, and Armstrongs were the most active competitors in building supplies. Sears and Armstrongs were the most serious competition in their respective areas; the discount stores were having little noticeable effect on the business.

MARKETING

Sales to commercial builders accounted for approximately 40 percent of total sales. Credit and delivery services were provided for volume buyers. The building supply department manager and Mr. Ross were experts in this area and were well known among local builders.

The second major market segment served was made up of individual craftsmen (carpenters, brick masons, plumbers, etc.). This market segment demanded quality tools and knowledgeable sales personnel. Normal made a special effort to meet these requirements; craftsman-quality tools were a company specialty.

The most heterogeneous market segment was comprised of home-owners, farmers, and do-it-yourselfers. The main approach to this segment was to staff the store with knowledgeable sales personnel ready to advise on appropriate products and techniques. These people were able to offer single items to solve problems, as opposed to prepackaged items in boxes or "blister" packages such as those sold by discount and department stores. The company also stocked items like screws, nails, bolts, and so forth for sale in bulk at lower unit prices than those prepackaged.

Spare parts were stocked for almost all items sold. Builders and crafts-men viewed this as a real advantage since they couldn't afford lengthy down-time or time wasted "chasing around" for replacement parts. Most customers seemed to appreciate the company's liberal refund and exchange policy, es-sentially one of "no questions asked."

Additional customer service programs included: referrals to reputable repairmen and contractors; acceptance of popular credit cards; technical ad-vice to customers; credit to builders and volume customers as well as selected individual customers (this was not advertised but provided by special request). Bad debts amounted to 2 percent of gross sales.

PROMOTION

All advertising and promotion was geared toward enhancing the company's image of "being customer and community oriented." "The most effective advertisement is a satisfied customer" was the motto for sales personnel. The advertising budget approximated $5,000 annually, most of which was spent on community service projects such as: advertisements in high school year-books, athletic programs, scout activities, etc. (see Exhibit 1); purchase of trophies for high school competitive activities; and support of community fund drives and community improvement projects. The company also offered

EXHIBIT 1 · Sample Advertisement from Athletic Program

For All . . .

BUILDING MATERIALS
HOME HARDWARE

NORMAL
Hardware Co.

"The Old Fashioned Hardware with
Old Fashioned Prices"

1328 Prince Avenue   Phone 543-5238

a $2 discount on first purchases to all "newcomers" through the Pan American Greeting Service. (Exhibit 2 is a sample page from the weekly report submitted by this service.) Cost of this service was approximately $600 annually.

Little newspaper advertising was used. Some advertisements were placed in the home builders' section of special newspaper editions; a limited number of cooperative advertisements were prepared from suppliers' "mats" (see Exhibit 3). However, these advertisements were thought of as "too artificial" and as contributing little to the company image. The only broadcast medium used was some radio advertising, used to project the company name and image to listeners.

Mr. Ross was extremely active in community service and church activities. He served as: (1) chairman and/or active member of numerous community improvement drives and projects, (2) member of the County Board of Commissioners for twelve years; (3) county representative to the State Legislature; and (4) lieutenant colonel and active member of the U.S. Army Reserves.

RECENT DEVELOPMENTS

Mr. Ross had identified several trends and specific developments which were troubling him. He wondered what changes, if any, were needed in overall

EXHIBIT 2 · Sample Page from Pan American Greeting Service Confidential Report

NAME, ADDRESS, TELEPHONE	INFORMATION
Dr. & Mrs. Paul Greco 121–12 Ashley Drive	U. Ga., Veterinary Medicine Moved from Italy (Torino) 1 boy: 12 2 girls: 5, 7
Mr. & Mrs. R. Golden 1345 Sandstone Circle	Sales—Textile Fibers Moved from Wilmington, Del. 2 girls: 6, 9 Catholic
Mr. & Mrs. Charles Hall 301 Greentree Drive	U. Ohio, Graduate School, Vocational Educ. Moved from Columbus, Ohio 1 girl: 3 1 boy: 1 Methodist
Capt. & Mrs. Thomas Miller 1175 Archer Street	So. Illinois Univ., Graduate Student Moved from Fort Harrison, Ind. 1 girl: 1 Baptist
Mrs. Charlotte Morton 255 Ruston Avenue	Widow—School Teacher 1 son—grown, lives on west coast Episcopalian
Dr. & Mrs. Donald O. Newton 430 Palmer Drive	Dentist—Newton Dental Clinic Moved from DeKalb, Ill. 2 girls: 6, 8 Methodist
3/Class & Mrs. B. T. Powell 102 Westchester Lane, Apt. 12	Navy—Steward Moved from San Diego, Calif. 1 girl: 1 Catholic

marketing strategy. For example, he had read several articles about the growth of shopping center trade and had been approached by a local developer about leasing space in a new shopping center. He knew about the growth of the discount business, especially since daily he drove by one discount store doing an apparently large business and past another under construction. According to other articles he had read and statistics published by the government, women were responsible for an increasingly large percentage of family purchasing, and inflation was making them more price conscious than ever.

These trends had raised several questions. For example, Mr. Ross wondered: Do the image and practices of Normal Hardware appeal to women customers? Would "loss leader" advertising improve profits? Was the shortage of parking space near the store causing Normal to lose business to the shopping centers?

Mr. Ross had narrowed the alternative courses of action down to five. These were:

EXHIBIT 3 · Sample Cooperative Newspaper Advertisement

1. Open a new and modern store in a shopping center.
2. Modernize the present facilities. Install a low ceiling with recessed lighting and checkout counters. Stock more prepackaged and fancy gift items to attract women shoppers. Improve window displays.
3. Eliminate slow-moving items of inventory. Stock only the fast-turnover items and require each item to "pay its own way."
4. Increase newspaper advertising. Use loss leaders and "specials" to get customers into the store. Obtain professional assistance in planning advertising.
5. In cooperation with adjacent stores, increase available parking space by buying and converting nearby vacant land.

Questions

1. What were the problems of the Normal Hardware Company?
2. What were the advantages and disadvantages of each of the alternatives under consideration?
3. What changes, if any, should Mr. Ross have made in the business?

1–3

MANHATTAN HANDBAGS, INC.

Reorganizing marketing after merger

Robert Jones and Jim Gallagher had founded Manhattan Handbags, Inc., in New York to manufacture better-quality ladies' handbags. Initially, Gallagher managed the manufacturing operation, Jones handled sales and served as president, and the two men designed the products jointly. Later on, as the company grew, design and sales personnel were added. Currently, the company faced several organizational problems tracing to its recent acquisition of the Ideal Handbag Company.

At its inception Manhattan made approximately 1,250 handbags per week, but recently its production had reached 2,000 per week. Annual dollar sales were now $1.1 million, and management estimated next year's sales volume at $1.7 million.

Manhattan sold its branded products direct to prestigious retail stores. When competitive accounts in cities where Manhattan already had distributors indicated an interest in handling the line, Manhattan sold them private labels. For example, in Chicago, Josette sold the Manhattan brand, whereas Carson Pirie Scott sold Manhattan-produced handbags under its own label. Seventeen large customers accounted for approximately 97 percent of Manhattan's sales (see Exhibit 1).

Jones began expansion of his marketing organization five years ago when he hired Barbara Smith, a young designer of handbags. Up until that time Manhattan was known primarily as an evening bag house with elegant taste. Customers were demanding additional bag styles, and Miss Smith worked toward expanding the product line to include the more fashionable bags. Before joining Manhattan, Miss Smith had attended a design school and had then served as an assistant designer for a competitor. Her duties at Manhattan

EXHIBIT 1 · Manhattan's Major Accounts

CUSTOMER	NUMBER OF STORES	LOCATION	TYPE OF BUYING	APPROXIMATE DOLLAR VOLUME
Bullock's	14	Los Angeles and suburbs	Decentralized	$ 330,000
Saks Fifth Avenue	22	New York and nationwide	Centralized	180,000
Josette	7	Chicago and suburbs	Centralized	176,000
B. Altman & Co.	6	New York and suburbs	Centralized	72,000
Neiman-Marcus	12	Texas and elsewhere	Centralized	72,000
Label's	2	San Francisco and Seattle	Centralized	45,000
Samuel's		New York	Centralized	30,000
Joske's		Houston	Centralized	26,000
Jaffee's		Minneapolis	Centralized	22,000
Milgrim, Inc.	3	Cleveland and Detroit	Centralized	21,000
Sakowitz		Houston	Centralized	18,000
Garfinckel & Co.		Washington, D.C.	Centralized	13,000
Josette (Oak Brook)		Oak Brook, Ill.	Centralized	11,000
Carson Pirie Scott & Co.		Chicago	Centralized	11,000
Smith's		Philadelphia	Centralized	11,000
Gidding-Jenny		Cincinnati	Centralized	10,000
R.H. Stearn Co.		Boston	Centralized	10,000
Total				$1,058,000

included designing four major lines a year and style-and-color coordination. Now she had become one of the industry's leading designers, providing Manhattan handbags with a high-fashion image.

Jones recognized that his duties and responsibilities as president kept him from providing the company with adequate sales coverage. He showed particular concern for service and sales coverage in the West and Southwest, areas with great potential, and with this in mind, he had hired Thomas Berle three years ago.

Berle, age 28, was a junior college graduate. His previous experience included three years as an assistant handbag buyer in a major department store and five years as a handbag sales representative on the west coast. He was married, had no children, and enjoyed traveling. Jones hired Berle on the recommendation of buyers at Bullock's stores in Pasadena and San Fernando, both of whom knew him as a sales representative.

Berle received a 10 percent commission on his sales plus a 5 percent commission on house accounts in his territory. Jones personally serviced *all* Manhattan house accounts, but some, such as Saks Fifth Avenue, operated stores in Berle's territory. Berle paid his own traveling expenses except for three trips a year to New York and one to the National Ladies Handbag Show in Chicago. Jones assigned Berle eleven accounts with an estimated sales potential totaling $265,000 (see Exhibit 2).

THE ACQUISITION.   By last year Manhattan could produce two thousand handbags weekly at full capacity. Then the company took over the Ideal Handbag Company and increased the production capability to four thousand bags weekly. With the expanded productive capacity, management's attention shifted to the sales organization.

Jerald Hametzstein had organized the Ideal Handbag Company in Philadelphia thirty years earlier. Ideal produced high-grade handbags; sales peaked at $2.5 million ten years ago, and its seventy-five accounts were among the industry's best. However, Ideal's sales then gradually declined and at the time Manhattan acquired the company only twelve accounts remained (see Exhibit 3).

Management felt that the Ideal purchase strengthened its production capabilities, added a popular brand, extended its distribution, and provided several additional prestige accounts, such as Lord and Taylor and Bonwit Teller.

John Grant, a sales representative for Ideal for twenty years, was asked to stay on. Although Grant would retire in three years, he knew Ideal's accounts intimately, and Manhattan wished to retain as many of them as possible. Grant called upon all of Ideal's accounts except Lord and Taylor, which Jones classified as a house account. Grant visited his accounts four times a year and saw them twice a year at handbag shows. He received a $500 weekly salary and full reimbursement of expenses.

Berle had recently suggested to Jones that the territories be reorganized on a geographical basis. Jones sensed a need for territorial reorganization but was hesitant to act upon Berle's suggestion. He was not certain that Manhattan and Ideal brands could reach their full potential in any territory with one person servicing both groups of accounts. Although Berle increased his sales

EXHIBIT 2 · Thomas Berle's Accounts

1. Bullock's—San Fernando	6. Nordstrom—Seattle,
2. Bullock's—Pasadena	Nordstrom—Portland
3. Bullock's—Westwood	7. Joske's—Houston
4. Bullock's—Santa Ana	8. Krupp & Tuffly—Houston
5. Label's—San Francisco	9. May—Denver
	10. Paul's—Fresno
	11. Hull's—Pasadena

EXHIBIT 3 · Ideal's Accounts at Acquisition

ACCOUNT	LOCATION	SALES VOLUME
1. Lord & Taylor	New York	$300,000
2. Robinson's	Los Angeles	92,000
3. Bonwit Teller	Philadelphia	53,000
4. Marshall Field	Chicago	38,000
5. J.L. Hudson	Detroit	20,000
6. Halle Bros. Co.	Cleveland	15,000
7. Frederick & Nelson	Seattle	15,000
8. Woodward & Lothrop	Washington, D.C.	14,000
9. Joske's	San Antonio	12,000
10. Joseph Horne	Pittsburgh	11,000
11. Titche-Goettinger	Dallas	12,000
12. Foley's	Houston	7,000

EXHIBIT 4 · Thomas Berle's Performance Chart with Manhattan

ACCOUNT	VOLUME GIVEN TO BERLE	FIRST YEAR SALES	SECOND YEAR SALES	THIRD YEAR SALES
Bullock's				
San Fernando	$ 33,739	$ 84,300	$ 75,480	$ 65,940
Pasadena	43,421	70,350	68,010	47,475
Westwood	34,320	47,340	53,805	47,325
Santa Ana	7,680	41,550	58,935	26,370
Lakewood*		53,760	38,865	35,025
Del Amo*			33,285	26,370
Downtown*				26,280
Hull's	5,220	3,315	2,295	1,665
Joske's	16,785	11,430	23,070	15,645
Krupp & Tuffly	6,240	2,820	6,270	6,765
Label's	56,565	67,485	45,720	35,745
Nordstrom	15,630	10,110		
Sakowitz*		6,570	16,890	
May	22,980	15,030	6,525	6,000
Paul's	22,520	4,530		
Neiman-Marcus*		7,980	67,650	163,245
Total Sales	$265,100	$426,570	$496,800	$503,850

*Accounts opened by Thomas Berle.

volume by more than $230,000 in three years, he had only limited success in securing new accounts. He had started with eleven accounts and now had only sixteen (see Exhibit 4). Jones doubted that Berle could handle the Ideal accounts in his territory. He also doubted that any sales representative in any territory could adequately handle both brands.

Questions

1. Should Jones have reorganized the sales organization along geographical lines?
2. What other organizational changes, if any, should have been made by Manhattan?

2–1

PHIDIPPIDES

Strategy adjustments at a specialty retailer

Dr. Ben Malcolm, owner of Phidippides, a running supplies shop, was assessing the performance of his business. Although sales had proceeded as planned, Dr. Malcolm was seeking to identify additional ways to increase sales.

COMPANY HISTORY

Dr. Malcolm was an associate professor of physics at Cornell University up until two years ago. For ten years he had been running. Spurred on by an interest in running, his daughter's study of exercise physiology, acquaintances at work and in the community who were "into" running, and his desire to try "something new," he left Cornell to start up his own business. Prior to opening his franchise in Ithaca, New York, Dr. Malcolm worked for several months at a Phidippides franchise in Syracuse, New York.

When the Ithaca Phidippides store opened, Dr. Malcolm was responsible for handling vendor arrangements, facility location, staffing, promotional policy, and other decisions associated with starting a retail business. The cost of the franchise was an initial $5,000 with additional monthly royalty payments of $3\frac{1}{2}$ percent of the gross. (Recently, Phidippides has switched its procedure to provide franchises with "turnkey" operations.)

The Phidippides chain was founded as a specialty store dedicated entirely to the sport of running. As a franchisee, Dr. Malcolm provided his customers with reliable equipment and current information tailored to the individual runner's needs. This included all manner of running gear as well as marathon race information and running seminars. The overall purpose was to stimulate local interest in running and thereby increase store traffic.

COMPETITION AND THE MARKET

Phidippides' competition came primarily from sports stores. Competitors carried the full line of sports equipment compared to Phidippides' specialized line. Two exceptions were the Athlete's Feet and Footlocker franchises—both emphasized running shoes, yet they provided little local direct competition as they were both several miles from Phidippides. The main source of competition was Seneca Sporting Goods, located just down the road, whose strength came mainly from its size and ability to carry a large inventory in the shoe department. Seneca also priced running shoes 10 percent under Phidippides.

Dr. Malcolm was uncertain as to market demographics, but he felt that the "string street" location near the university caused a larger than normal clientele of university students. Moreover, by having ample parking facilities in an area of high traffic flow, Phidippides was well positioned to attract nonstudent customers. Dr. Malcolm believed that he had an appropriate mix of student and nonstudent customers. Beyond this, the customers were, for the most part, either serious runners or people who ran regularly.

STORE OPERATIONS

Exhibit 1 shows the Ithaca Phidippides store layout. The store carried a complete assortment of running paraphernalia, not just shoes. The inventory was approximately $13,500 at cost; inventory turnover was 3.96 times per year. A large portion of the cost of goods sold was in shoes, while the inventory was in large part composed of slow-moving clothing items.

In the past two years, the store had succeeded in becoming profitable and Dr. Malcolm was reinvesting 40 percent of the profits. Lack of sufficient capital and the expense of carrying a large inventory had kept Dr. Malcolm from providing the depth of merchandise assortment to which he aspired. Storage space in the store was more than sufficient to stock larger quantities of inventory. In the meantime, only the most popular sizes of shoes (sizes 8½–10) were carried in any substantial quantity, while vendors were relied upon to make timely deliveries of special orders. Delivery times of the various shoe vendors were:

Nike	4–6 weeks
Brooks	7–10 days
Adidas	7–10 days
New Balance	6 weeks
Asics	2–3 weeks

Markups varied by product line. The markup on shoes was 40 percent when sold at suggested retail prices. This was lower than other items carried yet turnover was more rapid than for other items. Miscellaneous running accessories—sweatbands, socks, shoelaces, and so on—had markups of 50 percent. These items were positioned near the front of the store by the cash register (see Exhibit 1). Store practice was to give a 10 percent discount on all purchases by repeat customers.

EXHIBIT 1 · Store Layout, Phidippides—Ithaca

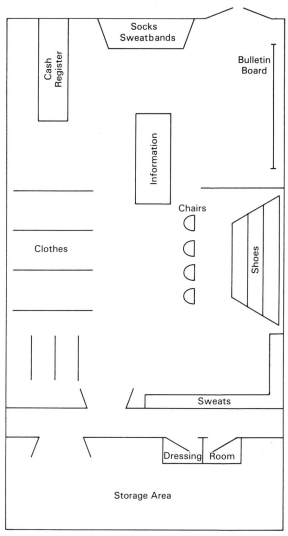

The store's hours of operation were 9:30–5:30 Monday through Friday and 9:30–5:00 on Saturday. This was consistent with the operating hours of the other three stores in the shopping center. Dr. Malcolm worked these hours with the exception of two hours each afternoon and a half day on Saturday. He spent this "off" time making business contacts and attending to details related to upcoming marathons and other community running events. In Dr. Malcolm's absence, part-time employees were used. The basic prerequisite for being employed part time was an interest in running and familiarity with the store's stock. Wages accounted for 13 percent of total expenses.

Dr. Malcolm believed that in a small business it was important for the customer to relate to the owner. He felt that the customer would be more apt to become a "steady" if the same individual were available each time the customer entered the store. Dr. Malcolm prided himself on his ability to establish rapport with customers and to be familiar with their levels of accomplishment as runners. This was consistent with the basic concept of the Phidippides chain—success depends largely upon the return business of steady customers.

MARKETING APPROACH

Dr. Malcolm did not subscribe to the "better mousetrap" theory. He felt that continuing success would depend upon offering more than just a good product. So he decided to provide running information as well as good merchandise. He felt this would get people interested in running and that, ultimately, they would become customers.

Dr. Malcolm cosponsored marathons with well funded local businesses. After nine marathons, Phidippides' visibility had increased tremendously. The expense was covered by the cosponsoring firms; Phidippides coordinated and set up the course to meet marathon standards (this acounted for much of the time Dr. Malcolm was away from the store). Phidippides received company exposure in the marathon brochures and on posters announcing the event. The store was an official registration "dropoff" point which helped increase store traffic.

In addition to cosponsoring marathons, Phidippides served as a registration point for other marathons in the Ithaca area. Race registration forms were made available to customers free of charge; this service was viewed as a means of attracting potential customers. An in-store bulletin board provided other information regarding news of interest to runners (see Exhibit 1).

The store scheduled regular running information seminars to inform runners of the sport's finer points. These sessions were held every other Thursday night at the store. They featured local running luminaries as well as podiatrists and other sports health specialists. It was felt that these sessions would develop happier and longer term customers by helping them to avoid injuries and/or to correct potential running problems.

Lack of working capital restricted other promotional efforts. Phidippides ran infrequent advertisements in the local newspaper and the university newspaper. Other advertising consisted of regional Phidippides Company promotions and advertising promotions sponsored by vendors. Dr. Malcolm hesitated to expand the advertising appropriation not only because of lack of capital but because he was uncertain as to the effect on sales. Still, he was considering increasing advertising from early to late December and from mid-June to mid-September, periods with low sales. He believed these slumps traced directly to Christmas and summer vacations at Cornell, and hoped increased advertising would remedy this problem.

All things considered, Dr. Malcolm was pleased with the success of Phidippides and looked forward to continuing growth. His thoughts were interrupted as a regular customer jogged through the front entrance of the store and shouted "Hi there!"

Questions

1. Should Phidippides try to attract the business of novice runners and, if so, how?
2. What changes should be made in the store's marketing strategy?
3. What changes are necessary, if any, in the store layout?

2–2

MICROGRAPHIC SYSTEMS DIVISION

Reacting to a growth opportunity

Kevin Pressman, general manager, Micrographic Systems Division (MSD), commented:

> The Insurance Service Organization is discontinuing sending its fire/casualty information on computer printouts to the 125,000 offices of the Independent Insurance Association. They are going to start using microfiche cards instead, effective next month. Since the Insurance Service Organization is the only source of fire/casualty information available to members of the Independent Insurance Association, each of their 125,000 offices is going to have to buy a microfiche reader. As a result, there will be tremendous competition among equipment sellers and resellers to secure as many of these offices as they can.

Pressman was not sure of the most effective way to reach this new market. Neither he nor MSD had faced such an opportunity before. If MSD could sign up 20 percent of the 125,000 potential accounts, the sales would be twice that of MSD's largest account.

COMPANY HISTORY

In 1969 *Dun's Review* described the micrographics industry:

> The microfilm industry's sales now run between $300 to $500 million a year. Insiders expect volume to top $1 billion by 1975 and $5 billion by 1980. Microfilm's rapid growth has been sparked by three things: improved hardware and other equipment, development of the whole broad field of micropublishing, and the marriage of microfilm to the computer. No one is quite sure where micrographics is going, but there is no question that it is coming to play a

larger part in American life every year. Already microfilm is in hospitals, law offices, department stores, churches, banks, automobile service centers, factories, offices, police stations, schools, and government offices. By the end of the century, it is estimated that less than half of our records will be on paper. Micrographics may well become a prime factor in education and a fairly new means of bringing information and entertainment into everybody's home. Also the film itself costs only about 15 percent as much as paper and has only 2 percent of the latter's bulk.[1]

General Micrographics, a computer output microfiche company, started in 1969. Its initial business was to take tapes from a customer's computer and use specialized equipment to transfer information from the tapes first onto microfiche recorders and then onto microfiche cards. Each card held up to 269 pages of regular computer printout. Banks and companies with large accounts payable/receivable were prime users. The company later became a wholly owned subsidiary of Anacomp Micrographics.

Anacomp had two divisions: (1) the service company that converted computer tapes to microfiche cards, and (2) the micrographic system division (MSD) that bought microfiche equipment from manufacturers. Microfiche equipment was used both internally at Anacomp Micrographics and was sold to customers converting their records systems to microfiche.

COMPANY OPERATIONS

Anacomp Micrographics had sales last year of $21 million, a 148 percent increase over the previous year; profits were up 99 percent. MSD had sales of $7.5 million, and was the United States' largest distributor of micrographic products.

The thirty-six Anacomp offices around the country converted customer computer tapes to microfiche records. Each office was treated as a profit center with a general manager in charge. Each general manager received a base salary plus a bonus based on the office's performance. Working out of each office were two salespeople who received commissions based on their gross sales. Anacomp headquarters established quotas for the offices and salespeople. The company had no marketing department.

MSD, based in a large southeastern city, sold microfiche equipment to Anacomp for internal use and for resale to microfiche accounts, and also sold through its own dealer network. Dealers bought from MSD for several reasons: the manufacturer would not sell to dealers unless they could meet minimum order requirements; MSD could buy at lower prices due to quantity purchasing and a dealer could buy from MSD for less than from the manufacturer; and manufacturers sold to MSD for less because of past business and the possibility of large future orders.

MSD had no sales force of its own but relied on the Anacomp Micrographics sales force. Approximately 65 percent of MSD's orders came from Anacomp Micrographics, and normally the equipment was "drop shipped" from the manufacturer to the customer. The other 35 percent of the orders came from dealers serving customers at sites without Anacomp offices. There were thirty-five of these dealers.

INDUSTRY STRUCTURE

Three computer output microfiche companies competed directly with Anacomp Micrographics. In addition, several large corporations, such as Kodak, Minnesota Mining and Manufacturing, and Bell and Howell, made and sold micrographic equipment. Bell and Howell, for example, made equipment which both Bell and Howell representatives and private dealers sold. Seven manufacturers of micrographic viewers and supplies sold their lines through dealers. MSD carried some products from all seven manufacturers, but did not carry the complete line of any one manufacturer. MSD had the largest sales of any of the equipment suppliers, but it had fewer offices than the second largest company, U.S. Data Corporation.

Three major trends affected the industry. First, the increasing use of sophisticated data processing equipment meant that companies with growth aspirations needed to offer "state of the art" products and to remain abreast of advancing technology. Second, profit margins were depressed because of increasing competition and a sluggish general economy. Third, a recent wave of acquisitions was changing the market structure, as small suppliers were being taken over by larger competitors with more extensive office networks.

PROMOTION

Neither MSD nor its competitors were very innovative in their advertising. MSD promotion included: advertisements in trade magazines, exhibits at trade shows, and equipment advertisements in local newspapers and Yellow Pages. At national trade shows equipment manufacturers set up exhibits and Anacomp Micrographics ran a hospitality booth and entertained guests. At local trade shows, Anacomp Micrographics and its competitors had equipment exhibits.

The only unique MSD promotion was a product catalog. This was a comprehensive catalog which included complete product descriptions and ordering systems so that customers could order products directly, using catalog order forms. Anacomp was the only industry member with such a catalog and management felt that it was a tremendously useful tool for the sales force. Between the calls of salespersons, customers used catalogs to order new equipment or for reorders.

MSD depended on the 108 Anacomp salespeople (thirty-six offices with two salespeople and thirty-six office managers who also made sales calls). This sales force was well trained, and in many cases was sought out by customers. Through careful prospecting and insightful probing, it could be quickly determined whether potential customers needed Anacomp's services or not. If they did, the lure of reduced handling and storing and lower costs was usually sufficient for a customer to buy. Once the basic "service" was purchased, selling the microfiche equipment was easy.

The typical sales approach was based upon the advantages of microfilm over paper. The overall cost of microfilm was less, storage space was significantly reduced, and microfiche was faster to use than sorting through files. For the average customer, switchover to the microfiche process could be done in a day. Viewer equipment costs were recouped in under ninety days. The system's only real disadvantage was that it was not possible to write on microfiche cards.

MSD carried a large assortment of equipment and supplies so that customers had a good opportunity to choose the product best fitting their needs. Management believed that product assortment along with size and volume advantages allowed MSD to meet its objective of maximizing possible sales.

PRICING

The MSD approach to pricing was simple. Equipment sold through MSD was first marked up 10 percent over cost to cover "the cost of doing business." Additional markups averaged 25 percent but varied by order size. Table 1 shows the price schedule. Discounts were calculated for monthly cumulative quantities. Terms were net 30 days. For discount purposes, MSD equipment and Anacomp services were combined for any given month. Anacomp's services were also priced to include an average 25 percent markup. Salespersons had some flexibility in selling below the 25 percent margin to get orders, but they were restrained by the fact that commissions diminished markedly on prices below the 25 percent level. Most of the company's business came from repeat customers, and most orders were larger than $1,000.

TABLE 1 · MSD Pricing Schedule

ORDER SIZE/MONTH	CUSTOMER DISCOUNT
Below $1,000	Net
$1,000–$2,500	9%
$2,500–$7,500	12%
Over $7,500	15%

THE OPPORTUNITY

As of August 1, the Insurance Service Organization (ISO) discontinued sending its fire/casualty information on computer printouts to the 125,000 offices of the Independent Insurance Association (IIA). This information was vital to the IIA because ISO was the only source of these data used for setting insurance rates. Effective August 1, the ISO began sending out the information on 4" x 6" microfiche cards only and no longer made printouts available. Each microfiche card contained up to 269 pages of printout and required a microfiche reader or viewer. To use the cards, each of the 125,000 IIA offices would need at least one viewer. Tremendous competition developed among micrographic equipment suppliers to secure as many as possible of these offices.

ISO did not recommend an equipment supplier to IIA, and IIA had no expertise in this area. Nor did IIA recommend an equipment supplier to the various state associations.

There were different types of IIA organizations in different states. Some state associations allowed their members to buy from any company they wished. Other associations, seeking profits from buying and reselling equipment, closely monitored members' purchases. Still other associations, while not seeking profits from equipment sales, wanted to distribute readers through a central distribution system. There was no uniformity among the states. What worked in one state might not work or even be applicable in another.

Pressman, MSD general manager, felt that competition among the 300 distributors of microfiche equipment was wide open. He conceded that the "Mom and Pop" suppliers would get many small town accounts, but he felt that MSD should be able to sell one-fifth of the 125,000 offices.

ISO began its changeover from paper to microfiche, region by region, beginning November 1. It was estimated that the changeover would be completed by November 1 of the next year. The changeover began in the northeastern region of the United States.

Pressman did not learn of the changeover at IIA until October, so he did not have time to act effectively in the northeastern region. He was not sure if this would hurt MSD's chances in other regions, but he felt that a company satisfactorily handling early accounts might gain an edge in securing business in regions converted later. After all, satisfied customer testimonials and word-of-mouth were powerful promotional devices.

Pressman did not know how MSD's competitors were reacting. He thought they would probably use simple price enticements and discounts, but did not rule out the creative use of service arrangements or "package deals." People in the IIA offices had little or no expertise in purchasing microfiche equipment and had no bases for judging quality, price, or service. MSD had sold microfiche equipment to the state associations of Georgia and Texas prior to the ISO announcement that the entire nation would switch to microfiche, but Pressman knew he would have to act quickly to secure business from additional states over the one-year period from November to November.

THE MSD STRATEGY

Pressman decided that MSD would offer a "package" to IIA offices and associations. The package would be called "ISO Microfiche Implementation for IIA of America." The package provided a substantial price discount on a combination of viewers and accessories. It offered five different readers depending upon individual needs and tastes, two reader-printers which allowed for variation in the number of prints required, and a host of accessories for handling different demands. The equipment selection was based on reliability and cost. Pressman believed that the IIA offices would neither require nor want high-priced viewers with many attachments of high sophistication.

Pressman sent a letter, the package description, and price information to every state association headquarters (see Appendix). In the letter accompanying the package description, Pressman stated:

> All of the items are provided to each state association at very competitive prices. You also may notice the large gaps between association cost and the member price. This deliberate difference has been provided so that the association (and consequently its membership) may profit from the sudden shift on the part of the ISO. Members now can extract benefits from the association's extra revenue in terms of enhanced services, reduced membership costs, etc.

Pressman did not know what to expect from this package, but he felt that the variety in the package and the lower costs would appeal to IIA members. He wanted MSD to be perceived as a quality company, trying to suit its clients' needs with competitive prices.

Pressman mailed the offer to the state associations the first week in October. A week later, he scheduled Anacomp Micrographic salespersons to make calls on state associations. There were only 108 salespersons so he could reach some but not all local offices in states without state associations doing centralized buying. Sales personnel were instructed to concentrate on state associations first. By mid-October he did not have but was trying to obtain a mailing list of all IIA members. He had a mailing list for Florida, a state which was allowing each office to buy independently.

Pressman had invited all fifty executive directors of the state associations to an MSD dinner and party at the IIA convention that was held in October. However, the date selected conflicted with a previously scheduled executive directors' meeting, and attendance was sparse. But Pressman made contact with several executive directors during the convention.

Therefore, Pressman had opted to compete for the IIA business by sending a package offer to state association headquarters with a follow-up sales call about one week after the package arrived. The offer was designed so as not to emphasize price, even though a significant discount was offered; but rather to stress availability of various equipment selections to satisfy customers' needs. Pressman now wondered whether this was the best possible strategy and what should be done next.

Questions

1. Do you think Pressman's strategy will be effective?
2. What are your suggestions for improving the strategy?
3. If you were marketing manager of Micrographic Systems Division, what changes would you make in the company?

APPENDIX: THE PACKAGE

The equipment package we recommend is all-encompassing. We are offering five different readers to cover individual needs and tastes, two reader-printers which allow for variance in the number of prints required, and a host of accessories to round out particular demands.

The three desk-top readers (two are portable units) are manufactured by Northwest Microfilm. These readers were selected because they incorporate the best features for reliability and viewability in the marketplace. The various models are the 14 for full-size viewing of the ISO fiche, the 75 for three-quarter viewing with less desk space, and the 85 with tilted screen for bifocal wearers.

Each reader will be imprinted with the IIA logo, and packaged with a spare lamp. More importantly, each carries a two-year warranty on parts and an 800-number to obtain replacement parts and service assistance. Additionally, a fiche storage panel will be included to keep the ISO microfiche accessible and will have our *Use and Care Booklet* enclosed. This pamphlet provides basic information for your members about microfiche and their reader, answering many questions before they arise.

IIA Equipment Packages

RECOMMENDED READERS	MEMBER COST	ASSN. COST
A. 75% Blowback NMI 75/48x	$ 199.00	$ 165.00
B. 85% Blowback—front projection NMI 85/48x	229.00	185.00
C. 100% Blowback NMI 14/48x	239.00	190.00

ACCESSORY PACKAGE (INCLUDED WITH ALL READERS)

IIA logo/spare lamp
Use and Care Booklet/Fiche panel

OPTIONS		
Dual lens mechanism (w/o lens)	25.00	20.00
Dual lens (2/lens)	75.00	65.00
Dual carriage	25.00	22.00

INDIVIDUAL ACCESSORIES		
Spare lamp	12.00	9.25
Eichner binder	10.00	5.90
Eichner 9200–670 panel	5.90	3.50
Wilson-Jones panel holder	9.00	6.75
Aigner file box	6.10	5.85
Dust cover	5.50	4.50
Turntable	20.00	16.00
Cleaning kit	6.00	5.00
Spare lens	50.00	45.00

RECOMMENDED READER-PRINTERS		
A. MDI RP-555/48x	1,445.00	1,150.00
B. DatagraphiX 1500DL w/48x, Dual lens mechanism, image rotation, spare lamp, and starter kit	2,080.00	1,825.00

SUPPLIES		
MDI 11″ paper (2 rolls/case)	52.00	35.00
MDI toner (12 qts./case)	48.00	30.00
DatagraphiX 11″ paper (4 rolls/case)	90.00	70.00
DatagraphiX toner (6 qts./case)	30.00	20.00

PORTABLES		
Micro 44	149.00	139.00
MDI portable	269.00	239.00

2–3

ARMSTRONG CORK COMPANY

Vendor-rating system

The Armstrong Cork Company's vendor-rating system varied both with the types of products it purchased and with the quantities required by its individual plants. The Fulton, New York, plant, for example, used a quality inspection program for buying raw materials and fuels, and "stockless" purchasing of MRO (maintenance, repairs, operations) items by means of data-phone; the Lancaster, Pennsylvania, closure plant used a quality certification system in selecting tinplate suppliers; and the Lancaster flooring plant applied a categorical-rating system in buying corrugated cartons. The company, in other words, had no company-wide formal vendor-rating system.

Armstrong Cork Company had four major product lines: (1) flooring products, including plastic and roto-vinyl floor coverings, asphalt rubber and cork tiles, linoleum, other resilient flooring, and installation and maintenance sundries; (2) building materials, including acoustical ceiling materials, wall coverings, and thermal roof installations; (3) industrial specialties, including friction materials of cork, felt, and synthetic rubber composition, gaskets, seals, filters, noise-damping insulation, and various adhesives (used by the automotive, textile, shoe, electrical and household appliance, air-conditioning, and furniture industries); and (4) packaging materials, including glass and plastic containers, plastic vials and prescription ware, metal and plastic caps and crowns—sold to companies marketing: (a) food items, (b) medicinal and health products, (c) household and industrial chemicals, (d) toiletries and cosmetics, (e) beer and soft drinks, and (f) wine and liquor. Armstrong emphasized both basic and applied product research and development, and more than half of the sales volume came from products introduced in the past ten years.

Armstrong Cork, headquartered in Lancaster, Pennsylvania, employed roughly nineteen thousand people, domestically and overseas. It had eighteen U.S. plants and five foreign plants. Sales offices were located in trading centers across the United States. The company had affiliates in Canada, England, Australia, South Africa, Spain, Switzerland, India, and West Germany.

As a manufacturer and distributor of diversified products, Armstrong bought a wide range of raw materials, shipping and packing materials, electrical and mechanical equipment, and other items. The firm had a decentralized purchasing system, but centralized functional control. Armstrong's purchasing department procured major equipment, handled general contracting, and bought for the central engineering department. It also served as a functional control center and advisory unit for plant purchasing agents. Each plant had one or two purchasing agents of its own and a stores/inventory person. All purchasing agents handled their own expediting.

SYSTEM AT THE FULTON PLANT

The Fulton plant made various flooring felts and fabricated industrial felt products for automotive, aircraft, air conditioning, and similar applications. It bought three categories of items:

1. Raw materials: asbestos, fillers, pigments, pulpwood, synthetic rubber, and lattices.
2. Shipping and packing materials: corrugated cartons and strapping.
3. Machinery: electrical equipment, motors, instrumentations, paper and board machinery, office equipment, and other supplies and services.

The Fulton plant negotiated for the supply of the majority of its raw materials through twenty-five blanket order contracts; all other items were procured through thirty blanket order contracts.

The Fulton plant had no formal vendor-rating system. Its purchasing personnel compiled case histories when they believed a supplier's performance was becoming unacceptable. They collected documents, such as receiving reports, inspection reports, expediting notes, purchase orders, invoices, packing lists, and freight bills, and informally evaluated the supplier's overall performance.

The plant purchasing agent said that this informal procedure served the plant's best interests for three main reasons. First, most large purchases (high dollar volume) were from single sources for product uniformity or because of market conditions. If Armstrong, for example, purchased a certain chemical from two different suppliers, quality differences might occur if Company X aged the chemical differently from Company Y. Market conditions (relative transportation costs, for example) varied for certain items, and it was safer to buy such items as rags (cloth scraps) from one local source than from numerous distant apparel firms.

Second, Armstrong depended on technical assistance from its suppliers, especially in the chemical field. The value of service and technical assistance was difficult to quantify; however, the plant purchasing agent believed that a good sole supplier served as a "partner" in making Armstrong's products. Sole vendors often devoted product research and development effort to the solution of Armstrong's problems.

Third, the corporate accounting department acted as a central data bank, making all documents available for informal audit. This department maintained purchasing files, classified by vendor. The files, for example, contained documents, arranged chronologically, for all transactions with each vendor.

At the Fulton plant two aspects of purchasing were formalized. First, the plant purchasing department received inspection reports on raw materials and fuels. The raw materials test center prepared these reports (including a detailed analysis of incoming materials and the date received). The plant purchasing agent used these reports as "first indicators" of unacceptable performance. Second, a local industrial supply house stocked many items and could supply the plant within twenty-four hours. The purchasing agent prepared punch cards for high-turnover items and initiated needed orders by inserting the appropriate cards into a data-phone.

The Fulton purchasing agent listed two advantages of data-phone ordering: (1) reduced cost of possession (lower inventories, less physical space to maintain inventories, and fewer personnel needed to handle inventories), and (2) lower acquisition cost (less paperwork through bypassing some steps in ordering, such as supervisory checking and approving). A purchase-analysis computer printout showed the number of purchases during the past month and the cumulative six months' total. Comparisons of quantities ordered with minimum inventory levels provided evaluations of delivery performance and indicated proper inventory levels for each supplier's products. Invoice statement printouts showed current prices, and when checked against previous invoices, permitted price comparisons.

SYSTEM AT LANCASTER CLOSURE PLANT

At the Lancaster closure plant, the production of packaging crowns and caps required large-volume purchases of tinplate. The suppliers (steel companies) all quoted similar prices and offered nearly identical delivery schedules, but product quality varied. Therefore, management set up a weight-point rating system for ascertaining tin quality (see Exhibit 1). The receiving department

EXHIBIT 1 · Vendor Rating—Crown Tinplate, Month of September

		VENDOR A				VENDOR B			
SUPPLIER		95#				95#			
BASE WEIGHT									
SIZE		20 DIE		22 DIE		20 DIE		22 DIE	
FINISH		MATTE	BRIGHT	MATTE	BRIGHT	MATTE	BRIGHT	MATTE	BRIGHT
No. skids examined		0	23	232	0	44	0	107	0
Rating:	Points								
Net weight	10	6.8		7.9		4.6		6.4	
Dimensions	20	20.0		20.0		20.0		−40.6	
Squareness	30	30.0		29.2		30.0		30.0	
Appearance	20	20.0		20.0		20.0		20.0	
Bowing, wavy edges	10	10.0		10.0		10.0		10.0	
Sheet count	15	8.6		8.8		10.0		10.5	
Total		95.4		95.9		94.6		36.3	

Penalty points*   0   −50 (150 bowed sheets)
Adjusted overall average   95.6   40.5

*Production problems: Any difficulties encountered in production, such as lamination, poor fabricating characteristics, etc., or rejectable defects as noted above but not originally detected when sampled, shall result in the following penalties:

If one-half skid or less is involved, deduct 50 points.
If over one-half skid is involved, deduct 100 points.

Third-quarter weighted average (July, August, September):   Vendor A = 98.3 points
Vendor B = 86.5 points

Distribution of fourth-quarter tonnage: Vendor A = 100%
Vendor B = 0

inspected shipments and assigned ratings. Management compiled a quarterly composite with point differentials among suppliers, thus apportioning its business for the next quarter (see Exhibit 2). For example, if Vendor C received 95.0 points and Vendor D 97.5 points, a differential of 2.5 points, Armstrong would buy 39 percent from C and 61 percent from D. If a differential exceeded 5 points, the leading vendor received all the orders for that particular item.

SYSTEM AT LANCASTER FLOORING PLANT

At the Lancaster flooring plant, corrugated cartons, used for packing finished products, were purchased in large volume. The plant purchasing agent applied a categorical vendor-rating system (see Exhibit 3). This system incorporated the judgments of others in departments directly involved with the suppliers. The plant purchasing agent used this evaluation to allocate business among vendors.

EXHIBIT 2 · Basis for Distribution of Business

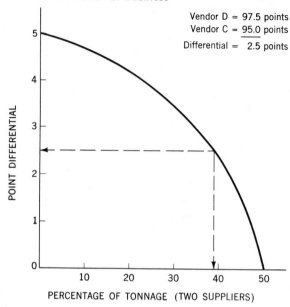

PERCENTAGE OF TONNAGE (TWO SUPPLIERS)

Questions

1. Outline the pros and cons of the vendor-rating systems used by the three plants.
2. Under what conditions is stockless purchasing by data-phone appropriate? Inappropriate?
3. Would it have been wiser for Armstrong to centralize all purchasing activities at corporate headquarters? Should the company have used a standardized vendor-rating system?

EXHIBIT 3 · Flooring Plant Vendor Rating

VENDOR EVALUATION SHEET	Vendor_____ Date:_____ Code P —Purchasing E —Engineering R —Receiving & Traffic A —Accounting QC —Quality Control	ALWAYS	USUALLY	SELDOM	NEVER		PRIMARY RESPONSIBILITY
THE ABOVE VENDOR		6	5	4	3	2	1	0	
1. Delivers per schedule									P
2. Has good quality									QC
3. Delivers per routing instructions									P&R
4. Supplies answers readily									P
5. Advises us of potential trouble									P
6. Not a chronic complainer									P
7. Helps in emergencies									P
8. Delivers without constant follow-up									P
9. Free of labor problems									P
10. Replaces rejections promptly									P
11. Acts upon correction action requests									QC
12. Furnishes necessary technical data									E
13. Has a good packaging									R
14. Invoices correctly									A
15. Issues credit memos punctually									A
16. Furnishes affidavit or certifications									QC
17. Cooperates on design problems									E
18. Has adequate Engineering representation									E
19. Maintains technical service in the field									E
20. Accepts our terms without exceptions									P
21. Keeps promises									P
22. Does not ask for special consideration (Purchasing)									P
23. Prices are generally competitive									P
24. Does not ask for special financial consideration									A
Other points 25.									
26.									
TOTAL GRADE									

Purchasing   Engineering   Quality Control   Receiving   Accounting

BE FAIR IN FILLING OUT THIS FORM. DO NOT BE PREJUDICED. CONSIDER ALL FACTS. MARK CODE LETTERS IN PROPER GRADE COLUMN.

2–4

CAB CHEMICAL COMPANY

Policy on gifts to buyers

Ten years ago C. A. Stringer and Robert Wilder formed the CAB Chemical Corporation, a producer and distributor of inorganic chemicals. Two years ago stiffening competition resulted in a reevaluation of the marketing program, particularly the approach used to tap the market segment made up of municipalities. Management wanted to develop a more effective approach to increase its sales to municipalities.

CAB Chemical, with annual sales of over $50 million, made and marketed special paints, paint removers, soaps, detergents, cleaning fluids, and a variety of janitorial chemicals. The home plant at Burke, California, made most of the products. To increase paint production capacity three years ago, the I. M. Holder Paint Company of Reno, Nevada, was purchased; management planned soon to shift all paint production to the Reno plant.

When Abraham Mitchell joined CAB as vice president of sales two years ago, he found it selling to municipalities through widely dispersed manufacturers' representatives. Although sales had increased each year, he suspected that vast market areas did not receive adequate coverage. Consequently, he analyzed the company's marketing system, compared it with competitors, and concluded that CAB needed its own sales force. The next year he developed plans for a company sales force which would operate under his direction. Top management approved his plan after reviewing the ineffectiveness of its agent system. Mitchell reported directly to Wilder, executive vice president.

Mitchell divided the United States into three regions and hired a regional sales manager for each. He began immediately recruiting a sales force, but continued relationships with most of the manufacturers' representatives until early last year. CAB now had 150 sales representatives "on board." The eastern regional sales manager supervised 75 sales representatives; the western manager, 50; and the southern manager, 25 (see Exhibit 1). ┼ ~

Regional managers recruited field sales personnel from competitors and through newspaper advertisements. Sales personnel sold directly to public-paid employees of municipalities and received a straight commission of 33⅓ percent on net sales, from which they paid their own expenses. One-half of the commission was paid when the sales representative wrote an order; the rest after the company received payment, usually about eight weeks later. Sales representatives also had weekly drawing accounts, the amounts drawn being later deducted from commission checks. Sales quotas differed among sales representatives because of variations in territorial sales potentials; the average quota was about $6,500 per week. Therefore, if he or she reached quota, the average sales representative could expect to gross about $2,167 per week.

Last July Ed Jones, eastern regional sales manager, phoned Abe Mitchell.

EXHIBIT 1 · CAB Chemical Company—Organizational Structure

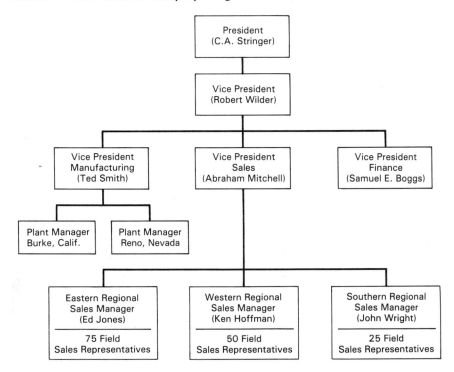

Ed: Hello Abe, this is Ed, I'd like to talk to you a minute or two on a few problems in my area that I think require some attention.

Abe: OK—shoot, Ed.

Ed: I've been getting reports from the field that we are consistently being undersold on our aerosol products and paint solvents. As you know, these items account for about 75 percent of our business and we're getting clobbered in our area. It seems our products are consistently higher priced than competitors' and my reps say it's hard for them to get their foot in the door. I guess you know our sales reports haven't been too encouraging recently.

Abe: I know. . . . I'm not surprised to hear what you're saying, however, John and Ken are having the same problems. I'll tell you what. . . . I'm going to set up a meeting here for next Saturday morning and I want you to attend. I'll contact John and Ken today. I want to present a new promotional technique, and I want your opinions.

Ed: OK, Abe, I'll plan to be in your office this Saturday at nine. . . . Is that OK?

Abe.   That's fine; I'll see you then.

The following Saturday morning Abe Mitchell met with the three regional managers and the president, C. A. Stringer. Mitchell opened the meeting.

Abe: I called you together because I've been getting some alarming reports from the field. Our gross sales for the last two months have increased only 3 percent and we've hired three new reps during this period. Now, all of you have been telling me we're being undersold on our money-making items.

The way I see it we're doing one of two things wrong: One—we're selling our products either too high or our competitors are selling theirs too low. I'm inclined to think our products are priced higher. Or two—our reps are not aggressive enough to sell the products. I'm ruling this out because it seems all our people are having difficulty. As you can see, I'm inferring that our products are too high priced for the market.

Stringer: Yes, that's true, but that's been my policy. As you know, our strategy is to maintain high gross margins. Our production costs can't be reduced much lower, so we have to maintain our present pricing. If we reduce our pricing, we may increase our sales; but you can't convince me that we can still maintain our present dollar margin. What we have to do is increase our sales and maintain our present pricing.

Ed: That's fine, but how are we going to do it? I've had my reps say it's next to impossible to make a sale to a municipality that's already been covered by a competitor. It seems to me the only way we're going to sell our products is to cut our prices.

Ken: I agree with Ed.

John: So do I.

Abe: I'll have to agree with Mr. Stringer concerning our operating margin. I think I have an answer to our problem. You see . . . our customers are mainly commissioners of public works, town superintendents, or town clerks. Now, they have to keep within their yearly budgets, but they probably won't buy more than $30,000 a year from us, so keeping within their budgets is only secondary to them. Now, if our reps were to approach a prospect and offer him a gift for doing business, I'll bet you anything he would bite.

Ed: Wouldn't that be illegal?

Abe: No. The concept isn't much different than a retail store giving trading stamps.

Ken: How about the cost of this promotion? Wouldn't it lower your margin?

Abe: No. I have considered using a 5 percent limit in gift value for each order. If a rep made a $3,000 sale, he would give away a gift worth $150. The $150 would come out of the rep's commission. He would then gross $850 instead of $1,000.

Ed: I don't think my reps are going to go for it.

Abe: I think they will. They're now burning up gas trying to make a sale. If they have a gift in their car trunk, they will probably have a jump on our competitors. You must also consider the customer. I think if you bait the line, he'll bite every time.

Ed: We could at least give it a try. Are you sure we won't get into any legal trouble?

Abe: No, I'm not!

Questions

1. Do you agree with Mitchell's size-up of the behavior of buyers for municipalities? Why? Why not?
2. Evaluate Mitchell's proposal to present buyers with gifts.

3–1

TEXIZE CHEMICAL, INC.

Product concept and product development

Texize Chemical, Inc., manufactured liquid detergents, other household cleaning and laundry products, specialty chemicals for the textile industry, and industrial maintenance and metal treatment compounds. Texize management was excited over the success of the division's new extrastrength household cleaner, "Janitor-in-a-Drum." Henderson Advertising Agency of Greenville, South Carolina, assisted Texize in developing the product concept, in collecting and interpreting marketing research information, and, subsequently, in introducing the product. In an effort to capitalize further upon the success of the 32-ounce size, management had tried adding a half-gallon (64-ounce) size (see Exhibit 1), but both the Texize management and the ad agency executives were dismayed by its disappointing sales. Both groups sought reasons for the poor showing; they began by reviewing the original product concept.

In working on the original product concept, Texize and its agency directed their effort toward developing an industrial-strength cleaner market segment within the household cleaner total market. A product study was undertaken and the following concept statement written:

> A super-concentrated liquid cleaner, formulated for industrial use, now is available to homemakers. It's the strongest cleaner ever sold in stores. It will handle extremely difficult cleaning jobs like grease-soaked garage floors, even car engines caked with greasy dirt, as well as those tough cleaning chores inside the home, including wax stripping. Just mix with water as directed. No rinsing necessary. Ideal for preparing surfaces for painting. Gives your detergent a boost when laundry is heavily soiled. Rubber gloves recommended for prolonged use.

EXHIBIT 1 · A Half-Gallon Container

A professional independent research firm showed the concept statement to a random sample of 1,000 housewives located throughout the United States (see Exhibit 2 for some results). Forty-two percent of the users of household cleaners expressed interest in purchasing an industrial-strength cleaner; 36 percent of the nonusers indicated buying interest. Among users of Spic-N-Span, the leading powdered cleaner, 41 percent were interested in buying an industrial-strength cleaner (see Exhibit 3).

EXHIBIT 2 · Household Cleaner Usage and Types of Products Used

HOUSEHOLD CLEANER USAGE

PERCENTAGE CONSUMERS USING	HEAVY DUTY	LARGE JOB	SMALL JOB	TOUCH UP
All-purpose liquids	51	54	53	51
All-purpose powders	50	44	25	21
Sprays	25	33	48	56
Pine oils	19	16	16	10
Scouring powder	20	18	31	20
Aerosol bathroom	19	16	16	10

TYPES OF HOUSEHOLD CLEANING PRODUCTS CURRENTLY USED

Scouring	99%
Liquids	80
Powders	67
Pine oil	59
Sprays	57
Bathroom aerosol	37

The average consumer used four kinds of cleaning agents in the home.

Source: Independent research firm.

EXHIBIT 3 · Some Concept Test Results*

BRAND NOW USING	PERCENTAGE
Spic-N-Span	41
Ajax	35
Mr. Clean	22
Top Job	17
Fantastik	15
409	13
Lestoil	8
Dow	6
Crew	3
Other brands	13

*Percentage of consumers using each brand who were interested in buying industrial-strength cleaner. Random sample of 1,000 housewives.
Source: Independent research firm.

When the concept test results came in, management decided to undertake product "use" testing. Therefore, it had the research agency place the product in 501 homes in five key market areas. Prior to using the item, 49 percent of the housewife respondents had expressed an interest in buying; after using it, 51 percent had buying interest. (See Exhibit 4 for other test results.)

Texize arranged for independent studies of the proposed name and

EXHIBIT 4 · Usage of Industrial-Strength Cleaner*

USE	PERCENTAGE
Floors	84
Woodwork	87
Walls	85
Cabinets	92
Grease-soaked floors	79
Stripping	83
Laundry	78
Bathroom	92
Kitchen	85
Tiles	91

*Percentage of consumers who found industrial-strength cleaner effective on specific uses. Sample of 501 housewives. Test cities: New York, Chicago, St. Louis, Dallas, Los Angeles.
Source: Independent research firm.

package. Texize already owned the proposed name, Janitor-in-a-Drum, which appeared on an industrial cleaner. Henderson Advertising Agency listed three reasons for using the Janitor-in-a-Drum name: (1) it reinforced the product image, (2) it was memorable, and (3) it was distinctive. An independent research organization, one not used for the earlier studies, reported the results of its "name research" (see Exhibit 5). The package, a replica of a 55-gallon drum, according to a study by the same research firm, provided several advantageous features relative to the packaging of competitive products:

1. It reinforced the product strength concept.
2. It contained 32 ounces, whereas major competitive packages contained only 28 ounces.
3. It had a distinctive color and shape.
4. It was easily gripped.
5. It was easy to use.
6. It possessed good stability (the product inside would not easily deteriorate).
7. It had excellent shelf visibility.[1]

Management decided to bypass national test marketing, choosing an area for initial market introduction extending from Maine to Philadelphia. This region had higher per capita household cleaner sales than any other; it contained 22 percent of the United States population and accounted for 29 percent of household cleaner sales. Texize began introducing the product in this area in July, obtaining excellent market acceptance (see Exhibits 7 and 8).

During the initial market introduction, Texize sent 8,000 sample bottles to retail grocers and food brokers. It also furnished both types of middlemen

[1]See Exhibit 6.

EXHIBIT 5 · "Janitor-in-a-Drum" Name Research*

ASSOCIATED WITH	PERCENTAGE OF RESPONDENTS
Heavy-duty liquid cleaner	23
Powdered floor and wall cleaner	22
Liquid drain opener	22
Scouring cleanser	21
Other associations	12
	100

*Sample size: 700.
Source: Independent research firm.

EXHIBIT 6 · Package Research*

ATTRIBUTE	PERCENTAGE INDICATING
Large job cleaner	68
Cleans quickly	68
Effective	54
Convenient	49
Easy to use	45
Modern	42
Economical	38

*Janitor-in-a-Drum name and package tested against four other exclusive designs. Sample size of 240 in Chicago and Atlanta.
Source: Independent research firm.

EXHIBIT 7 · Janitor-in-a-Drum Consumer Acceptance, Introductory Market Area, October

	RETAIL DISTRIBUTION	(MARKET SHARE) NIELSEN
Boston	54%	3.2%
Philadelphia	70	4.5
New York	63	4.5

AVERAGE SALES PER STORE STOCKING

		AUGUST	SEPTEMBER	OCTOBER
Boston	Ajax	31.1	33.7	38.0
	Janitor-in-a-Drum	6.1	22.2	40.8
Philadelphia	Ajax	36.6	49.7	44.8
	Janitor-in-a-Drum	2.7	36.0	54.0
New York	Ajax	46.9	53.6	53.5
	Janitor-in-a-Drum	4.6	35.4	71.3

Source: A. C. Nielsen.

EXHIBIT 8 · Janitor-in-a-Drum—Attainments vs. Objectives

	OBJECTIVES	ATTAINMENT
Housewife brand awareness	60%	59%—6 weeks
	Year 1	62%—14 weeks
Housewife brand trial	14%	11%—6 months
	Year 1	
All commodity distribution		
(food stores)	75%	
	Year 1	83%—6 months

Sources: Company records, A. C. Nielsen, and independent research firm.

with comparison sheets showing consumer cost per application, profitability per unit, and lineal shelf space occupied by Janitor-in-a-Drum and its two major competitors (see Exhibit 9). Retailers were urged to stress average cost per application to potential users.

The market introduction of Janitor-in-a-Drum was extended nationally the next January. At that time retailers and brokers received 42,000 trade samples. In March Texize launched a heavy TV advertising campaign. In April newspaper advertisements for Janitor-in-a-Drum across the country carried "twenty-cents off" coupons.

In June the 64-ounce size was introduced. An existing container, made for another product, was utilized so as to hasten delivery to retailers. Texize sales personnel and brokers immediately experienced difficulty in selling the new size. Although retailers received about the same profit margin as on the 32-ounce size, shelf space for the 64-ounce size proved difficult to obtain. Sales were below expectations, and management considered withdrawing the 64-ounce size from the market.

Questions

1. What additional marketing research information might have been requested by management when it first considered introducing Janitor-in-a-Drum?
2. What should Texize management have done about the half-gallon (64-ounce) container?
3. How, if at all, could Texize have improved its approaches to product development and market introduction?

EXHIBIT 9 · Consumer Cost/Application

	28 oz LEADING LIQUID	33 oz LEADING POWDER	32 oz JANITOR-IN-A- DRUM
Average retail price	$0.692	$0.590	$0.890
Consumer cost/ounce	$0.0247	$0.0179	$0.9278
Ounces/use	2.0	3.7	2.0
Number uses/package	14	9	16
Average cost/application	$0.0494	$0.0656	$0.0556

PROFITABILITY UNIT SALE

Profit margin	17.4%	16.7%	25.4%
Profit/sale	$0.1201	$0.0985	$0.2261

LINEAL SHELF FEET

Single facing width	4.0 in.	4.9 in.	4.2 in.
Facing/shelf foot	3.00	2.45	2.86
Profit/unit	$.1201	$.0985	$.2261
Profit/shelf foot	$.3603	$.2413	$.6466

3–2

SHUFORD MILLS, INC.

Research for market targeting

Mr. David Taylor, markets and products manager, Pressure Sensitive Tape Division, Shuford Mills, Inc., faced a critical decision on future strategy. He was responsible for all the division's product planning and promotional activities, including market and product analysis in terms of competitive position, product line, product application, merchandising, and product packaging. Plans for building a new plant costing over $1 million were complete. The new plant would house more than $4 million worth of the most advanced tape manufacturing equipment available, and would enable the Tape Division to triple its output.

Thus far, 90 percent of the Tape Division's sales were to the industrial market, 10 percent to the consumer market. Company sales had grown at a faster rate than the tape industry, but Mr. Taylor felt that future market policy required attention. Should the 90/10 percent ratio for industrial and retail sales be maintained, or should more attention be directed toward the consumer market? Realizing this issue's importance, he was considering doing a detailed study of the pressure-sensitive tape market.

COMPANY BACKGROUND

Shuford Mills, Inc., began in 1880 as Shuford, Gwyn, and Company. Abel A. Shuford and N. H. Gwyn started by making bunch yarn for hand looms and warp carpets. Although expansion was broad and rapid, the operation remained a family business. Over the years several plants were built or acquired, and Shuford Mills, Inc., evolved into a textile manufacturer with multiple operations in the Carolinas and Georgia.

Shuford Mills entered the pressure sensitive tape market, using a small experimental machine which turned out paper masking tape. After registering success in this market, the company entered the cloth tape market. Then the division entered the packaging equipment market when it started to sell carton sealing equipment that used "Shurtape" pressure sensitive tape.

The Tape Division made a wide range of pressure sensitive tape products, which it distributed worldwide under the "Shurtape" name. The line included: paper masking tape, cloth tape, crepe paper masking tape, filament reinforced strapping tape, film flat back paper, foil and printable tapes, rope stock paper tapes, and specialty items. The products saw use in the automotive, textile, printing, garment, aircraft, construction, and agricultural industries; Shuford pursued a differentiated strategy toward each of these market segments.

The Tape Division operated in competitive markets where innovations and development of new products were frequent, so close attention was paid to research and development. The Research and Development Department had the mission of developing new products and improving present products. It conducted continuing research on new and improved materials, seeking to assure the division's competence in the pressure sensitive tape and allied industries. Like its competitors, Shuford management knew that it couldn't afford to stand still while others were searching for new and better products. Mr. Taylor commented: "Marketing executives bear a special responsibility for keeping abreast of the major opportunities being opened up by technological market change."

THE INDUSTRY AND SHUFORD MILLS

Sales for Shuford Mills Tape Division last year were close to $24 million, and the company ranked seventh among the industry's fourteen major producers. The total pressure sensitive tape market in the United States was approximately $400 million and was largely dominated by such industrial giants as Minnesota Mining & Manufacturing Company, Mystik, Borden, and Tuck Industries.[1] Some European imports also were sold in the United States.

Most competitors belonged to the Pressure Sensitive Tape Council (PSTC), an association of U.S. tape manufacturers. Its purpose was to educate distributors and consumers about pressure sensitive tapes. It encouraged proper use of pressure sensitive tapes, developed standards of nomenclature and test methods, and maintained liaison with government agencies and other organizations.

Shuford's ratio of industrial sales to retail sales was about the same as the current industry ratio, 90 percent/10 percent. But the industry ratio had changed considerably over the past three years. It had moved from a long-

[1]See Exhibit 1 for industry sales.

established 95 percent/5 percent to 90 percent/10 percent in this period, and retail sales were expected to double again during the next three years.

DISTRIBUTION

Shuford distribution of tape was through 400 distributors scattered throughout the United States. Most distributors served sparsely populated market areas and called on the smaller industrial and retail accounts. Shuford field sales personnel handled direct sales and called on the distributors. The largest accounts, however, such as the giant paper and plastics distributors and industrial suppliers, were serviced either by Mr. Taylor or the field sales manager. And two agents in Michigan and Texas represented the Tape Division's product line in their areas.

    The company delivery standard was seventy-two hours for stock items and three to four weeks for special orders not currently in stock. The distributors and agents played a key role in delivery, so their locations and

EXHIBIT 1 · Tape Industry Sales (previous year)

COMPANY	SALES	PERCENT OF MARKET	INDUSTRIAL SALES AS % OF TOTAL SALES	RETAIL SALES AS % OF TOTAL SALES
Adhesive Tape Corporation	$ 3,700,000	1	100	0
Anchor Continental, Inc.	15,100,000	3	75	25
Armak Tape Division (part of Akzona, Inc.)	27,000,000	6	90	10
Arno Adhesive Tapes, Inc.	27,600,000	6	75	25
Ideal Tape Company	4,200,000	1	100	0
Kendall Company (Polyken Division)	12,500,000	3	100	0
Minnesota Mining & Manufacturing Company	180,100,000	50	60	40
Mystik Tape (division of Borden Chemical, Borden, Inc.)	27,400,000	6	75	25
Permacel (division of Johnson & Johnson)	25,100,000	5	90	10
Shuford Mills Tape Division	24,300,000	6	90	10
LePage's	3,400,000	1	10	90
Nashua	18,000,000	5	90	10
Tuck Industries	25,600,000	6	60	40
Hampton	4,000,000	1	90	10
TOTAL INDUSTRIAL SALES*	$398,000,000	100%		

*Industry ratio 90–10.

facilities were important. The company had two warehouses in Iowa that stocked Shuford tape and additional tape was in inventory at the manufacturing plants.

PROMOTION

The Tape Division's sales force was headed by Mr. W. H. Little. It consisted of seventeen salespersons including one in Europe, a west coast field sales manager, a southern regional field sales manager, and two Packaging Equipment Department regional sales supervisors, one each for the east and west coasts. Sales personnel were based in the areas of highest economic activity.

Mr. Little directed and coordinated all field sales activities. He had responsibility for both direct sales and agency sales, for day-to-day supervision of the division's own sales representatives, and for maintaining close and continuing contact with agents and their sales forces. He worked with Mr. Taylor in establishing sales policies and plans, including pricing, sales quotas, sales territories, distribution channels, sales personnel requirements and compensation, short- and long-run sales objectives, and the development of sales forecast data. He coordinated agency sales activities through personal contact with agency sales personnel, keeping them informed on objectives, special promotions, and so forth. He developed, along with the production manager, special sales promotions and directed all field sales activities related to their implementation.

Each regional sales manager's general function was to direct and coordinate regional sales activities to reach sales and profit objectives set by division management. The two Packaging Equipment Department regional sales supervisors directed and coordinated field sales activities of the Packaging Equipment Department.

The advertising effort was negligible. Sales promotion took the form of sales presentations (packaging equipment) and free samples. Sales meetings were held to describe company products, exchange ideas, and stimulate the sales force to greater effort. The Tape Division annually participated in several trade exhibitions, which were important since they resulted in making many initial contacts with prospects.

PRICING

Pricing was targeted to return a 12 percent profit on sales before taxes. This was an average long-run target profit, leaving sales personnel some room for price negotiation. Actually, Shuford had little pricing flexibility since Minnesota Mining & Manufacturing Company, with a market share of 50 percent, served as the price leader in the industrial and consumer markets. Shuford, accepting this pricing situation, relied on superior service, products, sales personnel, and established distributors to reach its share objectives.

MARKETING RESEARCH CONSIDERATIONS

Mr. Taylor realized that marketing strategy needed reappraising. Should the Tape Division continue to stress industrial sales? Was the company ready to expand its consumer market share? Mr. Taylor had always defined the basic application of pressure sensitive tape as that of an aid to manufacturing and processing. He realized that this application was important only to the industrial market. It was likely that the consumer market warranted a broader definition, especially if the company wanted to participate in the rapid growth of this market. The fact that the company had no marketing research department complicated matters.

Mr. Taylor wondered if his assistants should be held responsible for collecting data on new products, competitive products, market potentials, and the like. He wondered, too, what other information was needed and where it could be found, if at all. He also wondered whether the division should contact an outside organization to advise on a research program.

Questions

1. What information was needed to facilitate the decision of whether or not to expand consumer sales?
2. Should the company have relied on an outside research firm or should it have conducted its own study?
3. How might a marketing information system have been of help to Shuford Mills Tape Division?

3–3

ROBERTSON'S DEPARTMENT STORE

Determining demand for a new retail outlet

Recently, several black leaders discussed the economic situation in their small rural Mississippi town. They were frustrated by the black community's slow political and economic progress. This had led them to begin negotiations with the town's white merchants to employ black sales personnel. Little progress had been made, and many black customers were driving to Meridian (about thirty miles away) to shop.

Black consumers and black leaders alike recognized that most of the town's merchants were not interested in improving the local economic situation if that meant changing traditional business patterns. Thus, the black leadership concluded that an excellent opportunity existed for a new local retail outlet. Although several options were discussed, it was agreed that a clothing store (two members of the group had retail clothing experience) should be considered and the market potential in the community investigated.

PROFILE OF THE COMMUNITY

A marketing committee was set up to investigate the area's market potential. The group enlisted the local Chamber of Commerce to help in the study. The town had been almost totally dependent upon the agricultural and lumber industries until 1965. Then it began to attract more diversified industry and of late had become a thriving center of industrial growth. The town, a county seat, was in east-central Mississippi, thirty miles from Meridian and seventy-five miles from Jackson. As a trading center for the surrounding area, it was accessible by Interstate 20, two U.S. highways, and two Mississippi state highways. The Southern Railroad provided rail transportation service. A city-county airport was three miles north of town, and commercial airlines served both Meridian and Jackson.

The town's population in 1960 was about 5,000 and the county's 13,000. By 1980 town population had grown to about 9,500, county population to 22,000. Growth since 1980 averaged 7 percent per year. By 1980, total employment in the county was approximately 9,975 and was increasing at a 5 percent average annual rate.

There were sixteen manufacturers in the area. Exhibit 1 shows products and employment statistics of the major manufacturers.

Per capita income in the county, as of 1980, for males 16 years old and over was $8,841. For professional and managerial people it was $18,747; for craftsmen, foremen, and farm managers, $15,020. Per capita income for females 16 years old and over was $6,136; for clerical workers, $7,034; for operative workers, $5,750. The 1980 unemployment rate was 6.7 percent.

The marketing committee ran an independent marketing survey, which was conducted by local high school students. Its purpose was to determine local consumer buying habits. The town was divided into four sections with the railroad tracks serving as an arbitrary dividing point. Every sixth house in the selected survey area was contacted for a personal interview. The study covered only adults over 18, with most interviewees being between 21 and 40. Three hundred people in all were surveyed. Exhibit 2 shows the survey instrument, and Exhibit 3 presents the final results of the survey.

DECISION POINT

The marketing committee now was trying to determine if the group should go forward with the project or if more information was needed. They regarded the survey results as favorable, but they recognized that opening a new retail outlet was risky since statistics showed high failure rates for new retail ventures.

EXHIBIT 1 · Product and Employment Statistics: Major Manufacturers

PRODUCT(S) PRODUCED	1980 EMPLOYMENT
Canvas footwear	2,015
Men's slacks	1,117
Prefabricated homes	857
Synthetic fabrics	230
Pine lumber	223
Hardwood flooring	178
Crushed stones	141
Boxes and crates	111
Lumber	94
Pressure treated lumber	71

EXHIBIT 2 · Market Survey

Hello! My name is _____ . I am conducting a marketing survey to gather information regarding clothes buying behavior. Would you please answer a few brief questions? This will only take a few minutes of your time.

How many times do you shop for clothes annually?	____
Where do you buy most of your clothes?	____
How much do you spend per month on clothes?	____

Would you rather shop at a specialty store or a complete line department store?	Specialty	____
	Complete line	____
What time of day do you prefer to shop?	Mornings	____
	Afternoons	____
	Evenings	____
Do you prefer self-service or assistance?	Self-service	____
	Assistance	____

What is your age?	____
What is your race?	____
What is your occupation?	____

Thank you for taking the time to answer these questions.

Questions

1. What problems, if any, were there in the research design?
2. Identify the problems inherent in the questionnaire (see Exhibit 2) and design a new questionnaire to overcome those problems.
3. Should the new retail outlet have been opened? Why or why not?

EXHIBIT 3 · Market Survey Results*

How many times do you shop for clothes annually?	3–6 times 50%	9–12 times 25%	
Where do you buy most of your clothes?	Whites† 17%	Belk 13%	Sears† 8%
	Penney's† 9%	Federals 12%	Jordans 10%
How much do you spend per month on clothes?	$0–$50 77%	$51–$100 15%	$100 and up 8%
Would you rather shop at a specialty store or a complete line department store?	Specialty Store 37%	Complete Line 63%	
What time of the day do you prefer to shop?	Mornings 44%	Afternoons 38%	Evenings 18%
Do you prefer self-service or assistance?	Self-Service 56%	Assistance 44%	
What is your age?	18–21 11%	21–40 57%	Over 40 32%
What is your race?	Black 19%	White 79%	Other 2%
What is your occupation?	White Collar 26%	Blue Collar 39%	Unemployed 35%

*This was the only information tabulated from the survey.
†Nearest store located in Meridian, Mississippi, which meant that 34% of those surveyed were driving sixty miles (round trip) to shop for clothes.

3–4

PRESSURE SENSITIVE TAPE DIVISION

Analysis of research data for market targeting

Management of the Pressure Sensitive Tape Division (PSTD), Shuford Mills, Inc., was considering the feasibility of altering its sales ratio from 90 percent industrial/10 percent consumer to a ratio on the order of 80 percent industrial/20 percent consumer or conceivably an even higher consumer percentage.[1] To help determine the feasibility of this move, marketing research data were gathered (see the accompanying exhibits). Mr. David Taylor, the PSTD products manager, knew that expansion of sales (either consumer or industrial) was needed to utilize the new production capacity about to come on stream. The plant was capable of nearly tripling PSTD's output. Mr. Taylor and his staff were seeking clues from the data that might be helpful in developing an effective marketing strategy.

STUDY OBJECTIVES AND METHODOLOGY

The primary objective of the marketing research study had been to gather data from retail stores selling tape and from consumers who bought tape. From the retail stores, data were sought on:

1. types and volume of pressure sensitive tape sales
2. merchandising and promotion of tapes by retail stores
3. growth of pressure sensitive tape retail sales

---

[1] See Shuford Mills, Inc., for details regarding company history, product lines, competitive situation, and so forth.

Information from consumers was sought on:

1. consumption of tape
2. knowledge and importance of tape brands
3. types of retail stores where tapes were purchased
4. importance of price versus product quantity

Data were gathered through personal interviews with 3,837 tape customers, and owners and managers of 281 retail stores. Exhibit 1 shows the number and location of the consumer interviews, and Exhibit 2 shows the number, location, and type of retail store contacted.

STUDY FINDINGS

EXHIBIT 1 · Location and Number of Consumer Interviews

LOCATION	NUMBER	PERCENT
New York	806	21
Atlanta	729	19
Kansas City	690	18
Seattle	729	19
Los Angeles	883	23
Total	3,837	100

EXHIBIT 2 · Number and Type of Retail Store Surveyed

TOTAL	TOTAL 281	N.Y. 57	ATLANTA 57	SEATTLE 55	K.C. 56	L.A. 56
Department stores:						
Stationery dept.	17	3	4	4	4	2
Hardware dept.	19	3	4	4	4	4
Building materials	24	5	5	4	5	5
Stationery stores	28	6	6	5	5	6
Food stores	20	5	4	4	4	3
Art supply	23	5	4	4	5	5
Auto supply	22	5	4	4	4	5
Variety stores	27	6	5	6	5	5
Hardware stores	26	5	5	5	5	6
Paint & wallpaper	23	4	5	4	5	5
Drugstores	26	5	6	5	5	5
Discount stores	26	5	5	6	5	5

EXHIBIT 3 · Retail Tape Sales by Package Type

PACKAGE TYPE	PERCENTAGE
Display size	72.7
Bulk pack	26.3
Total	100.0%

EXHIBIT 4 · Retail Tape Sales by Tape and Package Type

	PACKAGE	
TAPE TYPE	DISPLAY (%)	BULK (%)
Cellophane (other clear film)	27.8	2.6
Paper (masking)	19.7	57.2
Electrical	12.5	4.9
Cloth	10.6	4.9
Translucent	9.2	—
Paper (packaging)	7.4	23.1
Double faced	6.2	1.4
Fiber reinforced	3.1	2.5
Insulating	1.5	.8
Metal foil	.7	1.2
Freezer	.6	—
Duct	.4	2.5
Hair	.3	—
Total	100.0%	100.0%

EXHIBIT 5 · Average Annual Tape Sales by Type of Store

STORE TYPE	AVERAGE ANNUAL SALE*
Discount store	$4,120
Hardware store	3,280
Stationery store	2,816
Building materials store	2,017
Variety store	1,996
Houseware store	1,816
Department store:	
Hardware department	1,476
Stationery department	1,381
Paint & wallpaper store	1,254
Drugstore	1,012
Auto supply	964
Food store	746
Art supply store	708

*Average sale per all store types—$1,878.

EXHIBIT 6 · Percent of Store Customers Requesting Tape by Brand Name

	STORES	
REQUEST TAPE BY BRAND NAME	#	%
None of our tape customers	159	56.4
1% to 5% of our tape customers	35	12.2
6% to 10% of our tape customers	26	9.1
11% to 20% of our tape customers	17	6.4
21% to 30% of our tape customers	7	2.5
31% to 50% of our tape customers	8	3.0
51% to 75% of our tape customers	13	4.6
Over 75% of our tape customers	16	5.8
Total	281	100.0

EXHIBIT 7 · Percent of Retail Store Sales of Tape by Type, Brand, and Package (N = 281 stores)

BRAND	PACKAGE	CELLO. (%)	TRANSL. (%)	MASK. (%)	CLOTH (%)	ELECT. (%)	DOUBLE (%)	REINF. (%)	PACK. (%)	FREEZER (%)	FOIL (%)	FOAM (%)	HAIR (%)	DUCT (%)
Scotch	(Display)	68	52	31	13	24	30	21	19	2	2	1	1	—
	(Bulk)	4	2	18	1	1	2	2	3	—	—	—	—	—
LePage	(D)	7	4	—	—	—	Neg.*	Neg.*	3	—	—	—	—	—
	(B)	—	—	—	—	1	—	—	—	—	—	—	—	—
Mystik	(D)	4	10	9	33	4	4	4	2	Neg.*	2	2	—	—
	(B)	—	1	7	1	Neg.*	Neg.*	1	1	—	—	—	—	—
Tuck	(D)	9	4	7	1	1	Neg.*	—	1	—	—	—	—	—
	(B)	—	—	9	2	1	—	Neg.*	1	—	—	—	—	—
Permacel	(D)	—	—	—	—	—	Neg.*	—	—	—	—	Neg.*	—	—
	(B)	2	—	—	—	1	Neg.*	—	—	—	—	—	—	—
Arno	(D)	—	1	1	2	Neg.*	7	2	1	—	4	Neg.*	—	—
	(B)	—	1	7	1	Neg.*	Neg.*	1	1	—	Neg.*	1	—	1
Bear	(D)	—	—	1	—	Neg.*	—	—	—	—	—	—	—	—
	(B)	—	—	2	—	—	Neg.*	—	—	—	—	—	—	—
Anchor	(D)	—	—	—	—	Neg.*	Neg.*	Neg.*	—	—	—	—	—	—
	(B)	—	—	—	—	—	—	Neg.*	—	—	—	—	—	—
Dutch	(D)	—	—	—	—	Neg.*	—	—	—	—	Neg.*	—	—	—
	(B)	—	—	—	—	—	—	—	—	—	—	—	—	—
Polyken	(D)	—	—	—	—	—	—	—	—	—	—	—	—	—
	(B)	—	—	—	—	—	—	—	—	—	—	—	—	—
Private Label	(D)	18	6	17	9	31	19	7	21	1	7	14	—	Neg.*
	(B)	—	2	18	8	11	8	5	6	—	3	4	—	3
Imports	(D)	Neg.*	—	1	—	2	—	1	—	—	—	—	1	—
	(B)	—	—	—	—	—	—	—	—	—	1	—	—	—
TOTAL	(D)	81	65	56	57	58	59	35	43	3	14	16	1	1
	(B)	7	3	44	8	11	7	8	13	—	1	2	—	1

*Neg. means less than 1% (negligible).

EXHIBIT 8 · Importance of Tape to Retail Stores

	STORES	
IMPORTANCE	#	%
"Very important. We need it in our line."	140	49.9
"It's important, but not a strong sales item."	69	24.6
"We carry only as a customer convenience."	72	25.5
Total	281	100.0

EXHIBIT 9 · Retail Display Space Allocated to Tape

	STORES	
SPACE ALLOCATED	#	%
No display. Keep in drawer.	3	1.2
1 to 3 square feet	69	24.5
4 to 7 square feet	75	26.8
8 to 10 square feet	47	17.3
11 to 15 square feet	36	12.6
16 to 20 square feet	22	7.9
Over 20 square feet	29	9.7
Total	281	100.0

EXHIBIT 10 · Consumer Use of Tape by Type (*N* = 3,837)

TYPE OF TAPE	% *OF CUSTOMERS USING*
Cellophane	73
Masking	67
Invisible	59
Electrical	51
Packaging	32
Reinforced	24
Cloth	23
Double faced	18
Foam	12
Metal foil	8

EXHIBIT 11 · Retail Expectations of Tape Sale Trends by Package Type

		% *RESPONSE REGARDING* 5-*YEAR PERIOD*	
EXPECTATION	*PACKAGE TYPE*	*PREVIOUS*	*FUTURE*
Increase	Display*	71.5	79.0
	Bulk†	76.0	76.0
No change	Display	27.7	20.6
	Bulk	23.3	24.0
Decline	Display	.8	.4
	Bulk	.7	—

*Average display pack increase was 21.4%.
†Average bulk pack increase was 22.9%.

EXHIBIT 12 · Consumer Knowledge of Tape Brands

BRAND	% OF CONSUMERS MENTIONING
Scotch	72
Mystik	19
Tuck	13
LePage	11

EXHIBIT 13 · Consumer Perceived Importance of Price Versus Quantity Purchased

PRICE/QUANTITY COMPARISON AMONG BRANDS	% OF RESPONDENTS (N = 3,837)
Never compare	74
Sometimes compare	22
Always compare	4

Questions

1. Should PSTD have expanded its emphasis on the retail market?
2. If PSTD were to try expanding its share of the retail market, what should have been its marketing strategy?
3. What additional information should have been available in making this decision?

4–1

WORLEY-SEWELL COMPANY

Addition of a new line

Five years ago Jack Worley, vice president and salesman for the Warren-Sewell Clothing Company, organized the Worley-Sewell Company of Bremen, Georgia. He believed that the Sewell name, well known for suits and sports coats in the men's clothing trade, would carry over to Worley-Sewell's line of men's jackets and all-weather coats. Two years later Worley-Sewell expanded its line to include ladies' and children's outerwear. Management was now considering adding a new line—boys' suits and sports coats.

Initially, an out-of-state contractor made Worley-Sewell's products. However, Worley and George Turner, an employee of Hubbard Slacks, also a Bremen Company, had organized T and W Manufacturing Company to make the Worley-Sewell line. The T and W plant, located in Waco, Georgia, finished piece goods furnished by Worley-Sewell. Title passed to Worley-Sewell upon completion of "trim" work, and the finished items were stored in warehouses in Bremen. Sales volume had grown to $2 million, causing management to expand both Bremen warehouses and the Waco plant.

Worley-Sewell regarded Campus and Cambridge Original as its principal competitors. Campus offered a wider product line and had annual sales of approximately $50 million. Cambridge Original of Duluth, Georgia, was about the same size as Worley-Sewell, had roughly the same territory coverage, and had a similar product line.

Worley-Sewell sold most of its output to retailers in small towns and in the smaller cities. Retailers in large cities were regarded as difficult prospects requiring excessive selling time. Competition was also more intense in the larger metropolitan areas. Management believed that middle-aged people constituted its largest customer group, as they were not particularly brand conscious and generally shopped for medium-priced quality clothing. Worley-Sewell did not attempt to set fashion but produced current styles; however, Jack Worley frequently visited various large cities to study fashion trends.

Currently, the product line included jackets, all-weather coats, three-quarter-length corduroy coats, parkas, men's formal wear, ladies' coats, and children's outerwear. Men's jackets came in sixteen colors and in sizes from Prep-6 to 54, and they retailed from $27 to $45 depending on size and type of lining. All-weather coats were made in five colors and in men's and ladies' sizes from 6 to 54, with retail prices ranging from $42 to $105. Wholesale prices were usually lower for ladies' coats than for men's. Corduroy coats came in three colors and twenty-five sizes. Formal wear for men included pants and dinner jackets in five colors. Every item in the line was offered in two qualities of material. Jackets and all-weather coats were the largest sellers, accounting for more volume than any other items.

Worley-Sewell's nine-person sales force covered the southeastern United States. Salespersons traveled their territories in September and October selling the spring offerings and in February through May selling the fall offerings. They received a 6 percent commission on all sales made in their territories, whether they personally wrote the orders or customers ordered from the home office. Salespersons earned an average of $30,000 to $36,000 annually. Although many carried noncompeting lines, such as men's hats, ties, and umbrellas produced by other makers, all were regarded as Worley-Sewell employees.

Mather Muse managed the company's sales force and personally called upon "prime" accounts near Bremen. He received an annual salary of $40,000 and a 6 percent commission on his own sales. His job involved selection, training, compensation, and supervision of sales personnel. New salespersons were recruited rather informally; most were former shipping clerks.

Worley-Sewell used very little advertising. It provided "plates" and "slicks" to retailers for use in local newspaper advertising. Most such advertising emphasized Mister 365, the brand name used on all company products except for the formal wear, which carried the name Black and White. On request, the company often sewed on a store's own label. Some sales personnel gave away pens, pencils, tape measures, and other novelties imprinted with their name and the company's. Sales personnel were not reimbursed for novelty costs and expenses incurred by them at trade shows.

Worley-Sewell sold its products to retailers at prices under the industry. Its markup for retailers averaged about 35 percent on the selling price as compared with other makers' markups of 45 percent. Unlike most of the industry, however, Worley-Sewell did not grant quantity discounts. It usually extended credit on a "net thirty days" basis, but "net sixty days" terms were allowed to those placing early orders. The company adhered to industry practice in selling ladies' clothing, granting an 8 percent cash discount for prompt payment.

When sales of formal wear dropped and the company had idle capacity among the formal-wear workers, Worley considered adding a new line. He believed that addition of boys' suits and sports coats would solve the idle capacity problem; therefore, he recommended that T and W tool up for production. He was aware of the intense competition in the new field; in fact, two other suit manufacturers in Bremen had already introduced similar lines. He also realized that customers for children's clothing were often price conscious; however, the idle capacity problem at T and W demanded immediate attention. He assumed that the new line could be sold through the present sales force and would not involve additional promotional expenditures. Therefore, he recommended to Turner and Sewell, and to Muse, the sales manager, that production begin on boys' suits and sports coats for the fall season coming up.

Questions

1. Should W-S have added the new line?
2. Evaluate the company's approach to structuring the product line.
3. Assuming that the company adds the new line, what should be the overall marketing strategy?

4-2

BEARDEN'S PIANO COMPANY

Loss of franchise

James Bearden, president of Bearden's Piano Company of Decatur, Georgia, an Atlanta suburb, was wondering how to compensate for the loss of one of his dealer franchises. Bearden's dealt in new and used pianos, but currently most sales were of used and rebuilt pianos. A short time ago, the firm had severed relations with Yamaha International Corporation, its major supplier of new pianos, and had not yet found a suitable replacement.

Since its founding Bearden's had specialized in selling new and used grand pianos, but it also carried a narrow line of vertical pianos. From time to time it stocked a few organs, even though the company considered itself a piano specialist. Bearden's also offered piano tuning and repair services, both of which became increasingly important sources of revenue after discontinuance of the Yamaha line. Bearden's did not provide piano-moving service, since it used hired trucks and part-time workers for its own deliveries. A music teacher worked part-time on a commission basis, instructing neighborhood children in piano. Sales of new and used pianos constituted about 70 percent of total sales.

James Bearden looked upon the Atlanta metropolitan area as a good market for musical merchandise, particularly DeKalb County. This fast-growing county, in which Bearden's was located, ranked second in population only to Fulton County in the heart of Atlanta. Per household incomes in DeKalb County were among the highest in Georgia, nearly $4,000 above the state's average, and $3,000 higher than the U.S. average.

To keep pace with Atlanta's booming economy, Bearden's had recently enlarged its building, adding showrooms and offices; also housed were rebuilding facilities and a small music studio. Before losing the Yamaha line, business was good in the *string-street* location, although James Bearden knew that a significant amount of business was being lost to outlying shopping centers.[1]

Twenty-seven competitors, including Atlanta's two major department stores—Rich's and Davison's—sold pianos and related products in the metropolitan market. Except for Rich's and Davison's, central city piano retailers had experienced declining sales as more and more buyers bought at shopping centers and from suburban dealers. Alexander Piano Sales and Honey Music Company provided major competition for Bearden's in DeKalb County; both operated stores in nearby shopping centers. Generally, prospects visited all three stores before buying.

Bearden's management classified piano buyers into three groups:

1. those searching for a piano to use as a piece of furniture
2. those hunting for a fine musical instrument
3. those looking for some combination of numbers 1 and 2

"Furniture" prospects were interested mostly in style, appearance, and size. "Instrument" prospects sought performance and therefore regarded name brands as highly important.

Management believed that buyers thought of a piano as a "culture" item. Typical buyers wanted their children taught how to play; piano buyers were usually middle-aged, but piano players were generally young. Most buyers were members of white, middle- to high-income groups, many of them professional or management people. Most often, purchasing was a family decision, with husbands and wives doing the prepurchase shopping together.

Bearden's handled two types of pianos, grand and vertical. Grand pianos ranged from the most popular models (five or six feet long) to concert grands (nine feet long) for professional musicians. Upright pianos (those containing vertical plates and strings) included studios, spinets, and consoles. Bearden's sold studio models to institutions; spinets and consoles, available in numerous styles and colors, were sold to private households. Grand pianos carried a higher dollar profit margin per unit than uprights.

Over the years Bearden's had handled various piano and organ lines. First, management took on the Starck line, a medium-quality, medium-priced piano. A few years later a little-known yet high-quality and high-priced line, Krakauer, was added. Bearden's had also carried, at one time or another, Gulbransen, Lowrey, and Thomas organs, although none were "pushed." Bearden's stock was high quality, but not composed of name brands until it added Yamaha pianos and organs ten years ago.

---

[1]A *string street* is a street on which businesses locate with little or no effort to coordinate their merchandise offerings as in planned shopping centers.

THE YAMAHA STORY

Nippon Gakki Company, Ltd., of Hammanatsu, Japan, maker of Yamaha (although better known by the U.S. general public for its motorcycles), was the world's largest piano manufacturer. Organs, guitars, band instruments, skis, boats, and archery equipment were also made under the Yamaha name. The first Yamaha sales office in the United States opened its doors in 1960, and Yamaha, along with a rival Japanese company—K. Kawai—soon came to dominate the U.S. piano market.

Yamaha made two and one-half times as many pianos as Wurlitzer, America's largest manufacturer. Over fifteen years ago Story and Clark Piano Company, a highly respected U.S. manufacturer, contracted with Yamaha to make Story and Clark grand pianos. About the same time Baldwin Piano and Organ Company, another U.S. manufacturer, made a similar agreement with Kawai.

Yamaha produced a high-quality piano. Employing low-cost but highly efficient mass-production methods and utilizing patents acquired from Beckstein, long recognized as a top European piano maker, Yamaha gained worldwide prominence. Numerous universities, churches, and individuals endorsed the Yamaha piano; it was purchased by such leading musical educational institutions as the Toronto Conservatory of Music, Oberlin College, and the University of North Carolina.

Bearden's sales increases during the three years it had the franchise traced directly to the Yamaha line, although occasionally it "special ordered" a Starck or a Krakauer. Previously specializing in *rebuilt* grands, the Yamaha dealership now allowed Bearden's to offer a complete line of *new* grands, opening up new opportunities to sell to restaurants, night clubs, schools, and churches. Bearden's continued to rebuild pianos but reduced its emphasis on this phase of the business. Yamaha's grand pianos were similar to other makes, but its vertical pianos were available in a variety of styles for which preferences existed in the American market: Early American, French Provincial, Italian Provincial, European, Contemporary, and Traditional.

Bearden's concentrated its promotion on the Yamaha products, advertising in local newspapers, neighborhood publications, high school annuals, and telephone directory "Yellow Pages." It also set up a Yamaha exhibit at Atlanta's Southeastern Fair, generating high interest and resulting in numerous inquiries and sales. Personal selling was aided by Yamaha sales brochures and pamphlets.

Yamaha suggested retail prices for all models (Exhibit 1). Bearden's margin averaged 45 percent. James Bearden believed that on a quality-for-the-money basis Yamaha was the best piano on the market. It was priced under all competitors except Kawai, which mirrored Yamaha's retail prices but allowed dealers a higher margin averaging about 51 percent.

In Atlanta, Yamaha dealers had exclusive community distribution but

EXHIBIT 1 · Retail Price Ranges for Yamaha and Similar Makes

	MAKE	SIZE	PRICE RANGE
Grands	Yamaha	5'1"–9'6"	$1,695–$ 6,195
	Chickering	5'1"–5'8"	2,275– 2,890
	Knabe	5'1"–9'	2,300– 6,550
	Steinway	5'1"–8'11"	3,325– 7,500
	Baldwin	5'2"–9'	3,018– 7,700
	Bechstein	5'6"–8'9"	5,300– 12,000
	Bosendorfer	5'–9'6"	5,600– 13,800
	Kawai	5'1"–9'2"	1,695– 6,195
Verticals	Yamaha	41–48"	$ 695–$ 995
	Chickering	40"	1,175– 1,480
	Knight	41–45"	1,495– 1,595
	Bechstein	45–50"	2,800– 3,400
	Steinway	40–46½"	1,495– 1,895
	Everett	41–45"	1,015– 1,170
	Kawai	41–49"	650– 995

not exclusive metropolitan-area distribution. Initially, Yamaha had three Atlanta dealers: Bearden's handled the line exclusively in Decatur; Maddox Music Mart sold in southwest Atlanta; and Waggoner Music, Inc., covered northwest Atlanta (Marietta).

Two matters caused friction to develop between Bearden's and Yamaha. The first was that Bearden's management did not want to emphasize organs as suggested by Yamaha (only two were ever ordered). The second was that James Bearden refused to sponsor and conduct a music course recommended by Yamaha for all its American dealers; he believed that the initial cost of setting up the course, approximately $2,800, was too high (Exhibit 2) and that Yamaha's "typical" operating budget was unrealistic because it was difficult to enroll as many as 300 students and even more difficult to hire qualified teachers, particularly at the rates suggested by Yamaha (Exhibit 3).

Yamaha's U.S. general sales manager contacted James Bearden and asked that he begin to offer the music course. Bearden refused. Four months later Yamaha's district sales manager visited Bearden and strongly suggested that he start the music course or face losing the dealership. Again Bearden refused, and two months later the association was terminated.

The dealership was moved to the Atlanta Piano Company, which had also recently acquired Maddox Music Mart, the Yamaha dealer in southwest Atlanta. Atlanta Piano planned to open two suburban stores in northwest Atlanta early the next year and agreed with Yamaha to offer the music course at all three locations. At about the same time the other Yamaha dealer in Atlanta, Waggoner Music Company, lost its dealership for selling to an out-of-state customer, a violation of its dealership agreement.

EXHIBIT 2 · Yamaha Music Course Specifications—Basic Course*

Equipment:	
Ten DS/49 Yamaha reed organs	$90.00 each
Kit of music materials	5.55
Rhythm instrument set	
1 small drum and beater	
1 tambourine, 7″ diameter	
1 set orchestra bells	
(glockenspiel with mallets)	
3 sets sleigh bells	
1 5″ triangle and beater	
1 wood block and beater	
2 castanets	
1 rhythmica	37.00
One magnet board (resembles	
blackboard with music notes)	12.50
Attendance record forms	.02 each
Student registration cards	.02 each
Mailing brochures (optional)	.04 each
Teacher:	
Qualifications	
Age 23–26	
College degree required	
Piano and singing talents	
Good worker with children	
References required	
Passing a Yamaha music test	
Four training seminars required	$300 cost to dealer

*Preschool children—ages four to six.

EXHIBIT 3 · Typical Operating Budget—Basic Music Course

Tuition received (300 @ $10 per month)		$3,000
Reserve for teaching (three teachers)	$1,200	
Royalty to Yamaha (10%)	300	
Reserve for church facility rental, if used	600	
	$2,100	
Remainder for administration and profit		900
Profit on material sales, average per month		50
Total average profit per month		$ 950

Subsequently, Bearden's found itself largely confined to the used piano business, since its stock of Starck and Krakauer pianos had also dwindled to nothing. Painfully aware of the seriousness of the situation, James Bearden explored the possibility of building up the offerings of Starck or Krakauer pianos, or of adding the Everett, Knight, or Kawai lines as possible replacements. Of these, the Kawai line seemed the best choice because it compared favorably with Yamaha in product offering, quality, and price. However, Kawai pianos could only be obtained through another dealer, a downtown Atlanta firm. This firm, headed by a personal friend of James Bearden, wanted a 5 percent commission on each unit ordered through it. But, since Kawai allowed a slightly higher dealer margin than Yamaha, Bearden was inclined to take on the line.

Questions

1. Was Yamaha justified in taking away Bearden's dealership? Why?
2. Should James Bearden have taken on a new line?

4–3

PALMER CORPORATION

Entering a new market

Palmer Corporation had headquarters and main manufacturing facilities at Beaver Falls, Pennsylvania. It made a complete line of gear-type power transmission equipment, automatic valve controls, linear actuators, and fluid mixers. The company custom built most of its products to users' specifications and manufactured for stock only a few low-priced items, such as replacement parts. Total yearly sales amounted to $54 million. During a ten-year expansion of the pulp and paper industry, the Palmer Corporation introduced a product line for sale to that industry; three years later management concluded that sales of this product line (fluid mixers) were not up to expectations.

All Palmer's product lines were marketed through a technically oriented sales organization. It consisted of twenty-four company salespersons working out of thirteen metropolitan sales offices, fifty-two manufacturers' agents using 127 salespersons to cover fifty-eight sales districts, and thirty-seven manufacturers' agents in thirty-one foreign countries. All the company's own sales personnel had either engineering degrees or a minimum of ten years' experience in the mechanical power transmission area. Prior to assigning them to the field, the home office required that each salesperson spend eighteen to twenty-four months as an inside sales engineer. This period of training stressed the acquisition of extensive product knowledge, and trainees were rotated through all corporate departments. The field salesperson's duties involved application, preliminary design, and, in some instances, product servicing.

THE MARKET

The pulp and paper industry was in the midst of a ten-year expansion. Industry capacity, however, had historically exceeded actual production by about 10

72

percent. The buildup of industry capacity was along three main lines: (1) "pure" expansion required to keep pace with rising pulp and paper demand; (2) modernization involving new technology, making existing machinery and equipment obsolete; and (3) replacement of worn-out equipment. An estimated 51 percent of predicted expenditures would be for "pure" expansion and 49 percent for modernization and replacement. Pulp and paper industry expenditures on gear-type products, such as fluid mixers, were forecast at roughly $10 million annually.

Personal relationships pervaded the pulp and paper industry, maintained and encouraged through trade journals, magazines, conventions, trade meetings, and joint committees and the "open-plant" policy of most mills. Information about a particular mill's solution of a problem quickly spread to other mills and was soon accepted as industry practice. Because of the open-plant policy, few developments, processes, or operating techniques remained trade secrets for long. This phenomenon carried over into selection and use of capital equipment—all industry members soon learned of specific instances involving a product's success or failure.

Zippy, Palmer's main competition, introduced its fluid mixers to the pulp and paper industry a decade earlier. Prior to Zippy's entry, the industry regarded mixing as more of an art than a science. Mixing knowledge and skills acquired over time by one person in using horsepower, speed, and propeller diameter were passed on to his or her successor. The end results of mixing operations often were not predictable and in many cases were unsatisfactory. Through application of chemical engineering and fluid dynamics principles, Zippy achieved consistent and predictable results in most mixing applications; consequently, its product line gained industry-wide acceptance and a commanding lead over competitors entering the market later.

THE PRODUCT

A fluid mixer was basically an electric motor coupled to a mechanical speed reducer which, in turn, was attached to a shaft and an impeller. The mixer was mounted on a tank so that the shaft and the impeller extended into the fluid(s) or material(s) being mixed. From this basic arrangement it was possible to substitute other prime movers for the electric motor, incorporate special seals between the tank and the reducer section, extend shafts, and make the components of almost any metal from carbon steel to titanium. Modifications of the basic arrangement were the rule rather than the exception.

At the time of its market entry Palmer offered four basic mixer designs, more than any competitor. Palmer was also the only company to manufacture its own mechanical speed reducer; competitors purchased reducers from transmission manufacturers. Management believed that offering four designs and "in-house" manufacture of the speed reducer component were significant competitive advantages. Mixer prices ranged from $700 to $50,000. Although Zippy mixers enjoyed wide market acceptance, prices and quality of Palmer mixers compared favorably with all major competitors, including Zippy.

MARKET ENTRY

Basing its decision on detailed market information and forecasts, Palmer introduced its mixers to the pulp and paper industry. The company had previously operated on the periphery of this market through selling speed reducers and valve controls both to the mills and to the many manufacturers of original equipment for the pulp and paper industry. Although Palmer was "known" in the industry, management recognized that the mixers required a sales approach different from that of other company products. In other words, to sell effectively, Palmer sales personnel would need to understand not only pulp production and papermaking and mixing methods and techniques but customers' objectives in using particular mixing processes. This contrasted sharply with circumstances met in selling the other product lines where customers normally specified machine requirements, and Palmer's engineering department came up with needed designs.

Competing in the pulp and paper market, it was necessary to accumulate certain industry information, to have management assimilate it, and to teach it to field and inside sales personnel. Mel Melrose, who had twenty-five years' experience as a paper mill superintendent, was hired to assist in this effort. His first assignment was to develop a design manual to serve as a reference source in mixer sales. This manual detailed proper methods of sizing mixers for different applications and provided related information on pulp and paper production. Next, he assisted in modifying existing mixer designs to meet specialized conditions in the pulp and paper industry, his role being that of adviser to the design engineers. He then visited numerous U.S. pulp and paper mills and wrote detailed reports on the industry's current problems for perusal by Palmer management. Finally, he was appointed as a manufacturers' agent for Palmer's mixer sales in the southeastern United States.

THE SALES FORCE FOR MIXERS

Mike Thomas, vice president of sales, next analyzed the existing sales force with respect to (1) geographic areas that would require more selling emphasis and (2) salespersons and agents capable of selling the mixer line after additional training. Initially, five manufacturers' agents covering eight areas and sales personnel from two company offices were selected for special training. These agents and company offices fielded twenty-four salespersons in all, but only thirteen actually received the special training.

The special training period varied in length from one to two weeks, depending upon the salesperson's background. The training was conducted at the home office under the direction of L. Cobb, senior application engineer, who later was to manage inside sales. Trainees were expected to learn the technical advantages of the Palmer mixer line compared with competitors' lines, mixing techniques, equipment applications, and pricing methods.

On completion of training, the salespersons knew they were to handle routine sales only. Cobb was to handle all situations involving extensive equipment modifications or unusual applications. Inquiries directed to the home office were quoted on directly to customers, and copies were sent to the area sales personnel, who would then follow up on quotes, answer questions, and, hopefully, get the orders. All Palmer quotations carried a guarantee that the mixer would perform as described or would be replaced at no charge. Two major competitors, including Zippy, used similar guarantees.

ADVERTISING

An advertising campaign started soon after sales training was underway. Models of the mixers were displayed at trade shows and conventions. Advertisements appeared in trade journals and magazines, and an attempt was made to promote a "showcase job" to point up Palmer's installation and operational efficiency and its industry know-how. This was partially achieved through an early contract Palmer obtained to supply all of the mixer requirements of Neptune Soap, a large detergent manufacturer, which had just begun producing facial and toilet tissue. However, Neptune regarded its manufacturing process as confidential, and since it was new to the pulp and paper industry, little testimonial benefit accrued to Palmer.

Despite its efforts, Palmer did not reach its goal of 10 percent of the mixer sales to the pulp and paper industry. Only a few mixer inquiries emanating from within the pulp and paper industry came to Palmer, and Cobb had written sales personnel several times urging them to generate more inquiries. One possible reason for the disappointing results was that Palmer delivered in from fourteen to twenty-two weeks and competitors in eight to twelve weeks. However, both Thomas and Cobb agreed that delivery was critical only for replacement sales, since most new construction programs had lead times well within Palmer's delivery schedule.

Questions

1. Should Palmer have initially entered the pulp and paper market? Why?
2. What advantages did Palmer have over competitors? What were the competitors' advantages?
3. What steps should Palmer have taken to attain its goal of securing a 10 percent market share in sales of mixers to the pulp and paper industry?

4–4

THE ALLEN-BRADLEY COMPANY

Addition of new products

The Allen-Bradley Company of Milwaukee, Wisconsin, pioneered in making motor control devices for industrial use. Its products were distributed nationally through its own sales force and a network of electrical wholesale distributors. District sales managers reported directly to the president, who was responsible for marketing operations and the sales effort. Voting control of the corporation was held by a foundation set up by the founders; consequently, company policy had been to expand through retained earnings rather than outside financing. In its quest for new products the company emphasized research and development (R & D) and made no move to acquire competitors or firms producing complementary products. Recently, this resulted in two new products not related to established product lines but believed to have strong marketing possibilities.

The backbone of the company's business had always been the manufacture and sale of high-quality motor control devices. One of the two major product lines included control relays, contactors, switches, rheostats, motor control centers, push buttons, pilot control devices, and control units for high-voltage equipment, such as those used in factories and utility installations. The second major product line consisted of condensers, resistors, and related highly technical and scientific devices used by the electronic equipment manufacturing industry. Both product lines were marketed through the same sales organization.

Direct sales effort was of two types. One type was through a small but select group of electrical wholesale distributors, each selling Allen-Bradley products on an exclusive basis within a specified geographical area. Each distributor was required to carry a complete line of stock items at an inventory level determined by the Allen-Bradley Company.

The other type was through the company's own sales force of highly trained, well-paid mechanical and electrical engineers. They sought out new accounts, performed required engineering work, and determined the indicated product applications. Normally, the sales personnel saw to it that most stock items were ordered through distributors, but in certain cases customers were allowed to order directly from the factory.

Company selling strategy, in other words, was that the sales force should complement the selling efforts of distributors by ensuring correct engineering applications and making the missionary calls and contacts that distributors' sales personnel were unable to handle. Where customers were disenchanted with distributors, the company sales force provided an alternative source of Allen-Bradley products. Prices quoted to customers were identical regardless of whether orders were placed through distributors or directly with the company. The company did not compete on a price basis but strived to manufacture and sell the highest quality products and to provide the best delivery time and service available.

In introducing new products to the market, company practice varied. The sales force attempted to pull new additions to the line of motor control products through the marketing channel by bringing them to the attention of architects and design engineers (who wrote the specifications for electrical installations), contractors (who made these installations), and industrial users (who paid for them). For example, a modular motor control center was introduced at a luncheon meeting with the executive committee of the Chicago Electrical Contractors Association. In other instances, sales personnel closely coordinated efforts with distributors to introduce new products to industrial users. New additions to the line of condensers, resistors, and related products were introduced directly by the sales force to electronics manufacturers, computer makers, and firms producing advanced technical devices.

The R & D department had just completed work on two new products. The first was a machine for sifting powders or particles, which compared with other sifters was much less noisy and required less maintenance. Market research indicated that the individual in a prospective customer's organization who would give the final sanction to such a purchase would be a physicist, chemist, or other scientist in charge of a large laboratory, a type of contact with which the company had no experience. Such laboratories were found in pharmaceutical, chemical, and other scientifically oriented companies.

The second new development was a decorative architectural building tile which was easy to clean and withstood the extremes of weather as well as any competitive product. Market introduction of the tile presented a sales problem because it lacked the engineering nature of the established product lines and seemed inappropriate for marketing through the established distributive network. Furthermore, the sales force, because of its engineering orientation, did not seem appropriate for introducing or selling the tile.

Questions

1. Should Allen-Bradley have attempted to market either or both of these new products? If so, how?
2. What should have been Allen-Bradley's product objectives? Product policies?

5–1

KELLY'S SEEDS, INC.

Problems with discounting and seasonality

Kelly's Seeds, Inc., a family-owned gardening and hardware business, was managed by the founder's sons, Tom and Bill Kelly. The firm had two retail outlets in a small central Ohio town and a wholesale horticultural supply outlet. Kelly's had met increasing competitive pressure from discount chains, and the gardening business was highly seasonal. In an effort to soften the seasonality and to come out in a market niche not dominated by discounters, changes had been made in the product mix, but as fall approached, Tom and Bill were dreading the annual lull in business.

COMPANY OPERATIONS

The downtown store (see Exhibit 1), managed by Tom Kelly, had been in the same location for a half-century and retailed gardening supplies and hardware items. Two-thirds of its annual sales were made during the gardening season (late April through August). The store had four full-time employees but, during the busy season, three part-timers helped handle the store traffic. Ten years ago, a line of fireplace equipment was added, primarily because no other retailers in town carried anything similar. Most sales in this line occurred between November and February. In the past few years several local retailers had added fireplace equipment lines and the market was saturated, although one item—gas logs—was still profitable.

The outlying Garden Center (see Exhibit 2), operated by Bill Kelly, was a different type of store. It featured a retail greenhouse, a complete nursery selection, a lawn and patio furniture department, and a Christmas shop/gift shop. The Garden Center did not carry hardware.

EXHIBIT 1 · Kelly's Downtown

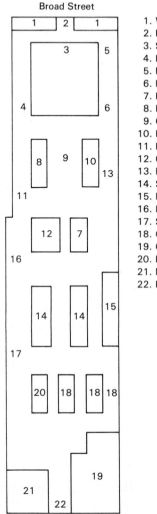

One inch equals thirty feet.

Products common to both stores were fertilizer, seeds, vegetable and flowering plants, fireplace equipment, and gardening tools. As fall approached, management considered adding a Christmas section at the downtown store—to increase "dead-season" business there. To do this, some of the downtown merchandise would be moved, warehoused, and enough Christmas merchandise purchased to stock the display. Considerable shifting of stock between downtown and the Garden Center occurred, so it would not be necessary to double the inventory of Christmas items.

The wholesale business, which accounted for 20 percent of company sales volume, operated out of the downtown store. Tom Kelly said that the primary reason for the wholesale business was to get better prices from suppliers for the two retail outlets. Tom Kelly did the buying for all three of the firm's operations. Items wholesaled included Chevron chemicals, Hudson sprayers, Wolfolk chemicals, Northrup-King seeds, W. R. Grace chemicals, Hydeberg bird feeders, Premier peat moss, Rapid-Grow fertilizer, Miracle-Gro fertilizer, and grass seed. The wholesale business also belonged to a buying cooperative, which enabled it to purchase hardware items at close-to-jobber prices.

The customers of the wholesale business included other area retail stores, some in direct competition with Kelly's retail outlets. The Kellys believed they transacted about 35 percent of the area's independent retail business. No estimate was available for garden-related sales of the discount/department stores.

Kelly advertising appeared in local newspapers and gardening magazines, and on local radio stations. Ad copy was oriented toward seasonal demand, and complimentary calendars were used for promotion. Occasional joint promotions were run with suppliers, and there were also end-of-season promotions and "clearances."

Retail markups varied with the product line. Hardware markup ranged from 33 percent to 40 percent, but distributors sometimes offered special deals which increased the markup. But for power equipment, the highest markup a retailer offered on a standard item was 25 percent, and usually discounters pushed this figure down ever further. Garden items, plants, shrubs, seeds, and the like carried markups as high as 80 percent (slow movers) and as low as $12\frac{1}{2}$ percent (fast movers).

COMPETITIVE ENVIRONMENT

The local market area was highly competitive. To illustrate, the local Toro distributorship (Toro was the power-equipment industry leader in quality) changed ownership three times in fifteen years. Entry of the discounters into the market resulted in low margins in power equipment retailing. The discounters promoted name-brand power tools as loss leaders to increase traffic.

Many manufacturers used dual distribution systems. They sold both to discounters, who sold at low markups, and to full-service retailers, who applied higher markups, and provided some product or service. Many consumers opted for the discounter distribution system and traditional retailers lost market share.

Traditional retailers were increasingly called upon to provide after-sale service (parts and repair) to the discounters' customers. Three local discounters sold Toro weed-eaters at a price only slightly above what Kelly's

EXHIBIT 2 · Kelly's Garden Center

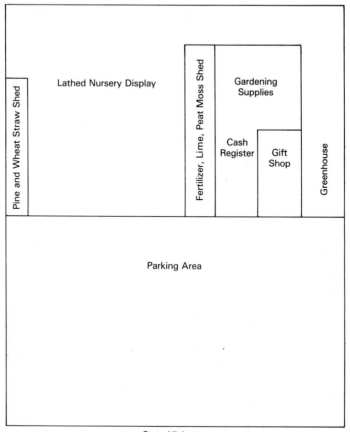

One inch equals sixty feet.

paid the distributor. Discounters' customers brought their weed-eaters to Kelly's for replacement strings and other parts, as the discounters did not stock these items. Markups on Toro parts were fairly high percentagewise, but these small-ticket items required much of the sales clerks' time and added little to Kelly's "bottom line."

There was also strong price competition in the premium fertilizer market. Scotts, a manufacturer of high-quality fertilizer which formerly catered to the "Cadillac trade," had recently begun selling to discounters. For years Kelly's and other full-service retailers pushed Scotts' complete program of lawn care, and, in return, received a 33 percent markup.

Recently, the discounters promoted Scotts as a loss leader/traffic builder and priced at 8 percent above Kelly's cost.

   Other characteristics regarding the competitive environment in the local gardening market were reported in a study at a nearby university:

1. In five years, the percentage of households with home gardens rose from 17 percent to 43 percent.
2. Fastest growth is in the sales of bedding plants, nursery products, and ornamental shrubs.
3. Getting enough good quality nursery stock to sell is the biggest problem.
4. The houseplant market is the fastest growing market.
5. Mass merchandisers had the most impact on the local ornamentals market. Ten years ago there were five fairly significant sales yards; now there is one. Mass merchandisers increased the dollar sales of nursery products by price competition, and at the same time made the market more concentrated. K-Mart usually got the lowest wholesale price and charged the lowest retail price. The quality of plants sold was comparable to that of other nurseries for the first two weeks. Then, because of inadequate maintenance, quality suffered.
6. Consumers believed Kelly's offered much better personal service, and the expertise of the salesperson had a tremendous impact on sales.
7. The best way to compete with the mass merchandisers is to imitate them. A chain of garden centers in Cincinnati has experienced tremendous growth through the use of loss leaders, weekend specials, and a large advertising budget.

The owner of Classic Nursery, a competitor of Kelly's, said:

Tom and Bill Kelly are excellent businessmen. They have certain advantages over their competitors because their business is the oldest in town and they enjoy much repeat business. We buy Ortho products from them wholesale and Bill does a good job servicing us. However, this is a highly transient town; there is a 20 percent turnover in population annually. New businesses can gain significant market share from newcomers who aren't loyal to Kelly's. The Garden Center, a Kelly operation, is "sandwiched" between Gold Circle and K-Mart, both of which have large garden departments and often use gardening items as loss leaders/traffic builders. These discounters advertise nursery items at low prices and make profits by increasing the markup on point-of-purchase items. Gold Circle takes business from both K-Mart and the Garden Center.

The total product is the sum of the physical product and the psychological product. The future for small businesses is to provide services, and Kelly's doesn't do that. Kelly's will have to sell high-quality merchandise so that it is not in competition with K-Mart and Gold Circle. We at Classic Nursery do not sell a shrub, we sell a beautiful setting for someone's home. We provide a complete service for the homeowner through our retail, lawn maintenance, and landscaping department.

Joe Costyn, a former Kelly's employee and a graduate horticulturist, managed the garden center at the local K-Mart. This garden center was open year round and sold a full line of gardening products. It was operated as a profit center with the local store purchasing its stock independent of other K-Marts. Costyn's philosophy was that price was the major determinant in the purchase decision for gardening supplies. He varied the markup of items in the department by article, time of year, and number in stock. He rarely priced items at cost and his department was profitable. Of Kelly's, he said:

> To many people, Kelly's is a synonym for high price. Sure people who come here are looking for a low price, but often I hear that Kelly's has too high a price. Overall quality of plants and hardgoods at K-Mart is equal to that of Kelly's but Kelly's indoor plants are probably higher quality. Kelly's serves a different clientele and has a wider variety in some areas, though these areas are so specialized that they are not profitable for K-Mart.

Mr. Norris, the garden center manager at Gold Circle, another discounter, described the local market as highly competitive. His philosophy was that the right items plus the right price equal a high profit. He viewed K-Mart as the primary competition and claimed Gold Circle was the area's low price leader. He reported that his first year had been "very profitable" and that corporate headquarters had been pleased with the reception and the small number of markdowns. He viewed his competitive advantages as low prices, high inventory turnover which insured freshness of plants, and economies of scale in purchasing and advertising. Gold Circle's strategy was to have a spring and a minifall season and to convert the space to toy sales for Christmas. Mr. Norris believed Gold Circle operated on a lower markup than Kelly's to increase inventory turns. The markups at Gold Circle were determined by centralized buyers operating out of corporate headquarters in a midwestern city.

KELLY'S RESPONSE

Tom and Bill Kelly disliked the "merchandising" techniques used by other retailers. They believed in having "honest markups" on all items stocked. They were convinced that discounters comparison-priced a few branded items, then sold inferior house brands at high markups.

They knew that something would have to be done if they were to survive. Tom Kelly outlined the alternatives as he saw them:

1. Meet K-Mart's prices, increase traffic, make no profit.
2. Price at regular markups, lose traffic, earn a normal per-unit profit.
3. Price at 10 to 20 percent markup, lose traffic, lose per-unit profit.
4. Carry only high-quality brands whose makers refuse to have them in discount outlets.

Tom Kelly believed also that the downtown store should be moved. He previously had considered locating on the town's east side, but that area seemed unpromising because of its many vacant retail stores. The contiguous adjacent counties on the east were all losing population, those to the west were gaining. The firm had also considered expansion to the Columbus, Canton, or Akron area if the local situation didn't improve soon.

Questions

1. Evaluate the alternatives outlined by Tom Kelly.
2. What other alternatives should have been considered?
3. How would you have gone about solving Kelly's problem(s)?

5–2

QUIK-THRIFT FOOD STORES, INC.

Expansion of a retail chain

Mr. Belcher, co-owner of Quik-Thrift Food Stores, was seeking ways to increase sales and profits of the company's newest and largest store. Located in Hilliard, Florida, it was the most recently opened of four stores operated by the company in the southeast Georgia–northeast Florida area.

The Hilliard store represented the largest investment Quik-Thrift had ever made. A market survey had indicated that the store would be profitable, but sales were much below the desired breakeven point, while operating expenses and inventory shortages were higher than expected.

COMPANY BACKGROUND

Mr. Belcher, a University of Georgia graduate, started his career as a store manager for Kroger. At Kroger he met Tom Sanders who was a meat market supervisor. Belcher and Sanders became dissatisfied with their jobs at Kroger and began looking for a store to purchase.

They pooled resources and made a down payment on a small supermarket in Smyrna, Georgia. With Belcher running the grocery operations and Sanders butchering the meat, the store's sales doubled in a year. Long operating hours, combined with Smyrna's rapid growth and the owners' philosophy of fast, friendly service, generated sufficient profit to buy a second store—this one in Austell, Georgia.

The Austell store also was profitable, and further expansion followed. Twelve years after the founding, the company operated five small supermarkets (7,000 to 9,000 square feet) and nine convenience stores (2,000 to 3,000 square feet). The Quik-Thrift stores had spread through metropolitan Atlanta (see Exhibit 1).

Mr. Belcher and Mr. Sanders, no longer working in the stores, managed the total operation from a small office in Smyrna. The office staff included a full-time secretary and seven part-timers handling various administrative functions. Two store supervisors oversaw daily operations.

INDUSTRY

The U.S. supermarket industry had limited growth prospects. U.S. population growth had averaged less than 1 percent, but certain regions (South Atlantic, West South Central, Mountain, and Pacific) had higher growth rates. Companies with operations in these regions had better expansion opportunities than their counterparts elsewhere. Grocery store sales as a percentage of disposable income had been declining. In addition, the growing number of one- and two-person households were inclined to dine out more than traditional family units.

Individual supermarket companies sought growth through increased market share or through expanded sales bases. Increased market share was most often accomplished by opening new units, but rising real estate and financing costs had made this alternative more expensive. Increased market share through increased utilization of existing facilities was both difficult and costly—changes in pricing and/or service strategies were quickly matched by competitors, causing sales to stabilize while margins fell. Some supermarket operators expanded their offerings of nonfoods, especially drugs and cosmetics; the emphasis on opening combination food–drug stores, or superstores, in expansion programs reflected this trend.

THE COMPANY'S SOUTHWARD MOVE

Quik-Thrift found its internal growth and expansion opportunities in the Atlanta area limited by the intense competition. Nevertheless, the company had been prosperous from the start and had built up substantial cash reserves. At this time Mr. Belcher was alerted to what seemed an extremely promising opportunity. The U.S. Defense Department confirmed Kings Bay, located in Georgia's southeast corner, as the site for its Trident Submarine Base. As a native of Kings Bay, Mr. Belcher visualized tremendous growth for the area.

A front-page article in the *Atlanta Constitution* discussed the impact that the Trident Submarine Base would have on southeast Georgia and northeast Florida. The submarine base would cost $1.5 billion for construction, and that much again for related off-base projects. An official was quoted as saying, "I think you'd have to say the Trident project is analogous to the space center at Cape Canaveral. It's just mind boggling to think how it will

EXHIBIT 1 · Quik-Thrift Store Locations

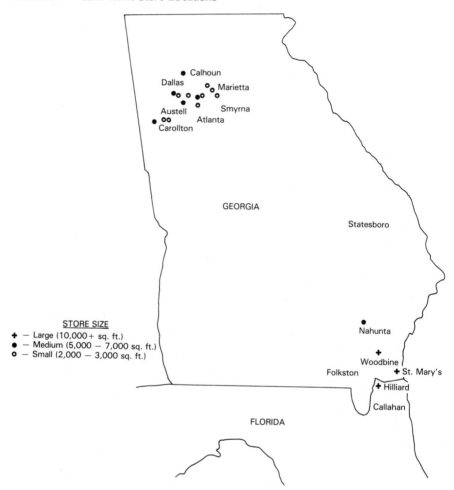

change this whole region." In addition, a significant spillover of increased economic activity was anticipated for Brantley, Charlton, Glynn, and Ware counties in Georgia and Nassau and Duval (Jacksonville) counties in Florida.

The company soon acquired a medium-sized supermarket in St. Mary's, Georgia (see Exhibit 1). It was ideally situated to capitalize on the expected business boom. The store moved up from initial weekly sales of $18,000 to $30,000 in less than a year. In an effort to discourage competition, the company announced plans to expand the store from the current 10,000 square feet to 15,000 square feet. The expansion was completed by the end of 1980 (at a cost of $200,000), and the expanded store reached average weekly sales of $60,000 in January 1981.

The company was also acquiring or opening stores in the close-by towns of Nahunta and Woodbine, Georgia. Nahunta was not expected to feel much impact from the naval base, but Belcher and Sanders felt that their acquisition of a modern 7,500-square-foot store ($250,000 cost) was justified. It was the only supermarket in town, and when acquired had weekly sales of $25,000. Under Belcher and Sanders, the Nahunta store reached weekly sales of $35,000 within a year. Woodbine had been growing and the naval base was expected to stimulate growth further—because Woodbine had no existing supermarket, Quik-Thrift built a 10,000-square-foot store whose weekly sales climbed to $35,000 the first year.

The three southeast Georgia stores were supplied by a Statesboro, Georgia, wholesaler. Each used the name "Foodliner." Operations of the three stores were closely monitored by a newly hired supervisor.

THE HILLIARD STORE

The need for a supermarket in Hilliard, Florida, first was articulated by an area newspaper—the *Nassau County Record*. In a front-page article, the paper cited the expected population increase to come from the nearby naval base, and the fact that the nearest supermarket was twelve miles away in Callahan, Florida. The paper said that a local supermarket would cause residents to shop in Hilliard and would attract additional residents.

Seeing this article, Belcher and Sanders decided the situation was "worth a look." After looking over the area personally, however, they were not convinced that Hilliard could support a supermarket. Nevertheless, they hired a marketing research firm to consider the feasibility of locating a supermarket in Hilliard. (See Exhibits 2 and 3 for the findings on trade area characteristics and characteristics of competition.)

The research firm also reported that the Hilliard residents made major grocery purchases at two supermarkets—Winn Dixie in Callahan, Florida, and Big J in Folkston, Georgia. It was believed that most of the supermarket trade was going to Callahan due to the lower sales tax in Florida and because the Callahan Winn Dixie had sales greater than its area's local potential.

The researchers concluded:

> It is our recommendation that a new supermarket of a size no greater than 16,000 sq. ft. overall be considered for the site in Hilliard, Florida. This unit should contain only conventional departments, with the possible exception of a bakery. First year average weekly sales should be $61,709 for a 16,000 sq. ft. store.

Based on this report, Belcher and Sanders decided that a new store in Hilliard would earn an adequate return on the investment. They decided to build a building, sell it to an outside investor, and lease it back. Inventory and equipment would be company owned.

EXHIBIT 2 · Trade Area Characteristics

LOCATION: Hilliard, Florida

GEOGRAPHIC LOCATION: Hilliard, Florida, is located in Nassau County approximately 11 miles northwest of Callahan, Florida, and 16 miles northwest of the Duval County (Jacksonville city limits) line. This city is approximately 135 miles from Statesboro, the distribution center.

TRADE AREA BOUNDARIES: The trade area extends 8.6 miles north, 5.0 miles south, 13.0 miles east, and 7.0 miles west. The trade area was determined to the north and west by the St. Mary's River and the state line. To the south and east, the trade area was determined by the use of Suelflow's Theory of Market Potential (traffic counts) and the analyst's judgment.

ECONOMIC AND DEMOGRAPHIC CHARACTERISTICS: The following is a list of some of the economic and demographic characteristics of the area based on the Census of Population:

	NASSAU COUNTY	FLORIDA
Persons per occupied housing unit	3.4	3.0
% homes owner occupied	76.6	68.6
Average income for families and unrelated individuals	$7,764	$10,120
% families income above $15,000	10.0	16.8
% families income below poverty level	15.7	12.7

POPULATION	1960	1970	1980	1985 (ESTIMATED)
Given year	3,053	4,136	6,126	7,166
Change				
Actual		1,083	1,990	1,040
%		35.5	48.1	17.0

Belcher and Sanders were contacted by the owner and operator of a successful carpet store in Hilliard. He was excited about the proposed supermarket for Hilliard and was eager to handle its financing and construction. After a check of this individual's financial capabilities, Belcher and Sanders decided he was the "right" investor.

The investor envisioned a beautiful, spacious store loaded with all modern "niceties." His plans called for a 19,000-square-foot store equipped with an 18-foot ceiling, automatic doors, numerous light fixtures, an $18,000 sprinkler system, and a massive marquee.

The Quik-Thrift owners believed this was "too much store" for a small country town. They did not like the plan for an extra 3,000 square feet over the recommended 16,000 square feet. But because the investor agreed to set the lease payments at the level of a 16,000-square-foot store, Belcher and Sanders agreed, and shortly thereafter construction began.

Belcher and Sanders wanted the store completed and open for business soon so cash inflows could begin offsetting their needed investment of $500,000

EXHIBIT 3 · Trade Area Potential

LOCATION: Hilliard, Florida

PCW: The trade area's average PCW (per capita weekly) expenditure for food at home is $14.76. This amount was determined by using the site county (Nassau) and the four contiguous counties and adjusting by income level and family size for the site county.

The following table shows the counties and PCW used:

COUNTY	CURRENT PCW
NASSAU, FLORIDA	$15.83
Baker, Florida	11.21
Duval, Florida	16.35
Camden, Georgia	16.57
Charlton, Georgia	21.84
Five-county average	$16.36

POTENTIAL: The trade area's average weekly food dollar potential is $90,420 (Population × PCW = Potential). The trade area's average FLOAT is 100.0% (FLOAT is the percent of the potential within an area that is not captured by the stores identified). While the area has a food dollar potential, there is no supermarket in the defined trade area to capture any of this potential. Therefore, the available food dollars are being spent outside the defined trade area. There are some convenience stores in the trade area, and they appear to have a higher than average volume for that type store.

in inventory and equipment. Belcher had reduced the inventories of the company's other stores by $150,000, but launching the Hilliard operation was straining working capital.

As the store neared completion, Mr. Belcher turned to hiring personnel. Seeking a manager with chain store experience, he hired a former Winn Dixie assistant store manager. Because an experienced meat department manager was important, Mr. Belcher transferred his best meat manager from north Georgia. The produce manager also was transferred from north Georgia. Belcher anticipated the need for thirty-five additional employees—stock clerks, bag boys, cashiers, department assistants, bookkeepers, and delicatessen helpers. With the exception of the bookkeeper, young and inexperienced help from Hilliard were hired to fill these jobs.

The grand opening finally came. Specials were advertised, and numerous activities were scheduled during the three-week grand opening. Sales climbed from $59,000 the first week to $64,000 the second week to $70,000 during the final week. Both owners were elated.

PROBLEMS

The joy was short-lived, however, as problems soon developed. The store manager was overwhelmed with training and supervising the store's many inexperienced workers. Productivity, store atmosphere, and customer service deteriorated. Sales plummeted to $50,000 in the tenth week. Finally, the store's first quarterly operating statement showed a $10,000 inventory shortage.

Belcher fired the manager and promoted the assistant manager. The new manager was an efficient, conscientious worker, but he was only 24 years old and had not quite four months of managerial experience. He had difficulty "taking control," and the situation worsened. The meat market manager, upset by the "disorganization" and lack of leadership, accused the cashiers and bag boys of being unfriendly to customers, "goofing off" at night, and giving "sweetheart discounts" to friends and relatives.

As the store approached its sixth month of operation, sales leveled off to $45,000 per week. The latest physical inventory revealed $5,000 of inventory missing, and pushed the total inventory shortage above $30,000. Energy costs for refrigeration, lighting, air conditioning, and store equipment use were above average at $9,000 per month. Wages, as a percent of sales, were at 12 percent; the company's other stores operated at 9 percent.

STORE POLICIES

Advertising for the Hilliard store was through circulars, newspapers, and road signs in front of the store. A two-page ad was run in the *Nassau County Record* (circulation 5,500) once a week. Those residents in the Hilliard trading area not subscribing to the *Record* received circulars containing the ad. A pair of road signs displayed the week's most attractive specials. Combined cost of the newspaper and circular advertising was $750 weekly.

The format of the ad was similar to Winn Dixie's with the standard department specials and major loss leaders heading the ad. Also patterned after Winn Dixie, the ad featured several coupons for use with $7.50 orders to obtain substantial savings.

Prior to the Hilliard store's opening, the Callahan Winn Dixie had a near monopoly. After a price check of major items, Belcher concluded that the Winn Dixie was using an above-average markup (24%). He concluded that the Hilliard store could afford to undercut Winn Dixie slightly, but anticipated that Winn Dixie would match prices if this move posed a serious threat.

The Hilliard store had not used special sales promotion programs, but Belcher believed one was needed. He had two alternatives under consideration—the Instant Bonus promotion and the Jackpot promotion. Quik-Thrift had experience with both plans—its south Georgia stores were using the Jackpot promotion, and its Smyrna store the Instant Bonus promotion.

The Instant Bonus promotion was designed to reward the customer for purchases. Under the Instant Bonus plan, a customer would receive one coupon, physically similar to a postage stamp, for every dollar spent at the store. The customer could receive additional coupons by buying specially designated items. The bonus would be either five, ten, or twenty extra coupons. If a customer bought $20 worth of groceries, including two items with stickers indicating five bonus coupons, a total of 20 + (2 × 5) = 30 coupons would be received.

To benefit from the coupons, the customer had to affix them to an Instant Bonus certificate. Once the customer had filled the certificate with its limit of 30 coupons, the certificate could be used to purchase one of six featured grocery items at an extremely low price. The six featured items were popular items and were changed weekly, markdowns on each ranging from 70¢ to $1.00. For example, a dozen large eggs (regular price, 89¢) could be purchased for 2¢ with a filled certificate. For the Hilliard store, total cost of the Instant Bonus promotion was estimated at $500 per week. From past experience, Belcher and Sanders predicted an Instant Bonus promotion would increase sales by 15 to 20 percent.

The Jackpot promotion was less complicated and cheaper, but less effective. With every purchase of $5 or more, the customer was given half of a card with a number on it; the store kept the other half. At the end of the week, a number was drawn from that week's collection of cards. The winning number was posted, and the person holding that number was given one week to claim a $100 prize. The Jackpot promotion was popular the first few months after the St. Mary's store opened, but thereafter customer interest declined steadily.

Questions

1. Given the negative factors affecting the grocery industry, how do you account for the relative success of Quik-Thrift?
2. What caused the Hilliard store's problems?
3. What actions should have been taken by management?

5–3

DRUG-X CORPORATION

Problems in a retail cooperative

Jane Tompkins, president, Drug-X Corporation, faced problem situations involving Drug-X's brand of ice cream, its advertising program, and its product mix.

DRUG-X CORPORATION

Drug-X was a wholesale drug distributor owned by member retail druggists who were also Drug-X's stockholders. It was organized twenty-five years ago to help small, independent drug stores compete with larger stores and chain stores. Drug-X members operated neighborhood drug stores and prided themselves on having an interest in their customers. Drug-X retailers offered services that distinguished them from most competitors. For instance, they offered free delivery and charge accounts.

Drug-X now had over 150 member stores and showed a substantial profit on its over $21 million in sales. Member stores bought from Drug-X at prices 10 percent under those of regular drug wholesalers. Deliveries to Drug-X stores were made three times a week. It was customary in the wholesale drug business for customers to place frequent orders, many of them for very small quantities.

Drug-X had four salespersons calling on member stores. Most orders, however, came in by telephone, but salespeople helped store owners get ready for special sales and seasonal promotions. Salespeople were paid salaries and received certain monetary incentives from manufacturers.

Drug-X advertised weekly in local newspapers. Generally, full-page ads featuring specially priced items were used. Drug-X members could participate in the advertising program by paying $50 a month. This entitled them to publicity material, such as shelf markers for "Advertised Specials," and window posters for attracting the attention of passersby. However, almost half of Drug-X's members did not participate in the advertising program.

Most items carried by Drug-X stores were those traditionally handled by retail drug outlets. They stocked a full line of prescription items and a wide assortment of nonprescription products, such as cold tablets, cough syrups, and so on. Also stocked were beauty aids from manufacturers such as Clairol, Toni, and Pond's. Drug-X members were free to buy merchandise from other wholesalers or from national producers (many of the stores bought Revlon products from the manufacturer's sales force). Drug-X did not stock toys or hobby items, although most of its members carried these items.

Drug-X carried only items that it could sell for less than "regular wholesale prices." For example, member stores used to buy cigarettes from a tobacco wholesaler, but Drug-X developed an agreement to buy cigarettes in quantities from the same wholesaler and to sell them at lower prices to its members.

Three people did the buying for Drug-X: the two sales managers and the advertising department head. They knew their lines, and were individually responsible for buying products from specified manufacturers. Successful buying meant knowing when to buy, when to reorder, and how much to buy. Many manufacturers offered "deals" for buying a certain quantity of the manufacturers' products. Deals might involve receiving a certain number of the items free or a free unrelated item that could be sold in the store (or taken home by the store owner). Many "deals" involved shipping the gift item with the merchandise; others, because of size or nondurability, were sent to the dealer after the special purchase was made. The key was to anticipate demand accurately. Deals were generally good buys for retailers, and Drug-X encouraged its members to accept them.

PURCHASING ISSUES

The three buyers did not agree on purchasing strategy. The sales managers generally stuck to name brand items—proven sellers that offered little risk. The other buyer, however, used a different approach. Before joining Drug-X he had been with a large drug store chain, and knew that many chain drug stores were practically department stores in that they carried clothing, cooking utensils, hardware items, gardening supplies, and more. For the most part, these items were not branded products, yet the buyer believed these items could attract customers to Drug-X stores through the low prices at which they could be sold. Some of Drug-X's managers, as well as many Drug-X members, store owners, disliked this approach. Although there was a generous markup on these goods, they were "risky" because of difficulty in estimating demand. In spite of the fact that many stores did not carry these specials, they were still purchased and some of each week's newspaper ad was devoted to promoting the "item of the week."

ICE CREAM PROBLEMS

Three years ago Drug-X stopped selling its own brand of ice cream, the "Topmost" brand. The ice cream operation had employed twenty people, six of them directly involved in making the ice cream. Topmost ice cream had been sold only in Drug-X stores. It was a premium ice cream sold at a lower price than comparable ice creams. It was made with milk containing 40 percent pure cream and contained granulated sugar to give Topmost a texture like homemade ice cream. Topmost also had an uncommon package, a round container with an easy-reseal feature.

Although ice cream sales were substantial, the main reason Drug-X stopped ice cream production was that it did not have modern packaging equipment. Each container of the product was packaged by hand. As the ice cream came out of the machine, a second worker would place the lid on the container, and a third would place the cartons in a shipping bag. If modern machinery had been used, only one person would have been needed (to place the cartons into sacks). Instead of buying the new equipment, management found a major ice cream producer who would make Topmost ice cream and sell it to Drug-X at a sizable savings. The product came in cartons bearing the Topmost and Drug-X names which were transferred to Drug-X for delivery to retailers. However, product quality suffered, as the producer did not use fresh milk, using instead imported frozen processed milk with a lower cream content than had been in the original product. Nor did this producer use granulated sugar, since liquid sweeteners were more easily used in automatic equipment. Last, the product no longer came in round containers— only rectangular packages with the "easy open tab" were used in the packaging machine.

A decline in Topmost sales set in as soon as the new product was placed on the market. Many retailers reported their customers saw no resemblance whatever to the original Topmost ice cream. Sales continued to decline and Drug-X cut its number of ice cream delivery routes by one. This discontinued route was absorbed by the remaining four routes.

The new Topmost ice cream simply did not taste as good as most other brands on the market. The flavor was described as not being distinct or "sharp." The retail price was $2.49 for a half gallon, the same as before, but the product now seemed to be in direct competition with brands sold in supermarkets, which sold for ten to twenty cents less per half gallon.

In hopes of correcting this situation, Drug-X arranged for another ice cream producer to manufacture the Topmost line. It was expected that the "flavor problem" could be worked out with a "more receptive company." During the transitional period, Drug-X did not take the older product out of circulation. It introduced the new product and continued to sell existing stocks of the older product. No effort was made to make the public aware that Topmost had been improved, management not wanting to draw attention to the previous quality problem.

Unfortunately, sales did not improve, but complaints about taste and flavor declined. It appeared Drug-X was losing a very valuable loss leader. Topmost ice cream for years had been sold monthly at a special price of $1.99 per half gallon, one cent below the actual cost to member stores. This sale was historically very popular with customers, and increased store traffic helped sell other items. After the second change in ice cream production, the special sales were not nearly as effective. The percent reduction in store sales revenue was even greater than the percent reduction in ice cream sales.

As Ms. Tompkins reviewed the ice cream problem and the product mix problem, she hoped to uncover some clues as to how to improve the situation. She also wondered how to get better participation in the company's advertising program.

Questions

1. What should have been done about the ice cream problem?
2. What should have been done about the inconsistency of retailer demand for nondrug items?
3. How could Ms. Tompkins have achieved better participation in the company's advertising program?

5-4

GUARD-LINE CUTTER COMPANY, INC.

Marketing program

Guard-Line Cutter Company, Inc., of Albany, New York, produced a unique hand-operated cutter designed for use with nonmetal sheet materials such as paper, vinyl, acetate, poster board, leather, and emulsion paper. This family-owned business had experienced little success in achieving sales volume, which barely reached $200,000 last year. Donald E. Showalter, sales manager and son of the owner, was seeking ways to increase sales volume. His most recent plan had been to secure wholesalers capable of performing the marketing tasks necessary to reach final buyers. Because of financial and manpower limitations, management regarded wholesaler distribution as the only feasible alternative, but this form of distribution had produced disappointingly small sales.

The company, essentially a one-product firm, made three models of slide-type cutters. Originally, an eighteen-inch model was designed and put into production by Showalter's father, who believed that the product's inherent safety features and high quality would require only minimum selling effort. The Guard-Line cutter consisted of a flat base board with a bar and sliding blade attached. The user placed the material to be cut under the bar, applied downward pressure to the bar, and moved the blade along the distance to be cut. Maximum cutting length depended upon the board's length; for example, an eighteen-inch cut was the maximum on the eighteen-inch model. Various precise angles were imprinted on the masonite base board, making it easy to cut any angle accurately. The maximum thickness that could be cut at a time was one-eighth of an inch. Besides the eighteen-inch cutter, twelve- and forty-two-inch models had been developed.

When Showalter's father conceived the idea of the cutter, no formal market research was conducted. A prototype was produced and displayed at a school suppliers' trade show. On the basis of favorable comments from the trade show attendants and encouragement from friends, management believed that the cutter could not help but be a success. The sales manager believed that the largest potential market for all three models would be public school systems. However, considerable delay in selling this segment was typical because of school system annual budgetary limitations and administrative red tape. He thought that other potential buyers would be architectural firms, photocopy finishers, blueprinters, general office suppliers, and art and photography schools.

List prices for the three cutter models were set at:

42-inch model	$109.95
18-inch model	$ 28.50
12-inch model	$ 19.95

These prices compared favorably with those of competitive products. Management did not attempt to exercise any control over retail prices but based the discounts allowed to distributors on a percentage of list price. List price was set by deriving the unit cost of a single cutter and multiplying by six—this formula had been devised by a producer of a similar product. Depending on the particular agreements made with individual distributors, they received discounts of from 40 percent plus 10 percent to 66 percent off list prices.[1] No distributor had yet ordered in large enough quantities to be regarded as doing anything but making a trial purchase.

Guard-Line had no sales force, but the sales manager attended trade shows in the hope of interesting distributors in taking on the line. However, company budgetary limitations prevented him from attending as many trade shows as he would have liked. Direct mail flyers had been used to contact distributors not reached at trade shows, and a large Chicago wholesaler, contacted initially through direct mail, had bought a fairly large number of cutters over the last two years, but nothing was known about its customers. The Chicago firm had been granted the right and the responsibility for contacting and selling retail outlets west of a line drawn from Washington, D.C., to Pittsburgh. East of this line no formal distributorship had been secured. Four mail-order wholesalers, known as *catalog houses,* carried the cutter in their catalogs, and all four served mainly the school and office supply markets.

The sales manager had never met or discussed the cutter with the Chicago distributor. Monthly phone conversations, however, were held to resolve difficulties. In the East, the catalog houses and other prospective customers were contacted initially at trade shows, but there had been little

[1]A discount of 40 percent plus 10 percent is the equivalent of 46 percent off list price. On an item priced at $100, for example, the 40 percent discount ($40) was deducted first. Then, from the remainder ($60), the 10 percent discount was deducted, leaving a net price of $54.

communication since, other than that necessary to get the product included in catalogs or to fill small orders. Direct orders were accepted and filled both from retailers (who received 40 percent discounts from list prices) and from final buyers (who paid list prices).

Originally, the company had turned over the problem of promoting the cutter line to a large advertising agency. This resulted in numerous articles and photographs of the cutter in trade magazines and journals. A few small orders came in from interested readers, but no repeat orders from this group had ever been received. At this point management realized that the cutter would not sell "on sight." The sales manager concluded that to make sales someone had to demonstrate the product's capabilities. Shortly thereafter, he began demonstrating the product at trade shows in New England and in New York City. While this promotional method limited the product's exposure to potential dealers, he felt this might be counterbalanced by volume sales to wholesalers attending trade shows.

Direct mail flyers, pictorially describing the cutter's specifications and its uses, were circulated throughout New York State. These were addressed to prospective final buyers, such as school systems and photographers. Management hoped to initiate a "pulling" effect on distribution—that is, when addressees asked distributors for the product.

Similar cutting devices were on the market, but none were exactly like the Guard-Line in function or in appearance. Management thought that primary competition came from the familiar "guillotine" cutter, but no market share data were availabe. Dangers in using the guillotine cutter, especially around children, were a feature on which Guard-Line hoped to capitalize. Four competitive products had safety features comparable to the Guard-Line, but little was known about their method of distribution, promotion, or marketing success. Showalter said that these competitive products were turned out by companies much larger than Guard-Line, so even if he could get such information it would probably be of limited utility due to Guard-Line's small size.

Question

What improvements should have been made in the marketing program of the Guard-Line Cutter Company?

5–5

WESTINGHOUSE ELECTRIC CORPORATION

Changes in distribution policy

Mr. R. J. Martin, national sales manager, Overhead Distribution Transformer Division (ODTD), Westinghouse Electric Corporation, found the escalating operating costs of the division's trucking fleet of increasing concern. Fuel prices had zoomed after the 1973 Arab oil embargo. If rising shipping costs forced ODTD to raise prices, substantial loss in market share could occur. Ideally, Mr. Martin wanted to satisfy customer demand, keep shipping costs down, and avoid a price increase.

Westinghouse Corporation was organized into three "companies": industrial products, power systems, and public systems. Power Systems Company made such products as meters and instruments, power transformers, large motors, relays, turbines, and generators. The Overhead Distribution Transformer Division was part of the Power Systems Company.

THE OVERHEAD DISTRIBUTION TRANSFORMER DIVISION

All Westinghouse overhead distribution transformers were designed and manufactured in the Athens, Georgia, plant. This facility turned out approximately 240,000 transformers a year which ODTD's truck fleet delivered throughout the entire United States. Large orders from the Athens plant also went to customers in India, Germany, Australia, Denmark, and elsewhere. ODTD was the world's leading supplier of power distribution transformers (see Exhibit 1).

ODTD's goal was "to remain first in performance . . . and first in the industry." Top management relied on its engineering staff to keep the products ahead of competition. The marketing department, also engineering ori-

101

EXHIBIT 1 · Westinghouse Advertisement for National Market

Volume with quality from the leader in distribution transformers.

We want you to expect a lot from us. Because we produce distribution transformers in volume, we want you to expect your order when you need it.

And because we build each transformer like it is the only one, we want you to expect only the finest in quality. And we also want you to expect us to keep

innovating ways to make our transformers even better. Producing quality in volume is what we are about. And that means a lot for you.

ented, included the traffic and shipping operations and fielded twenty-five sales engineers. The complex, technical nature of overhead transformers required sales personnel with extensive engineering backgrounds.

THE PRODUCT AND COMPETITION

Distribution transformers were devices employing the mutual induction principle to convert variations of current in a primary circuit into variations of voltage and current in a secondary circuit. Typically, they consisted of two separate coils with different numbers of turns wound on closed laminated iron cores. Power and utility companies used overhead distribution transformers to reduce the voltage of current flowing through main power lines to allow electricity to enter homes, schools, and other buildings. They also made it possible for utilities to use smaller power lines and save on costs of copper wire and other materials. Industrial demand was high because overhead transformers were needed to use electricity in high volume with minimum waste.

ODTD led the transformer industry—its products were known for excellent quality and design, and it designed custom products to meet specific requirements of different customers. The Athens plant turned out 10,000 distinctive types of transformers based on different power requirements, voltage specifications, and design features. The average transformer weighed four to five hundred pounds.

ODTD had a highly trained technical sales force. When these sales engineers conferred with prospective customers, they were equipped to provide detailed information as to which design features would best fit customer needs and how this design could be made available at the lowest cost. ODTD enjoyed the reputation of being able and willing to provide whatever the customer needed. Competition on standard product lines was fierce (twenty-three companies made overhead distribution transformers), but ODTD had the largest market share.

THE WHOLESALE MARKET

Most of ODTD's sales effort was directed toward electrical supply houses. These were establishments stocking electrical products of all kinds and serving as middlemen between electrical apparatus manufacturers and electric utilities. Unless customers needed a piece of apparatus requiring special production considerations, they placed their orders with the supply houses. The ODTD sales force spent a great deal of time working closely with supply houses.

The sales force provided product information to electrical supply houses. Sales engineers visited supply houses twice a week and made sure that their stocks included adequate supplies of all materials needed for installing and maintaining ODTD products. Sales management recognized the importance of the supply houses' operations, and sales engineers made every effort to offer the best service and quality.

THE TRANSPORTATION SITUATION

The 1973 Arab oil embargo set off inflation in trucking costs. As diesel fuel costs went up, ODTD executives recognized the potential negative impact on the transformer industry, which depended heavily upon long-distance trucking. Mr. Martin did not want to absorb higher trucking costs by raising prices of ODTD products. If ODTD prices went up, the smaller electrical manufacturers, many located nearer to certain customers, might take market share away from ODTD. High product quality and custom production would shield current sales levels only briefly if ODTD prices rose.

Mr. Martin had considered using alternate transportation modes for transformers. After reviewing the situation, he concluded that:

1. supply houses did not have the necessary unloading facilities for rail shipments and some trucking would still be required,
2. the finished products were too heavy for shipment by air,

and

3. the company had a sizable trucking fleet and abandoning it would not be cost-efficient.

THE SOLUTION

Mr. Martin believed that the key to the problem was better management of the trucking operation. ODTD trucks had been making deliveries in less than truckload lots and the trucks had returned to the plant empty. Orders had been filled and delivered randomly, not according to any fuel-conscious delivery plan.

The solution, developed by Mr. Martin and with other ODTD executives, was to set up a distribution system based on making regularly scheduled deliveries to electrical supply houses. The system was so designed that every ODTD truck making a delivery could travel a short distance farther and pick up a load of raw materials, or other items needed by the Athens plant. Where it was not possible to find return loads, ODTD would contract with commercial truck lines to make the delivery to the wholesalers; this would cut the total number of trips by ODTD trucks and would stop the practice of covering long distances with empty trucks.

Mr. Martin realized, however, that this new system could cause problems with the electrical supply houses, which were accustomed to receiving frequent orders and small quantities. The new distribution system would require them to order larger quantities and less frequently. Many electrical supply houses would accept this change only if given some extraordinary incentive.

Mr. Martin then put into effect a policy borrowed from the commercial truck lines. He offered quantity discounts on truckload orders (loads over 30,000 lbs.). Any customer ordering more than 30,000 pounds at one time would receive a 10 percent discount off the contract price. This made it possible for ODTD to receive price breaks from trucking companies (or to operate its own trucks more economically) and to pass on the savings to the electrical supply houses. ODTD sales engineers contacted all of the electrical supply houses and encouraged them to boost order sizes.

This policy change proved advantageous to the larger electrical supply houses but enraged the smaller establishments. The larger operations had lots of storage space to stock larger inventories of ODTD products, and the price break was sufficiently attractive to encourage them to carry larger inventories. But most small electrical supply houses did not have the extra storage space needed for larger inventories, and they complained bitterly that ODTD had handed the larger electrical supply houses an unfair selling advantage.

A few months after putting the new policy into effect, sales to the larger customers had increased, but many smaller customers were phasing out ODTD transformers and support products.

Questions

1. Should ODTD's distribution policy have been altered?
2. Was it illegal for Westinghouse to discriminate in price between large and small customers?
3. What should Mr. Martin have done next?

6–1

ENERGY-MIZERS OF VIRGINIA, INC.

Development of a marketing program

Energy-Mizers of Virginia, Inc. (EMVI), was organized to market the Mist-Mizer, a high-quality, energy-reducing unit that attached to commercial air conditioners. The manufacturer had granted EMVI exclusive distribution rights for Virginia. A large market was anticipated in Virginia for energy-saving devices because of sharp increases in utility rates and widespread use of commercial air conditioning equipment. Management desired to establish a quality image for Mist-Mizer and build a solid image as a quality distributor of energy-saving products.

The company was owned and operated by three principals. Robert Law, an engineering graduate, had worked as a computer security manager for a Richmond corporation. Tom DeVore, also an engineering graduate, had worked in the technical services division of a local manufacturing firm and now handled EMVI installations. Bill Wilder, a Ph.D. in public administration, had experience in both academic and business positions. Shortly after incorporating, EMVI hired a salesperson to sell the Mist-Mizer throughout Virginia.

THE ENERGY INDUSTRY

The Arab oil embargo of 1973 forced the United States to realize its dependency on foreign oil. This dependency, together with the belief that fossil fuel was running out, came to be known as the "energy crisis." The energy crisis, exacerbated by a high rate of inflation and practically no economic growth, forced reductions in energy consumption. This opened up opportunities to sell energy-saving devices.

Companies in the "energy industry" were uniquely situated. A tremendous marketing opportunity unfolded with passage of federal legislation creating tax incentives for buyers of energy-saving products. These tax incentives served to subsidize the entrance of many firms into the industry, some of them of questionable reputation, some selling low-quality products. This made it difficult even for reputable operators to establish credibility with target markets.

Because of the many companies marketing a diversity of products, EMVI, at least nominally, had numerous competitors. However, even though a host of companies sold energy-saving devices, EMVI actually encountered little product-specific competition for the Mist-Mizer. There was one similar product, the Aqua-Mist, but EMVI management evaluated it as of lower quality and efficiency than the Mist-Mizer. Even so, they were somewhat fearful that prospective buyers would perceive Mist-Mizer as similar in quality and efficiency to Aqua-Mist.

EMVI faced direct competition from Mist-Mizer distributors in neighboring states, who were free to sell in areas without authorized distributors. For example, the Florida Mist-Mizer distributor had sold to large commercial customers in Florida, then turned to "skimming the cream" of major commercial accounts in south Georgia.

THE PRODUCT

The Mist-Mizer was EMVI's only product. It was a patented water-spraying device that regulated the temperature of freon in air conditioning systems. When the freon reached a temperature of 95.5° F., the Mist-Mizer sprayed water on the freon coils, cooling them so that the system used less electricity. The product cut electricity usage from 15 to 50 percent while neither reducing cooling output nor harming the air conditioning system. Recent articles in both trade and science magazines provided testimonials to the Mist-Mizer's effectiveness. Also, several satisfied buyers had written letters to EMVI describing their savings and satisfaction with the Mist-Mizer. The following excerpt is from one letter:

> Last summer we ran some tests on the Mist-Mizer at one of our schools. We used rooms with the same square footage and identical air conditioning units to try and get a true and accurate test.
>
> The test was conducted over several days. Rating the temperature in both rooms, we found that the unit with the Mist-Mizer installed ran $1/5$ less than the unit without the Mist-Mizer, and also used about 2 amps less electricity.
>
> This coming summer we are hoping to install quite a few more of the Mist-Mizers to try to conserve energy and provide a more efficient system.

Another letter said:

> Upon installing your Mist-Mizer, . . . [we had] better than a 20 percent decrease in the overall power consumption. The installation of the Mist-Mizer in this instance not only decreased the power input but also provided a more economical solution to some other operating problems. Congratulations on an excellent product!

EMVI had switched guarantees on the Mist-Mizer three times. On the first few units sold, EMVI guaranteed a minimum of 15 percent savings in electricity. Later purchasers were guaranteed some savings, but not 15 percent. Recently, it was concluded that the product was gaining credibility and needed no guarantee.

PROMOTION

EMVI's promotion effort was confined to Virginia. Advertisements were run in trade magazines with state-wide circulations. Attendance at trade shows was emphasized, since they not only provided selling opportunities but gave exposure to other energy-saving products which might be added to the EMVI line.

The manufacturer of Mist-Mizer had plans for running national TV spots and a print campaign in national magazines, newspapers, and trade journals.

The only EMVI salesperson was a former IBM sales representative for computer software. Management appraised him as an aggressive, highly effective salesperson. He was paid a straight commission of 15 percent on the selling price and paid his own expenses. The typical installation was for more than 10 units, since most stores and factories had banks of several air conditioners which cooled the entire building. The first year's earnings potential for this salesperson was in excess of $30,000.

THE MARKET

EMVI's potential market consisted of large retail stores and factories with air conditioners. The private home market was not viewed as a potentially profitable segment since residential air conditioning units were neither as powerful nor as expensive to operate as the commercial units. Management regarded further segmentation as unnecessary. Consequently, no specific industries or types of air conditioner had been targeted as further bases for segmentation.

Nevertheless, EMVI was beginning to move into an additional application for Mist-Mizer—refrigeration, such as that used by dairies and cold storage warehouses. In the refrigeration application, the Mist-Mizer operated on the same principle as in the air conditioning application. If the company could move successfully into supplying supplementary energy-efficient equipment for refrigeration units, it could offset the seasonal demand problem associated with air conditioning units.

PRICE

The manufacturer set suggested resale prices on the Mist-Mizer as follows:

NO. OF UNITS	UNIT PRICE*
1–10	$475
11–50	440
51–100	415
101–500	395
501–Up	370

*Less discounts as follows:
4%—Prepayment
3%—COD
2%—10 days, 30 days net
10%—Customer installs Mist-Mizer(s)

These prices allowed the distributor 32 percent gross profit after commissions and discounts but before other expenses and taxes. Mist-Mizer distributors were not required to use the suggested resale prices, but most distributors, including EMVI, did.

EMVI had data showing that energy savings generated by the Mist-Mizer could "pay" for the device in under five years (see Exhibit 1). Nevertheless, the EMVI salesperson had difficulty using this information effectively as prospects were being bombarded with all sorts of wild claims by other sellers of energy-efficient devices.

EXHIBIT 1 · Mist-Mizer Energy-Savings Payback

Example:

Install Mist-Mizers on 5 air conditioners/freezers averaging 20 tons/unit. Current cooling costs are 5 × 20 × $68 or $6,800/year.

Cost of 5 Mist-Mizers installed	$2,375 (gross)
Energy savings/year	25% of $6,800 = $1,700
Years to pay back	$2,375/1,700 = 1.4

Assumptions:

Average annual energy cost/ton of air conditioning per season* (12 hrs./day, 5 days/week, 25 weeks/year: 1.6 kw./ton, $.03/kwh.).

Savings experienced by Mist-Mizer users are 15 to 50%; assume 25% for this example.

*Based on figures supplied by Virginia Electric Power Company (VEPCO).

Questions

1. What problems did EMVI face?
2. What should have been done by EMVI to insure early success in distributing Mist-Mizer in Virginia?
3. Prepare an exhibit to improve the credibility of Exhibit 1. Assume the customer: is in the 50 percent tax bracket (local and federal combined); uses 5-year straight-line depreciation, no salvage value; receives a one-time energy tax credit of 10 percent; receives an investment tax credit of 10 percent.

6–2

WOODBURY BUSINESS FORMS AND SYSTEMS

Managing the sales force

The general sales manager of Woodbury Business Forms and Systems was certain that many company sales branches were not selling all they could but he was not certain how to improve their performances. However, since he also served as sales manager of the Macon, Georgia, branch, he possessed some insights which he thought might be helpful in improving overall company performance.

COMPANY HISTORY AND OPERATIONS

Woodbury Business Forms and Systems (WBFS) was set up ten years ago by Woodbury Business Forms, which owned 50 percent of WBFS and was the major supplier of products sold through the subsidiary. Woodbury Business Forms had been selling most of its products through dealers who sold to commercial users; Woodbury had no control over final sales. If dealers could buy the forms elsewhere either less expensively or with faster delivery, they did so. Dealers had little loyalty to suppliers. Woodbury Business Forms hoped WBFS would develop close ties with Woodbury's manufacturing plant and operate similarly to brokers. (WBFS sales personnel received commissions and were allowed to buy items for resale from other manufacturers.)

The president was the only full-time WBFS officer; all other managers gave part of their time to other duties (see Exhibit 1). The general sales manager, who was also the Macon branch manager, had consistently made his branch the most profitable in WBFS. The two salespersons working out of the Macon branch had sizable accounts with hospitals. Hospitals were excellent prospects for business forms because they required personalized service and many custom forms, and because there was so much paperwork in the typical hospital, and hospital forms traditionally had carried the highest markups in the business forms industry. The Macon branch led the company in selling to hospitals.

WBFS sold a variety of printed forms including: four color process work, blind embossed, and continuous forms. It specialized in custom continuous forms because these required the greatest printing expertise and were items the WBFS sales force excelled in selling.

Personal service provided by company sales personnel was as important as the physical products. To illustrate, WBFS salespeople called on the Georgia Farm Bureau and found a paper flow problem—this organization was running invoices on the computer, separately "stuffing" the invoices in envelopes, rerunning the envelopes, and then making a follow-up run. WBFS sales personnel designed a form which, with one run, accomplished all these steps.

SALES FORCE OPERATION

The general sales manager believed that the key to WBFS' overall success lay in the sales force selection process. There had been several basic criteria for sales force candidates: age (25–40 years old), education (college graduate), experience (successful sales experience), knowledge (of the geographical area

EXHIBIT 1 · WBFS Corporate Structure

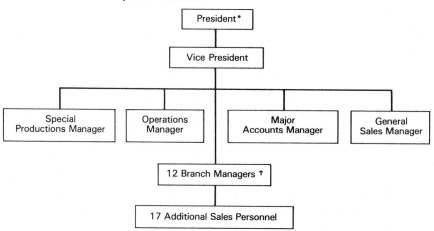

*The president was the only full-time corporate officer.
†Each branch manager was also a salesperson. The twelve branches were: Georgia—Athens, Atlanta, Columbus, LaGrange, Macon, and Savannah; Florida—Jacksonville, Miami, and Tampa; Chattanooga, Tennessee; Greensboro, North Carolina; and Spartanburg, South Carolina.

and of sales technique). Although candidates not meeting all requirements were sometimes selected, the general sales manager was convinced that candidates meeting only one or two criteria had little chance of success.

On finding an individual meeting these criteria, WBFS began a two-day program of psychological testing, both written and oral. As WBFS spent a lot of money and time in training sales personnel, management wanted to give offers only to individuals with psychological patterns similar to successful WBFS sales personnel. Among the traits sought were: intelligence, ambition, courage, and empathy. The general sales manager said, "To succeed in this business you need these qualities."

Sales personnel operated somewhat autonomously. Within their territories, the sales personnel identified markets that they believed suitable, usually ones in which the salesperson had considerable expertise. Market targets might be banks, hospitals, manufacturers, retailers, or other commercial users. "Hospitals," the general sales manager said, "are detailed and difficult to deal with, and require a great deal of expertise. I personally wouldn't have one!" Once a salesperson developed enough accounts in a particular geographic area, a new salesperson would also be assigned to the territory to open up new and different accounts.

In prospecting for new territories and accounts, WBFS people considered many sources of information (see Exhibit 2). In qualifying new accounts, they asked such questions as:

Does your firm buy locally?
Does it buy more than $25,000 worth of printing per year?
Who is the firm's present supplier?

When WBFS identified between fifty and sixty prospective accounts in an area, it considered opening a new territory.

The company supported its sales force with advertisements in two monthly magazines—*Business Forms* and *Data Processing*—and advertised in the local Yellow Pages. No other advertising was used.

As the general sales manager reviewed the outstanding sales record of the Macon branch, he wondered how the performances of other branches

EXHIBIT 2 · Sources of Prospects for New Accounts

1. Dun & Bradstreet reports
2. Directories of manufacturers
3. Telephone book Yellow Pages
4. Data processing magazines
5. Newspapers
6. Industry trade associations
7. Chambers of Commerce

could be improved. He knew that many types of commercial users were prospects for WBFS' products. Yet, comparing different classes of prospects (banks, insurance companies, manufacturers, hospitals, and others), he knew that those most suitable for WBFS were the hospitals. He wondered how he could encourage the other branches to focus on the hospital market, especially since he personally preferred nonhospital accounts?

Questions

1. Should WBFS branches have been encouraged to pursue hospital accounts?
2. Was the WBFS approach to the recruitment and selection of sales personnel appropriate?
3. Comment on the WBFS approach to prospecting.

6–3

Ajax Pump Company (A)

Promotion strategy for a new product introduction

Ajax Pump Company had developed a new product to complement its line of pumps—a gear reduction unit known as a "gear-box." Feedback from customers had indicated that a gear-box would sell well and be an attractive addition to the line. Many customers had used Ajax pumps with competing gear-box units.

To initiate promotion for the new product, a national sales meeting was held in October, but orders for gear-boxes were not to be written until June 1 of the next year. It was not possible to launch a full-scale promotional campaign at this time because of budgetary limitations. The marketing department had to squeeze promotion of the gear-box into existing promotion plans, but the objective was to make this promotion as effective as possible within the budgetary constraints.

COMPANY HISTORY, OPERATIONS, AND PRODUCT LINE

Ajax Pump Company's first products were single-force pumps for wells and two-cylinder pumps for fighting fires. Later Ajax had added a beer-and-ale pump, a garden-force pump, a noiseless-chain pump, a rotary-gear pump, a windmill pump, and other unique pumps.

Over the years Ajax modified its marketing strategy. Early on, Ajax had developed pumps for a wide range of applications, but more and more it concentrated on making and selling rotary-gear pumps for the industrial market. The product line gradually expanded but the product-market scope was narrowed to industrial applications. Ajax continued in the "fast lane" of pump technology as evidenced by its development of a lubricating pump for

116

the bearing joints of the platform assembly crawlers at the Cape Kennedy Space Launch Center.

Ajax products included three basic pump types: external rotary gear, screw, and progressive cavity. The external rotary-gear pump was Ajax's mainstay, as it was rooted in an established pumping technology where Ajax had long experience. Ajax started making rotary-gear pumps early in the twentieth century, later concentrating on industrial rotary-gear applications. This experience, coupled with Ajax's reputation as a quality pump producer, gave the company a strong competitive edge in this market. The rotary-gear pumps brought in substantial cash flows, and this "cash cow" provided funds for financing other endeavors.

Ajax's line of external rotary-gear pumps was divided into four subcategories. The first was a line of stainless-steel pumps for pumping industrial chemicals, especially highly corrosive materials. The second was a line of low-pressure pumps for pumping "clean" liquids at standard motor speeds, thick fluids at slow speeds, and fluids with low flow rates. The third line was made up of medium-pressure gear pumps for blending fuel supplies at standard motor speeds, pumping petroleum for bulk transport, and pumping liquids with high flow rates. The fourth line was made up of general purpose pumps used for mixing, blending, recirculating, and transferring a wide variety of fluids for heavy duty applications.

The second basic type of Ajax product was the screw pump used in hydraulic systems. Ajax had long experience in developing and making screw pumps for automobile lifts, bulldozers, and other heavy equipment.

The third basic type of Ajax product was the progressive cavity (PC) pump, a recent Ajax innovation. Management believed this pump had great potential in the transfer of industrial and municipal waste liquids containing solid particles, and in handling abrasive materials, slurries, low- and high-viscosity materials, and common sewage. The progressive cavity pump operated on a different principle than the rotary-gear pump, but produced the same result. The main moving part was a curved shaft or rotor similar to a drill bit and encased in a pump housing. The rotor and the housing formed pockets, or cavities, in which the liquid was transferred. Similar to the way wood or metal was transferred up the length of an operating drill bit, pumped material was transferred from one end of the PC to the other; this continual cavity made possible the pumping of liquids containing solid particles. A substantial investment had been made in PC production and sales in return for rather limited revenues. However, management expected future improvement in this situation.

DISTRIBUTION AND PROMOTION

Ajax sold its products through twenty-two manufacturer's representatives. Each representative had an exclusive sales territory in which to call on pumping distributors. The Ajax representatives covered the entire United States, portions of Canada, and Puerto Rico.

Ajax paid the representatives straight commissions ranging from 5 percent to 10 percent, and the representatives paid their own expenses. Ajax signed contracts with the representatives, but either party could cancel the working arrangement on thirty days' notice.

Manufacturer's representatives also set up original equipment manufacturer (OEM) accounts (firms that used pumps as components of larger end products). For instance, most U.S.-made locomotives had built-in Ajax lube pumps. Several large fast-food franchisors also used Ajax pumps as accessory equipment for the recirculation of cooking oil. After setting up an OEM or service account, the manufacturer's representative acted as a consultant to the account. But OEMs negotiated directly with Ajax to assure proper pump design and installation.

Ajax made sales to over five hundred pumping distributors through the manufacturer's representatives. The distributors were generally local businesses that resold to industrial users, which included firms buying for "single-shot" situations such as replacements for obsolete or worn-out pumps, and firms buying to improve or upgrade their pumping facilities. Distributors also sold to contractors building facilities requiring pumping applications or processes.

Ajax had good working relationships with the distributors, who recognized that the Ajax name meant quality and performance, translating into sales and profits for them. Most distributors valued the Ajax association. Ajax's main problem with the distributors was the long lead time between an order's receipt and its delivery, an average of 48 weeks. Distributors said many of their customers preferred to buy other makes rather than wait for delivery from Ajax.

Ajax used four main types of promotion: (1) selective media advertising, (2) trade show demonstrations, (3) direct mail, and (4) personal selling. In addition, Ajax shared the costs of Yellow Page ads with local distributors and provided logos for their use. Ajax's core theme in all types of promotion aimed for brand-name awareness and emphasized company and product reliability and performance. The media budget, amounting to 1.5 percent of sales, was spent on advertising in trade journals with readership in the petroleum, chemical, and tank truck industries.

Ajax, teaming up with its local distributors and manufacturer's representatives, made extensive use of regional trade shows. The company provided, at no charge, cutaway product models and informational literature to distributors and manufacturer's representatives wanting to demonstrate Ajax products at such shows.

Direct mailing and personal selling, handled by the manufacturer's representatives, played key roles in Ajax's promotional strategy. Manufacturer's representatives were responsible for setting up distributors in their territories and for securing OEM customers. Direct mail was a practical and effective way to build customer awareness of Ajax Pump Company, before making the first sales call, to obtain distributors, and to keep existing accounts abreast of new developments. The technical nature of the pumps required personal selling—face-to-face interactions between manufacturer's representatives and distributors to explain and to demonstrate new products and to answer questions about existing products.

Standard markups were used in pricing all catalog items (those items that distributors ordered from Ajax). While quantity discounts were not given on catalog items, discounts on quantity purchases were given to OEM accounts.

Ajax was forecasting a record year at the time of the new product introduction (see Exhibit 1) with net sales expected to exceed $24 million, an increase of 7.6 percent over the previous year. Demand for Ajax's products remained strong and several price increases on various Ajax products had been put into effect during the year. Net earnings of $1.6 million were expected, up 42 percent from the year before.

MARKET SITUATION

Ajax Pump Company sold its pumps in the United States, Canada, and Puerto Rico to the petroleum pump market, the industrial pump market (which included the chemical processing industry), and the sewage (abrasive liquid) pump market. Ajax did not sell pumps in Mexico, which had a law requiring potential pump buyers to buy pumps from Mexican manufacturers. Ajax sold pumps occasionally to buyers in other foreign countries, but its long lead time made arranging for export credit difficult.

Ajax's major competitors were Viscount Pump Company and Becker Pump Division of the Darvo Corporation.[1] While Ajax sold to multiple markets, its competitors limited their product-market scopes to one of the three markets mentioned. Ajax's management believed that the company's broader product line would contribute to the prime objective, that was, improving the "bottom line."

The petroleum pump market had two segments—bulk transport and home fuel oil delivery. The bulk transport segment bought pumps for use in refinery operations, storage, and pipeline movement. The home delivery segment bought pumps for use in making deliveries to residential and commercial users. Ajax had nearly 90 percent of the bulk transport market, while Becker had most of the remaining market share. The opposite situation held true in the home delivery market—Becker had 75 percent, Ajax 12 percent, and others 13 percent. Overall, however, the petroleum pump market was Ajax's strongest.

Ajax had a small share of the abrasive liquid pump market, the market

---

[1] The markets served by Ajax and its competitors were only a segment of the total pump market. The applications served by Ajax, Becker, Viscount, and others were restricted by flow rates, port size, horsepower ratings, pump revolutions per minute, and temperature limitations.

Exhibit 1 · Financial Report

	PRESENT YEAR (FORECAST)	1 YEAR PREVIOUS	2 YEARS PREVIOUS	3 YEARS PREVIOUS	4 YEARS PREVIOUS	5 YEARS PREVIOUS
NET SALES	$24,083,856	$22,392,611	$19,658,239	$17,241,311	$15,053,881	$14,651,012
COSTS AND EXPENSES						
Cost of products sold	16,707,375	16,072,239	13,222,983	11,109,328	9,520,315	9,325,186
Selling, general, and administrative	4,091,702	3,956,991	3,650,695	3,431,162	3,042,257	3,207,738
Interest	182,529	123,947	53,961	73,878	115,679	128,329
	20,981,606	20,153,177	16,927,639	14,614,368	12,678,251	12,661,253
EARNINGS BEFORE INCOME TAXES	3,102,250	2,239,434	2,730,600	2,626,943	2,375,630	1,989,759
INCOME TAXES	1,458,900	1,080,000	1,354,500	1,318,500	1,190,700	1,034,100
NET EARNINGS	$ 1,643,350	$ 1,159,434	$ 1,376,100	$ 1,308,443	$ 1,184,930	$ 955,659
AVERAGE NUMBER OF SHARES OUTSTANDING	929,871	929,871	932,613	935,087	935,445	936,872
NET EARNINGS PER SHARE	$1.77	$1.13	$1.33	$1.26	$1.14	$ .92
CASH DIVIDENDS PAID PER SHARE	$ .50	$ .50	$ .46	$ .43	$ .42	$ .42
STOCKHOLDERS' EQUITY PER SHARE	$11.95	$10.85	$10.17	$9.34	$8.51	$7.79

leader being Roswell Company with 80 percent, while Ajax had 2 percent and others 18 percent.

In the industrial pump market Viscount led with 50 percent of the market, Ajax had 30 percent, and others 20 percent.

DEVELOPMENT AND INTRODUCTION OF THE NEW PRODUCT

Top management encouraged the marketing department to search for and pursue promising product opportunities. Management believed the gear-box presented an opportunity to enhance the company's product portfolio. The gear-box was financially appealing, in that it involved a small investment relative to expected revenues. The marketing staff was convinced that the gear-box had high potential as a cash cow.

The marketing department did not know what market share the gear-box could be expected to obtain in its first year. But its first year's sales target was 1,800 units with 15 percent annual increases expected thereafter. Ajax management hoped that future pump customers needing gear-boxes would find it easier and less expensive to order pump and gear-box from the same source. Ajax planned, where feasible, to mount and attach the gear-box to the pump and deliver both as a single unit, further enhancing the chances of selling gear-box units.

The gear-box found its greatest potential application in the industrial pump market. However, Ajax's market share trailed Viscount, which had been selling gear-boxes for a long time. Viscount had the competitive edge in that its product enjoyed both visibility and recognition. Ajax would first have to overcome its product's perceived newness, then convince potential customers to buy its gear-box rather than Viscount's. Still, Ajax's reputation as a maker of high-quality equipment was expected to carry over to the gear-box. In fact, the impetus Ajax had for producing the gear-box came from existing customers who wanted to buy both pumps and gear-boxes from a single source.

Ajax marketing executives felt that the gear-box's introduction should begin with an aggressive promotional campaign. Target customers had to be made aware that Ajax had a gear-box whose quality was equal to or better than the competition. However, there was little room in the budget for the type and amount of advertising needed for the gear-box introduction.

Questions

1. What should have been the target market for the introduction of the new product?
2. How should the new product have been promoted in the near term, given the funding problem?
3. What should have been the long-run promotional strategy?

6–4

BETTER MACHINES, INC.

Motivating sales personnel

Better Machines, Inc., was an industrial distributor selling a broad line. It had three divisions: (1) the Machine Tool Division, which sold metalworking equipment, (2) the Materials Handling Equipment Division, which distributed specialized handling equipment, and (3) the Construction Service Division (CSD), which sold and serviced construction equipment. Ted Logan, CSD marketing manager, recently identified his division's most important problem as that of motivating sales personnel to perform effectively. He remarked, "Sales executives can give employees incentives, but motivation must come from within the individual." The division's sales personnel received considerably higher compensation than the average in the industry, but motivational problems persisted.

Last year CSD sold $46 million worth of equipment. It competed against thirty distributors serving the Indiana and southern Illinois market and attained a penetration ratio of 50 percent.[1] CSD's sales income came from equipment ($30 million), parts ($11.4 million), and service ($4.6 million). Sales of Goliath equipment, the leading line, amounted to $22 million.

CSD represented four manufacturers of graders, loaders, stone crushers, earthmovers, rollers, bulldozers, cranes, power shovels, and asphalt pavers. Prices of different pieces of equipment ranged from $20,000 for small loaders to $600,000 for larger, heavier products. Management made gradual changes in the items handled, discontinuing some pieces of equipment from time to time, but had dropped none during the last five years. The high quality of the equipment was a source of pride throughout the division.

---

[1] A *penetration ratio* indicates the relationship between actual sales and market potential.

Central headquarters were at Terre Haute, Indiana, and CSD's sales area extended over Indiana and southern Illinois. Branch offices, with parts and service facilities, were at Decatur and Mount Vernon in Illinois, and at Indianapolis, Fort Wayne, and Terre Haute in Indiana. Branches, each with a full-time manager, operated autonomously as profit centers.

Of the nineteen CSD field salespersons, five worked out of Terre Haute, five out of Indianapolis, four out of Fort Wayne, three out of Mount Vernon, and two out of Decatur. Each managed the assigned territory, made scheduled calls, prospected for new customers, developed mailing lists, and submitted weekly activity reports to the branch manager. Five specialists, with engineering and application knowledge of certain equipment lines, covered the entire market area, assisting regular territorial salespersons. While on field assignments, specialists were supervised by branch managers (see Exhibit 1—Organization Chart).

Sales in different sales territories ranged from $600,000 to $6 million annually. Territorial boundaries were drawn mainly on the basis of analyses of company and industry sales records indicating performances of both CSD and its thirty competitors. Further analysis of territorial sizes and potentials took into account the number of pieces of equipment already in each sales territory, their ages, and their models. After appraisal of these and other data, branch managers and the general manager determined market and sales potentials, made sales forecasts, and set the division's sales quotas. Experienced salespersons worked the larger-volume territories, newer salespeople the rest.

Management utilized a prospect classification system aimed toward improving control over field sales operations. All prospects for construction equipment were put into one of four categories:

1. Those who were *going to buy.*
2. Those who were *probably going to buy.*
3. Those *interested in buying.*
4. Those with almost *no interest in buying.*

Prospects in category 1 received the highest contact priority. Prospects stayed in category 2 for two weeks and in category 3 for three weeks; during these periods, contacts by sales personnel were used to qualify these prospects for other classifications. This system forced sales personnel to gauge the degree of buying intent in customers' minds. After a prospect bought equipment and became a customer, the division recorded the equipment's type, the date of sale, and the amount of sale. The company had recently computerized its prospect and customer classification system, utilizing the information to determine weekly routing schedules for the field sales personnel.

Management assigned quotas to all field sales personnel. Those failing to reach their quotas were required to submit written reports explaining the

EXHIBIT 1 · Organization Chart

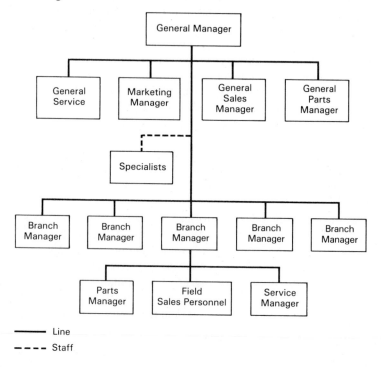

reasons for unsatisfactory performance. Branch managers reviewed these reports when considering salespersons' contract renewals.

Sales force compensation included a salary, averaging about 65 percent of the total income, and commissions on sales. Factors such as relative seniority, nature of territorial assignment, and recent performance compared with quota were used in determining base salaries. Commission rates varied according to the level of sales, and both rates and rate-break points differed among individual salespersons' contracts. In addition, certain product lines carried varying commission rates; for example, the contract of one salesperson provided on sales of Goliath equipment 1 percent commission up to $300,000, 1.25 percent from $300,000 to $450,000, and 1.5 percent above $450,000. Specialists also worked on a salary-plus-commission basis, sharing commissions on joint sales made with field sales personnel. Shared amounts varied with the type of equipment, the selling effort exerted, and the provisions of individual employment contracts.

CSD paid salespersons' travel and entertainment expenses in their entirety. In addition, all sales personnel participated in a profit-sharing plan which paid up to 17 percent of base salary, depending upon company profits.

Salespersons averaged between $28,000 and $34,000 in total compensation, compared with an average of from $18,000 to $22,000 for competitors' sales personnel. Sales executives received base salaries plus profit-sharing bonuses. Top management reviewed all compensation plans annually; however, only minor changes had been made in recent years.

Sales personnel reported to branch managers on their work plans, expense items, complaints and adjustments, and lost sales. They also submitted daily call reports. Copies of all salespersons' reports were sent to the central sales control unit, tabulated, and then forwarded to sales and marketing managers. Expense reimbursements occurred only after receipt of detailed expense reports. Selling expenses had expanded rapidly in the last two years, though executives had been unable to determine the reasons.

When salespersons lost two or more consecutive sales to the same account, branch managers immediately tried to determine if the reason was salesperson–customer incompatibility. On occasion, management reassigned certain customers to different salespersons. Branch managers, the sales manager, and the marketing manager all spent considerable time traveling with sales personnel.

CSD did not use sales contests or other devices involving special recognition for improved or outstanding sales performance. The management regarded such frills unnecessary in view of the high level of monetary compensation. CSD held seven formal sales meetings annually. Participants discussed such topics as new products, updating of sales techniques, and changes in company policy. "Improving morale" was a recurring and stated goal of such meetings.

CSD's annual sales force turnover rate was 12 percent; this compared with the industry's rate of 9 percent. The company did not conduct exit interviews, but management thought that most salespersons left because of greater monetary opportunities elsewhere. Three of the last five salespersons leaving the company, however, had gone to work for competitors.

Questions

1. What, if anything, should have been done to motivate CSD's sales personnel to perform more effectively?
2. Had you been called in as a management consultant to CSD, what would have been your recommendations?

6–5

Bristol Laboratories

Sales contests

Bristol Laboratories, a division of Bristol-Myers, was one of the world's largest manufacturers of antibiotics and pharmaceuticals. It had 725 salespersons deployed throughout the United States. Bristol faced managerial problems in motivation and in balancing the selling emphasis given its product lines. Management used sales contests to motivate and direct sales personnel. These ran continuously each month throughout the year.

Bristol's major brands included Tetrex, Saluron, Syncillin, Kantrex, Naldecon, Polycillin, Staphcillin, Prostaphlin, and Salutensin. Hospitals and drug wholesalers purchased direct from the company. Ultimate consumers bought Bristol's products from retail druggists on doctors' prescriptions.

Bristol's sales force was organized into ten regions containing sixty-five sales districts. Sales personnel were distributed within districts according to the sizes of individual territories and relative sales potentials. Their duties included calling on doctors, hospitals, and drug wholesalers, and making service calls on retail drugstores. Each salesperson visited an average of 120 doctors, ten hospitals, and two wholesalers per month.

The sales force compensation plan consisted of a small salary plus a 5 percent commission on territorial sales volume. K. J. Ryan, sales manager, believed the sales force was among the highest paid in the drug field. Salespeople averaged $26,000 annually, the top person earning $78,000 last year.

Through its sales contests, Bristol sought to direct sales personnel toward emphasizing all products in the line instead of only the high-commission, easy-to-sell items. While contests ran continuously, different products received emphasis each month. Ryan regarded money less important as an incentive than merchandise and travel awards, especially to a highly paid sales force. Sales personnel competed against predetermined territorial sales goals; management believed that using other bases for contests would have caused morale problems, as salespersons worked different territories and had varying selling abilities. In all sales contests, the closer a salesperson came to the established targets, the greater was the reward.

Maritz, Inc., a firm specializing in the organization and operation of sales incentive campaigns, planned and administered Bristol's contests. Four different drugs were promoted each month. One month these were Polycillin, Tetrex, Kantrex, and Naldecon. The marketing department estimated dollar sales and the percentage of each drug that should comprise a salesperson's total effort. December's target mix was 65 percent Polycillin, 23 percent Tetrex, 9 percent Kantrex, and 3 percent Naldecon.

The contest scoring system awarded prize points in two categories: (1) total sales of the four drugs and (2) performance relative to the target sales percentage mix. For each dollar of total sales, one-half of one prize point was awarded (for example, $12,000 total sales = 6,000 prize points). Points awarded in the second category, "mix points," were based on performance relative to the target sales mix. For example, salesperson X had actual sales as follows:

PRODUCT	TARGET MIX	TARGET SALES	ACTUAL SALES	PERFORMANCE RATING
Polycillin	65%	$ 6,500	$ 9,800	150%
Tetrex	23	2,300	1,650	72
Kantrex	9	900	360	40
Naldecon	3	300	360	120
Total	100%	$10,000	$12,170	

If X's sales had equaled the target sales, all the performance ratings in the last column would have been 100 percent. This column represented the percentages of drugs sold relative to the mix goal. Prize points ("mix points") were calculated by multiplying the lowest performance number by the "sales factor" set by management (see Exhibit 1). X's mix point total was 11,000 points (40 × 275 = 11,000). The lowest performance number was used in an effort to motivate sales personnel to make sales proportionate to management's target percentages. Total prize points earned by X were:

Total sales of promoted drugs ($12,170 ÷ 2) .... 6,085 points
Performance relative to target (40 × 275) .... 11,000 mix points
Total .... 17,085 prize points

Had X sold the exact targeted product mix, mix point total would have been 27,500, and total prize points 33,585.

"Prize-point" checks were mailed monthly, and were exchangeable for merchandise described in the Maritz catalog. Each prize point was worth

$.005 (17,085 points = $85.43). Management withheld the proper income tax each month. Points could be exchanged for almost any item imaginable, from airplanes to pearls. Travel awards consisted of trips to such places as London, Casablanca, and Tel Aviv.

Questions

1. Should Bristol have used sales contests? As many as it did?
2. What improvements, if any, might Bristol have made in its program for motivating and directing sales personnel?

EXHIBIT 1 · Memorandum—Bristol Laboratories

The contest items, product mix, and payoff for this sales month are:

	$	MIX
Polycillin	3,400,000	65
Tetrex	1,235,000	23
Kantrex	485,000	9
Naldecon	220,000	3
Total detail sales	5,340,000	100
Total sales estimate		$6,750,000
Total budget estimate		
(.9% of sales)		$60,750
Less ½ point per dollar sales		16,875
Mix payoff dollar budget		$43,875
Mix payoff in points		
($.005 × dollar budget)		8,775,000
Total detail items		5,340,000
60% of detail items*		3,204,000

$$\frac{3,204,000}{100} = \text{Sales factor} \qquad\qquad 32,040$$

$$\frac{\text{Mix points}}{\text{Sales factor}} = \frac{8,775,000}{32,040} = 275 \text{ Points/Sales Factor}$$

*Note: Determined by management.

7–1

AJAX PUMP COMPANY (B)

Pricing strategy for a new product introduction

Ajax Pump Company had developed a new product, a gear reduction unit called a "gear-box," in response to customers' requests (see Ajax Pump Company [A]). Prior to introducing the gear-box, management needed to develop an appropriate pricing strategy.

DETERMINATION OF PRODUCT PRICES

Ajax used a cost-plus approach in determining list prices for its catalog items.[1] The procedure was to take the item's production cost and multiply by a constant of 4.17. This constant included provisions for 25 percent margins for both the end user and the distributor and a 2 percent discount for payment within ten days of receipt of the invoice (2/10, net 30). The "net" multiple to Ajax after margins and discounts amounted to a constant of approximately 2.1 (see Exhibit 1 for a detailed description of the pricing procedure).

Ajax offered no quantity discounts on catalog items, as order size had practically no impact on prices. The company turned out thousands of pumps annually, each unit contributing a minute share to coverage of fixed costs and accounting for only a minute share of variable costs. Therefore, an order from any one distributor, regardless of order size, had an insignificant impact on total costs. As a result, the change in total cost per unit resulting from a large order was not sufficient to justify quantity discounts.

Management had another reason for not granting quantity discounts

[1]Catalog items came from the different product lines described in Ajax Pump Company (A). In effect, catalog items were those ordered from Ajax by distributors.

129

EXHIBIT 1 · Pricing Procedure

The formula used by Ajax determined the suggested price of catalog items by multiplying an item's cost by a constant of 4.17. The resulting price allowed a 56 percent margin for Ajax. In addition, it allowed discounts of 25 percent for both the distributor and the end user.

For example:

Assume Ajax had costs of $120 in producing an item, the list price would be:

$$\$120 \times 4.17 = \$500 \text{ (rounded)}$$

From the list price, discounts were computed. Starting with the end user and working backward, the distributor listed the item at $500, and could offer the end user the item at:

$$\$500 \times (1.00 - .25) = \$375$$

The distributor received a discount from Ajax as follows:

$$\$375 (1.00 - .25) = \$280 \text{ (rounded)}$$

Thus, Ajax received $280 from the distributor who resold the item for $375. The distributor's margin was:

$$(\$375 - \$280)/\$375 = .25$$

Note that the cost of the item to the distributor was 2.34 times the manufacturing cost; hence, the company realized a margin of 56 percent on the selling price. When cash discounts and commissions to the manufacturer's representatives were considered, this was reduced to a figure of 2.1.

on catalog items—not offering quantity discounts avoided connotations of inferior quality associated with discount pricing. Management wanted to maintain an image of superior quality. Shrewd purchasing agents were capable of manipulating the manufacturer's representatives into lower prices, but the no-discount policy eliminated the temptation to "give in" to such demands. Distributors, therefore, were encouraged to sell pumps at suggested list prices, and most did in "single-shot" transactions.

Ajax offered quantity discounts to original equipment manufacturers (OEM). OEMs were treated as special order situations since they generally did not order "standard" (catalog) items. Each OEM account required special production setups and designs because of individualized specifications. Ajax considered unit costs to be fixed (setup) costs plus actual production costs. Larger orders spread the fixed (setup) costs over more units, while variable costs (materials) decreased because of quantity purchases of raw materials. Therefore, each incremental unit ordered reduced per-unit costs by some amount. Larger orders incurred substantially lower per-unit costs than smaller orders, so management felt that quantity discounts were logically a part of the pricing structure for OEM accounts.

Questions

1. What questions should a company consider before pricing a new product?
2. What were the problems with Ajax's cost-plus pricing formula?
3. Should Ajax have used a penetration or a skimming strategy in pricing its gear-boxes?

7–2

ROANOKE RAPID ROOFERS

Determination of price strategy

As William Barnes sat in his rustic country home near Roanoke, Virginia (population 73,000), he wondered how he could get some of his large commercial bids accepted. His product and service were both better than those of conventional commercial roofing companies. But how could a relatively new process and business compete against established companies? He was reluctant to underbid the conventional roofers with a product which was more price efficient in the long run. On the other hand, he knew that he was competing with companies which had been doing business locally for years.

CONKLIN COMPANY, INC.

Roanoke Rapid Roofers was the area distributor for products manufactured by Conklin Company, Inc. The Conklin line contained approximately sixty products. Products formulated and manufactured by Conklin were cleaners, sealers, lubricants, wetting agents, micronutrients, and roofing materials. Other lubricants and hard goods were purchased by Conklin from other producers and resold to the distributors. The company's roofing material, RAPID ROOF®, was a latex product for coating roofs.

Conklin sold nothing direct to ultimate users, but confined its operation to selling through the distributors. All distributors purchased products directly from Conklin at the same unit prices, whether an initial purchase or subsequent purchase. The distributor relationship was expected to continue so long as the distributor complied with the rules and conditions set forth in the Conklin Distributor Agreement.

The agreement specified that Conklin would provide services in the areas of:

SALES AND MARKETING ASSISTANCE.   A Conklin field manager would provide orientation assistance to the distributor. This assistance would consist of advice and guidance on: (1) organizing the business, (2) products, pricing, and inventory, (3) methods of building customer confidence in the distributor, (4) methods of expanding the distributor's business, and (5) initial goals for the distributor. This assistance constituted the Conklin Orientation Program and usually took one working day.

ADVERTISING, TECHNICAL ASSISTANCE, AND PROMOTION.   Conklin did not use mass media advertising, but from time to time promoted Conklin products in media determined most effective and economical. Further, the distributor was required to submit all advertising to Conklin for approval prior to publication or use. Conklin had a promotion department charged with developing and offering for sale to distributors new or improved marketing and sales aids.

TRAINING.   Within sixty days after execution of the agreement, Conklin would make a Leadership Program available to the distributor. This consisted primarily of classroom lectures and demonstrations aimed to familiarize the distributor with Conklin Products, familiarize the distributor with Conklin operations, and present marketing and sales techniques and attitudes conducive to developing a successful business.

ROANOKE RAPID ROOFERS

Roanoke Rapid Roofers was a small commercial roofing company owned and operated by William Barnes, who bought the company when it was about a year and a half old. Shortly after acquiring the company, Barnes listed it in the telephone directory's Yellow Pages and arranged for the services of a local answering service. He also inherited a list of previous clients and the Roanoke area distributorship for Conklin Products. Mr. Barnes chose to concentrate initially on developing the commercial roofing business before moving into the other Conklin areas of operations.

Primarily through the previous owner's efforts, Roanoke Rapid Roofers continued profitable with the typical accepted roof repair bid ranging from $200 to $5,000. This business was sufficient for Mr. Barnes to keep a two- or three-person crew working most of the time.

Operations were profitable, but Mr. Barnes knew that to reach profit goals set, jobs in the $10,000 to $50,000 range were needed. The only difference between these jobs and current jobs was roof size. Roanoke had the personnel and equipment needed to complete jobs as quickly as competitors. However, Roanoke's pricing structure was slightly different, so bid prices were usually on the high side. Mr. Barnes, however, was convinced that the difference in bid price was more than justified by the increased roof life Conklin Products provided.

COMPETITION

Thirteen other roofing contractors were listed in the Yellow Pages of the Roanoke telephone directory. One of these, Perma Plastic, installed acrylic fiberglass roofs which were similar to those installed by Roanoke Rapid Roofers. The other roofing contractors advertised commercial reroofing, new roofs, and gutters as their major businesses—these consisted of conventional roofing techniques such as built-up roofing, asphalt shingles, and sheet metal. Except for one competitor, A-1 Roofing, all the companies listed had been doing business in Roanoke for ten years or more. A-1 had entered the market last summer.

THE MARKETING PROGRAM

Mr. Barnes used various techniques to market the services of Roanoke Rapid Roofers, including advertising, promotion, and personal selling. One small "continuing" advertisement was placed in the area's largest circulation newspaper, but failed to produce a single response and was canceled after a week. Little business had been generated by the Yellow Pages listing, so Barnes decided to reduce it to a standard one-line listing with the phone number.

Roanoke Rapid Roofers operated out of an office attached to Mr. Barnes' residence. He kept a small inventory of Conklin roofing materials at home, but for more extensive jobs materials were brought in from a regional Conklin warehouse in Greensboro, North Carolina, 100 miles away. Warehouse shipments were received twenty-four hours after the order was placed.

Mr. Barnes personally developed all quotes in response to bid requests. When a prospective customer contacted Roanoke Rapid Roofers, Mr. Barnes set up a visit with the prospect, measured the roof, and applied a standard-square-foot-pricing schedule to determine the amount of the bid. Once the roof was measured, determining the price was easy since the Conklin Company supplied a suggested pricing formula to its distributors. This formula had a "reasonable" profit built in for the distributor.

Mr. Barnes had tried to become active in the local Jaycees, believing this would provide opportunities to circulate among area business people. However, his industrial business largely consisted of repair jobs for local concerns; the only other industrial business was one small initial construction job and one complete reroofing job.

Mr. Barnes believed that the jobs Roanoke Rapid Roofers was doing were noticeably superior to those of competitors. He was convinced that the major strength of the enterprise was the quality of its work and that its reputation for doing fine work would spread by word of mouth. Nevertheless, he was disappointed at how long this process was taking.

Questions

1. What was the pricing objective of Roanoke Rapid Roofers? Was this appropriate?
2. Should Roanoke Rapid Roofers have priced above the competition, at the competitive level, or below competition to achieve its objectives?
3. How should Mr. Barnes have proceeded to become successful in the industrial roofing market?

7–3

DAYS INNS OF AMERICA, INC.

Pricing and the corporate image

In February of 1980, Roy B. Burnette, senior vice president of marketing and sales for Days Inn of America, Inc. (DIA), a chain of family-oriented budget motels, commented that DIA had two problems. One was that what guests experienced at one DIA motel, they expected of all. To a degree, this was desirable because with standardization of quality and service, DIA could ensure that guests associated the favorable impression received at one DIA motel with the next in another town. However, one thing could not be standardized—room rates. Management could not legally dictate an across-the-board rate to its franchisees, but it could set "guidelines," indicating a rate 20 percent to 30 percent lower than local competition. Widely varying rates adversely affected travelers' perceptions of DIA. "A tourist staying in a Fort Lauderdale Days Inn might pay $40 a night. How do you convince him that, in this area where the going rate is $60 and up, he is getting a real bargain? And how do you convince him that a Days Inn in Macon would not be as expensive?"

The second problem also concerned room rates. Under DIA's system, a one-franchise operation could be sold to a successor. As the franchise changed hands, the capital investment increased because of rising property prices, higher interest rates on loans, refurbishing costs, and other expenses. So, to obtain a reasonable return on investment, the new owner raised prices.

BACKGROUND

The Days Inns chain of "budget luxury" motels was founded in 1970 by Cecil B. Day, who had made a fortune in real estate and construction. He "retired" at age 35, intending to devote his life to his church and family. Shortly afterward, while traveling with his wife and five children, he became convinced that a need existed for inexpensive, family-oriented, quality roadside motels.

Driving through New England in 1968, Mr. Day concluded that motel rates were burdensomely high for the average vacationing family. This market segment needed a motel operation positioned in the niche between cheap, spartan motels, and high-priced luxury facilities. Day's target market, therefore, was the traveling, vacationing family. He wanted to provide quality lodging, fair and honest service, and a wholesome family atmosphere. Liquor was prohibited from any DIA property, and two Bibles were in every room.

Day's first unit, named "8 Days Inn" (because of the eight-dollar room rate) opened at Savannah Beach, Georgia, in 1970 with room rates 40 percent to 50 percent less than the competition. By eliminating costly lobbies and elaborate convention facilities, DIA has since kept its prices 20 percent to 30 percent under the competition, but as inflation pushed room rates up, the "8" was dropped from the logo.

DEVELOPMENT PATTERN

The chain expanded up and down the U.S. east coast, along the main highways from New England to Florida. Then it expanded westward and into the north central states. DIA licensed Canterra Development Corporation to develop "Days Inn" and "Days Lodge" motel–hotels in Canada and in 1979 one Days Inn in Cambridge, Ontario, was operating and five more were planned or under construction.

The majority of Days Inns—some 60 percent—were franchised, 27 percent were company owned, and 13 percent were owned by DIA-affiliated companies. The chain had 308 motels, making it the sixth largest motel chain in America. This ranking was based on number of properties owned—thus excluding Best Western (which would otherwise rank second), Budget Hotels, and Friendship Inns; these were referral systems operating national reservations systems but not owning motels.

During the 1973 oil embargo, DIA installed gas pumps at all its motels to ensure gas supplies for guests. Guests could plan their daily travel from one Days Inn to the next, and be assured of getting gas each morning. During the summer 1978 gas shortage, DIA lost 5 percentage points in occupancy rate while the industry lost 20 percentage points. DIA even managed to decrease its room occupancy breakeven point from a breakeven point of 60 percent in 1978 to 50 percent in 1979.

After Mr. Day's death in December 1978, Richard Kessler became chairman of the board. This was a nominal change, as Mr. Kessler had been given complete operational authority over the company years before. Mr.

Day, son of a Baptist preacher, was a very religious man and felt the need to spend most of his time directing the religious and charitable activities of the Day Company Foundation, a nonprofit organization that received 10 percent of the after-tax profits. During the chain's rapid growth (one room built every 20 minutes from 1971 through 1975), Kessler and Day stuck to the philosophy that good, honest, no-frills lodging was what people wanted.

By 1979, Days Inns had expanded as far west as Arizona. It operated in twenty-eight states and Canada and was planning further expansion into Colorado and California. In addition, a Days Inns affiliate, C. B. Day Realty of Florida, was planning to expand further into southeast Florida. DIA was working to saturate the Washington, D.C., area, building five DIA units in the Alexandria, Virginia, area.

Over the years, the target market changed and expanded to include not only vacationing American families, but vacationing foreigners, traveling business people, truck drivers, and senior citizens. The major thrust of the advertising and facilities' design, however, remained geared to the middle-income family with two or more children, two or more cars, and two or more weeks of annual vacation.

THE U.S. MOTEL INDUSTRY

Rapid expansion of the interstate highway system, coupled with cheap gasoline prices, encouraged a burgeoning of family vacationing travelers in the 1950s. "Tourist courts" mushroomed, and unlike downtown hotels, they were convenient, informal, and cheap—and the car stayed right outside the room's front door. Most motels were small, independently owned, and of variable quality. "Twenty years ago," said an industry observer, "you'd always go in first and look over the room, because many were kind of sleazy, and the beds were poor. Even if you took the room, you couldn't count on things like the air conditioning working."

Holiday Inns was the first to recognize the unfilled niche between motel accommodations of uncertain quality and expensive hotels. The first Holiday Inn opened in Memphis in 1952, letting children stay free with parents, and offering ice, a swimming pool, room telephone, and kennel service. The consumer appeal was the chain's assurance that what they knew about one Holiday Inn, they could expect of all. "You always know there'll be a Coke machine at the end of the hall and a certain standard of housekeeping," said one consumer, "and the rooms always have a work area."

Much standardization grew out of cost control. "There's a conscious effort to standardize," said Roy Burnette, "given maintenance and replacement costs, and the chance to buy in quantity." By the 1970s there were several competitive chains, each offering standardized accommodations and service. The 1973–1975 recession and gas crisis proved a watershed for the industry. Marginal mom-and-pop operations folded by the thousands, and the large chains applied sophisticated marketing techniques while scrambling for larger market shares. According to Dan Phillip, vice president, Market Group Research and Development for Holiday Inns, the marketing trend in the lodging industry was a cross between a consumer service and a prepackaged good. "The primary commonality," said Phillip, "is that the person getting a burger or renting a room en route has very little psychological commitment to the product, so you can have a standardized system of rules for delivering that product, whether it's a Big Mac, a Whopper, or a Holiday Inn room."

The industry's market research began to define, describe, and segment the market. Business travel was confirmed as the most steady segment, even during travel slumps caused by gas shortages, and provided the largest dollar volume. Family vacationers, even in summer, accounted for a quarter of the total volume. Industry insiders observed that the nation was taking shorter pleasure trips, and doing more "destination" travel. The number of women travelers—almost 30 percent of U.S. business travel—was increasing, according to Best Western. More women were also traveling with their children.

By 1979 chains controlled 29 percent of U.S. motel properties and 63 percent of the rooms. According to Standard and Poor's, 52 percent of the lodging industry's business was from business travel, 25 percent from pleasure, and the rest from conventions. Pleasure travel was aided by many factors, including increased leisure time, and the coming of age of the post–World War II baby boom. The dollar's weakness in foreign markets encouraged more foreigners to travel in the United States and kept more Americans vacationing at home.

Some chains began to court the business segment by locating units around airports and metropolitan locations, and providing convention facilities, lounges, and entertainment. Others focused on featuring their operations as destinations in themselves, going into resort properties, and later into gambling. In 1979 the *Los Angeles Times* noted that hotels and motels have come full circle, from one-story motels on the highway to high-rise hotels clustered around urban centers.

Since the 1973 oil embargo, motel chain growth (in terms of number of rooms) had been modest (see Exhibit 1). Chains focused on refurbishing old rooms and "pruning" marginal units from their systems, concentrating on airport and metropolitan locations. Ramada Inns and Howard Johnson reduced the number of motels in their systems. By 1980 new construction had picked up after bottoming out in 1975, but construction costs still rose rapidly. In 1979, the average cost of constructing a "modest" motel was $20,000 a room. Because of rising construction and financing costs, industry observers predicted a shortage of rooms by the early 1980s. In order to expand more rapidly, most leading chains franchised extensively.

EXHIBIT 1 · Worldwide Growth in Number of Rooms for Selected Hotel Chains (in thousands of units)

CHAINS	1970	1972	1974	1976	1977	1978	ANNUAL GROWTH RATE FROM 1970 (%)
Holiday Inns	182.5	222.7	267.0	278.1	279.0	286.5	5.7
Best Western	NA*	80.0	90.0	109.1	141.2	152.7	11.3
ITT Sheraton	59.6	71.5	90.2	97.2	99.2	102.0	7.5
Ramada Inns	35.6	60.0	91.6	94.3	95.0	92.5	12.7
Trust House	46.5	52.7	56.6	76.3	81.5	75.0	7.7
Hilton Hotels	46.5	47.7	56.7	62.8	62.9	66.7	5.2
Howard Johnson	39.5	46.8	58.1	59.2	59.2	59.1	5.5

*NA means not available.
Source: Service World International.

FRANCHISE OPERATION

DIA's franchise operation presented three important advantages. One was that franchising widened the operating area, providing the opportunity to cover more territory. A second was that each franchise paid DIA a minimum initial fee of $15,000 and monthly payments of 3 percent of gross receipts. This helped fuel the company's own motel development. A third was that franchising spread the risk—if a particular franchise lost money, the effect on DIA was minimal.

The main disadvantage of franchising was loss of immediate control over operating units. The room rates set by franchisees presented a problem, as DIA management had no way to dictate rates at levels 20 percent to 30 percent under local competitors—the competitive edge needed to preserve the budget luxury image. Persuading franchisees to post suggested rates was complicated by rising property values. As the original owners sold motels, buyers paid higher prices—new owners had to charge higher room rates than their predecessors to earn satisfactory returns on their investments.

DIA sold franchisees nonexclusive rights to build and operate Days Inn Plan facilities, and expected them to obtain their own debt financing. Franchisees had to have at least 25 percent equity investment, total cost. So with a motel of 122 rooms costing $20,000 per room to build the franchisee needed $600,000 in equity. Franchisees also were required to spend $6,100 minimum on promotion for two months before and three months after the motel opening.

The contract was filled with rules governing service quality. To maintain the Days Inns "image," no franchisee was "allowed to sell any materials deemed by franchisor as pornographic," or "to sell, serve, or apply for any license, permit or authority to sell or serve alcoholic beverages (or permit consumption of alcoholic beverages in any restaurant or public building area) on the premises or any other property adjacent or contiguous thereto, which is owned or controlled, directly or indirectly, by Franchisee."

In 1979 DIA received a total of 75 applications—46 met financial guidelines, and 38 were approved.

STATUS AS PRIVATELY HELD CORPORATION

Privately held DIA did not pursue profit maximization as a publicly held company might have. The outstanding stock was owned by thirty-one executives and motel managers who were interested in plowing back cash flow into such projects as installing solar heating panels and expanding the reservation center—both likely to prove cost effective. Short-term net income generation was a secondary priority.

The owners also leaned toward investing in unique projects with uncertain payback periods. DIA had paid a world-renowned painter to give lessons to a talented employee, and planned to receive royalties from future sales of the employee's art, once he became famous. A similar dream lay behind DIA's sponsorship of James Tillman, "The Voice of Days Inns." DIA executives recognized Tillman's extraordinary singing ability, so they regularly sponsored his performances; in 1979 he sang the national anthem, opening the 35th Annual National Cherry Blossom Festival Parade in Washington, D.C. Top management hoped he would get a chance to sing on the *Lawrence Welk Show*. If he "made it big" in the television and recording industry, DIA would earn a handsome return on its investment.

RESERVATIONS SYSTEM

DIA's reservation center was computerized and had one hundred reservation agents each using an on-line terminal to reserve rooms twenty-four hours a day for people calling a toll-free number. This system was leased from MICOR, Inc., a Ramada Inns subsidiary. The center was in Atlanta at company headquarters, and in case the system "went down" the agents used manually operated card files as backups. In 1979 the center took 3.4 million calls and made 1.8 million reservations, telephone charges exceeding $1 million. Plans had been finalized to expand the reservation facility from 8,000 to 15,000 square feet, and to increase the number of agents to from 150 to 180 the next year. Each reservation agent handled approximately 33,750 calls annually.

DIA ADVERTISING AND PROMOTION

DIA overall marketing philosophy was to meet the needs of five audiences. The first was the customers. All advertisements and promotions aimed to generate new customers, retain existing customers, and attract dissatisfied customers—recent advertisements, for example, aimed to alter dissatisfied customers' perceptions of the chain, to convince them of the Days Inns' "budget luxury" image, and to persuade them to try the chain again. The second audience was the business and financial community—DIA considered it important to project a sound financial image to banks, savings and loans, and insurance companies—sources for most of the company's funding. The third audience was made up of potential investors—DIA needed to convince potential franchisees that investments in the "Days Inns Plan" received strong support in nationwide promotions, local cooperative advertising, and motel-management expertise. The fourth audience consisted of existing franchisees. DIA advertisements sought to keep them favorably disposed to the franchise operation and to reinforce positive perceptions of the DIA's public relations efforts. The fifth audience was made up of 10,000 DIA employees—company advertisements aimed to make employees proud of their jobs and of the company. Employees who took pride in what they were doing, it was reasoned, would be better able to persuade customers of the value offered by DIA services.

DIA had its own in-house marketing department. It handled most production and placement of promotional material, including copy, layout, and graphic arts, while DIA's New York advertising agency placed national advertising. One of the largest marketing expenditures, and the most cost effective, was the $1 million spent annually on outdoor billboards and signs (see Exhibit 2). The first few years this was the only advertising the company could afford, but this still was an inexpensive and effective way to call travelers' attention to the inns. DIA signs, painted bright yellow, and all using the same format and "sunrise-in-the-cupola" logo, were distinctive and easy to see from highways.

The marketing department in 1979 spent $2.5 million on TV (Channel 17, Atlanta), radio (4,000 spots nationwide), and print media. TV spots were broadcast via satellite to stations throughout the United States, while radio spots were broadcast from stations along major interstate highways in the early morning and evening.

During 1979, DIA spent $30.1 million for replacement of almost everything in the motel rooms (see Exhibit 3). This was the third year of a four-year plan for upgrading every company-owned room. DIA replaced carpet in over 5,000 rooms, installed new wall vinyl in more than 2,000, and replaced color TVs in 9,500 rooms at a cost of $2.3 million. Other expenditures were for new bedspreads, bedding, drapes, lamps, chairs, vanities, pictures, and air conditioners.

To reduce the impact of energy costs on room prices, DIA installed solar heating panels (funded in part through federal grants) in eleven inns. A solar heating system for one motel cost $10,163 to install. The anticipated payback period was four years.

In 1975 DIA directed promotion toward senior citizens, a market segment not previously cultivated by the lodging industry. Free membership cards

EXHIBIT 2 · Days Inn Outdoor Billboard

in "September Days Club" were issued entitling holders to 10 percent discounts on food, gifts, gasoline, and lodging costs at participating motels. Though the program was originally intended to run in September only, the time limit was eliminated and the club grew from 75,000 members in March 1975 to 800,000 in January 1977.

Membership was no longer free in 1977, and members paid a $3 annual membership fee (or $7.50 for three years, or got a life membership "for yourself and spouse" for $15). In 1979 the annual fee was raised to $5 (for single or couple) and membership dropped back to 500,000. Besides getting discounts on motel costs, members received 25 percent discounts on Hertz Rent-a-Cars, cut rates at certain theme parks and attractions, a four-color quarterly magazine (*September Days*), and participation in club conventions.

The national director of the club, Tom C. Lawler, said club members "take good care of our rooms, they travel most often in pairs, and usually in the spring and fall off-seasons. They tend to eat where they stay, and take advantage of their discounts by eating at Days Inns in their home towns. They are a tremendous market!" By 1977 senior citizens were accounting for 15 to 20 percent of total DIA occupancy.

DIA at first paid commissions to travel agents only for group bookings

EXHIBIT 3 · Refurbished DIA Room

of ten or more. This was changed in 1977 when a prepaid voucher system, Travel Agent Nite Chek (TANC), was instituted. Through TANC, agents earned 10 percent commissions on rooms booked at any DIA properties. Bookings by travel agents increased by about 200 percent in the TANC system's first year.

Promotion of the TANC program was low key and accounted for 5 percent of total occupancy, but DIA planned to step up the promotion of TANC. According to Mr. Wright, "We look upon our travel agent customers as a market. Our business from bus tours has increased tremendously because of agent involvement." DIA had increased its advertising of TANC and planned to attend more trade shows to work with travel industry personnel. A thirty-two page directory of locations and rates was made available to agents and customers at no charge. The directory had recently been restructured and made available to the general public through a four-page supplement in the PARADE section of Sunday newspapers, enabling Days Inns to reach over 18 million U.S. homes. In addition, DIA's New York agency placed advertisements in *Time, Newsweek, People, National Geographic, TV Guide, Life,* and *Better Homes and Gardens* (see Exhibit 4).

FUTURE PLANS

Despite shifts in travel patterns of the American public, DIA management reaffirmed its commitment to market the chain to the family, the business traveler, and the senior citizen, while communicating the message of savings, comfort, and convenience. Roy Burnette saw Days Inns occupying the niche in the travel market that chains such as Holiday Inns abandoned when they built expensive high rises, resorts, and casinos. When asked if he saw Days Inn occupying that same niche ten or fifteen years from 1980, he said, "Yes."

In spite of the generally favorable outlook, DIA executives, most notably Mr. Burnette, had been unable to devise, yet alone implement, plans to resolve DIA's central dilemma. Rising interest rates and property values

EXHIBIT 4 · Typical Days Inn Magazine Advertisement

were continuing to escalate the prices of franchised units changing hands, forcing new owners to raise room rates which, in turn, threatened to change the DIA image from a "budget luxury" motel chain to a motel chain with "continually rising room rates."

Questions

1. What, if anything, should have been done about the escalating room rates?
2. What, if anything, did DIA have to sell besides low price?
3. Did DIA have the proper market segments targeted? Why or why not?

7-4

STADIUM COMFORT, INC.

Acceptance of private-brand order

Stadium Comfort, Inc., of Portland, Oregon, specialized in making blankets for spectator use at outdoor sports events. Distributing its output through selected dealers, both in large cities and in university towns, the company won recognition as a leading maker of sports blankets, and operations proceeded smoothly and profitably over the first several years. Recently, however, a general business recession had set in, causing sales to decline to the point where the production rate was cut to 55 percent of plant capacity. About this time a large retail organization asked Stadium Comfort to produce the identical sports blankets for it, but under a private label. Executives were divided on the question of whether to accept the order.

The founders, both of whom had considerable experience in textile manufacturing, set up the business to cater to the "comfort" needs of spectators at outdoor sports events, such as football and baseball games, track and field meets, winter sports carnivals, crew races, and rodeos. With continuing expansion of both intercollegiate athletics and professional sports, they visualized spectators as an already large and growing market segment for items designed to make spectatorship more comfortable, particularly in cold weather and at night events. While various products had been tried, such as stadium seats and cushions, eventually management decided to concentrate on making blankets of synthetic fibers (many of them in "team" colors), which spectators could use either for warmth or for sitting upon.

The large retail organization, which had never bought from Stadium Comfort before, offered to contract for fifty thousand private-label blankets for delivery over the next twelve months at a price of $5.50 each. It refused to accept the sales manager's counterproposal to supply the fifty thousand blankets under Stadium Comfort's label at the established selling price of $7.00 each. The retail organization operated a chain of sports shops and leased departments, mainly located in cities along the Atlantic Coast from New England to Florida.

Various executives pointed out reasons favoring or opposing acceptance of the contract. A few opposed acceptance on the grounds that the company had a long-standing policy against producing for private-label customers, since they might take business away from customers selling the Stadium Comfort label. The president and the production manager wanted to accept the order because, they said, it would make it possible to keep the plant operating and the skilled work force intact. The sales manager, in arguing against acceptance, emphasized that the offer was below the "hitherto uniform selling price" and would likely cause bad relations with established accounts. At an executive committee meeting called to discuss the chain's proposal, the controller presented the figures shown in Exhibit 1.

EXHIBIT 1 · Stadium Comfort's Cost Structure

Output level (in units)	100,000	150,000	200,000 (plant capacity)
Selling price/unit	$7.00	$7.00	$7.00
Cost/unit	$7.70	$6.50	$5.95
Margin/unit	($0.70)	$0.50	$1.05
Sales volume ($)	$700,000	$1,050,000	$1,400,000
Costs:			
General, administrative, and other fixed costs	$210,000	$210,000	$ 210,000
Factory overhead and other semi-fixed costs	150,000	285,000	420,000
Direct labor, materials, sales commissions, and other variable costs	410,000	480,000	560,000
Total costs	$770,000	$975,000	$1,190,000
Profit (loss)	($70,000)	$75,000	$210,000

Question

Should Stadium Comfort have accepted the private-brand order? Why or why not?

7–5

C. C. CHESTELLE COMPANY

Pricing wholesale produce

C. C. Chestelle Company, a fruit and vegetable wholesaler located in a Rochester, New York, suburb, sold to small-town retailers in an area extending from Rochester to Syracuse. Chestelle experienced pricing difficulties in competing with chains, supermarkets, and large-city wholesalers. Consequently, its selling strategy was to concentrate on serving the needs of retailers in the small towns and in the smaller cities rather than those of retailers in the two large metropolitan areas.

Two major factors influenced adoption of this strategy:

1. Established produce wholesalers, operating in the two metropolitan areas, had a strong local competitive advantage because they had cultivated both large and small retailers for many years.
2. City grocers customarily made daily early-morning visits to wholesale produce markets, buying directly from commission houses, various specialized wholesalers (such as banana specialists, lettuce and celery houses, and potato and onion dealers), and local growers and truck farmers.

In the small towns, Chestelle met its main competition from two firms. One operated out of Rochester, selling in the western part of Chestelle's selling area. The other, a Syracuse wholesaler, made calls in the eastern part of Chestelle's area.

C. C. Chestelle, the proprietor, set up four sales routes, assigning a salesperson and a helper to each. Salespersons bought produce to meet their customers' anticipated requirements from commission merchants and farmers at the Rochester regional market in the predawn hours each morning. They began making deliveries at 7:00 A.M., completing them by 2:30 P.M. Sales and deliveries were made routinely five days per week; "special" deliveries were sometimes made on Saturdays. Besides supervising general operations, Chestelle personally acted as the salesperson on one of the routes. He planned to hire someone to take over this route, but he had been unable to recruit an acceptable person.

Chestelle emphasized high-quality produce, selling low-quality items only when specifically ordered by customers. Chestelle based prices on the assumption that produce quality was more important than price to his clientele. He attributed much of the company's success to strict adherence to this pricing strategy plus its ability to provide individualized account service. Through Chestelle's personal selling efforts, his thirty-five years of experience in the wholesale produce field, and his managerial ability, sales increased from $400,000 ten years ago to $960,000 last year. He predicted a 10 percent sales increase for the coming year.

Chestelle sold to 175 retailers, with the greatest volume coming from nonaffiliated medium and large independently operated grocery stores and supermarkets. Many retailer accounts, however, were members of voluntary chains. Chestelle's other accounts included fruit stands, open only during the summer, and a few restaurants. During the winter, to maintain volume, Chestelle pushed sales to small neighborhood grocers.

The company's largest selling and most profitable produce items were bananas, lettuce, and potatoes. These three items accounted for 65 percent of the total sales volume. The average dollar markup on cost ranged from $0.25 to $1.50 on lettuce in eighteen- and twenty-four-head crates, $0.50 to $1.00 on bananas in thirty-five-pound boxes, and $0.50 to $1.00 on potatoes in one-hundred-pound lots.

Although bananas, lettuce, and potatoes were Chestelle's "bread and butter," other items, including apples, citrus fruits, onions, and watermelons, brought in substantial profits during certain seasons. For example, at harvest time Chestelle bought apples from local orchardists and stored them until sold. Last year Chestelle sold twenty-five thousand boxes of cellophane-packed apples. One year, during a heat wave, the company sold five thousand watermelons in a single week.

The firm handled other produce items, such as green onions, beets, radishes, cucumbers, mushrooms, endive, and escarole. As these were highly perishable items, spoilage sometimes wiped out low profit margins. However, since customers frequently wanted these specialty items, Chestelle insisted on handling them.

Markups varied widely; Chestelle gave four major reasons:

1. *Size of customer.* (Larger customers bought larger lots and demanded lower prices.)
2. *Market conditions.* (When wholesale buying prices rose above normal levels, Chestelle found it difficult to secure standard markups.)

3. *Produce type.* (High unit value items, such as cantaloupes and grapes, carried higher markups than lower valued items, such as locally grown cabbage and onions, because of both greater investment and higher risk of spoilage.)
4. *Intensity of retail account competition.* (When large supermarkets threatened serious price competition, lower markups were taken on certain items, particularly those sold to larger accounts.)

As a pricing goal, Chestelle aimed for an average markup of 20 percent on cost, but he actually realized only about 13 percent. He believed that his direct competitors, operating out of Rochester and Syracuse, had similar pricing goals and experienced comparable difficulties in pricing so as to permit their customers to meet retail price competition from large supermarkets.

For the most part Chestelle concentrated purchases with a select group of commission merchants and farmers at the regional market. This, he believed, resulted in his paying lower prices because he also bought in larger lot sizes. It also enabled him to strengthen business ties with a small group of sellers, leading to special discounts and improving his chances of getting supplies during market shortages. Frequently he bought staple produce items in advance, storing them in his own modern warehouse.

Buying practices of Chestelle's retail-level competitors varied. Chain outlets bought through central buying points, and large independent supermarkets bought direct from regional-market commission merchants. Typically, chain store buyers purchased full carloads of shipped-in produce, stored it in regional warehouses, and dispersed it to individual outlets. Fairly often, however, chain store produce managers received short shipments or shipments of items not ordered. Chain store produce managers also had little to say about produce buying and pricing, such decisions being made at chain central buying offices.

Chestelle's customers chronically complained about the low prices featured by chain and large supermarket competitors. These complaints increased when competitors promoted weekend, holiday, and other specials. In helping his larger accounts meet competition, Chestelle sometimes lowered prices on specific items. However, it did not always take a competitor's special promotion for a customer to complain, since supermarkets seemed always able to sell at lower prices. Chestelle's accounts argued that they could not maintain adequate margins if they cut produce prices to competitive levels.

Questions

1. To become more competitive, should Chestelle's policies on quality and price have been changed?
2. How appropriate was Chestelle's selling strategy?

7–6

CENTRAL SOYA

Pricing poultry

Central Soya, in Decatur, Indiana, was the largest domestic processor of soybeans, as well as a leading manufacturer and distributor of concentrated livestock and poultry feeds. Other corporate efforts included grain merchandising and poultry production and processing. The company had four operating divisions: (1) soya processing, (2) chemurgy, (3) feed sales and field operations, and (4) grain operations. Forty-four percent of sales traced to soybean processing, 37 percent to feed and poultry, and 19 percent to grain merchandising.

A few years ago Central Soya launched a poultry-processing operation, as did other diversified feed manufacturers. Management predicted rapid growth for not only the poultry industry but also the feed market. Management was attracted by the opportunity for increasing feed sales without increasing selling costs.

Soya faced three types of competition: (1) meat packers doing poultry processing, including Armour, Swift, and Wilson, (2) other feed manufacturers, such as Pillsbury and Ralston Purina, engaged in poultry processing, and (3) specialized poultry processors, such as Rockingham and Southeastern Poultry.

As Soya and other feed manufacturers became more involved in broiler production, they recognized the need for coordinating and controlling the various broiler-processing activities. Therefore they either combined or coordinated diverse activities formerly performed by separate organizations— breeders, hatching egg producers, hatcheries, broiler growers, feed dealers, and processors. Soya's management accomplished this through vertical integration and contractual arrangements.

152

Contractual arrangements reflected a continuing shift of management and risk from growers to contractors. Generally, growers furnished the land, buildings, equipment, water, electricity, and labor. Contractors provided other inputs, such as management services, medicine, feed, and labor to catch and transport the broilers to processing.

As the number of contracts increased, processors assumed an inflexible commitment. With a forty-week production cycle from establishment of a breeder flock to marketable broilers, and a two- to four-day optimum marketing period, processors had to forecast market requirements nine months ahead or suffer the consequences of oversupply or undersupply. If insufficient demand existed during the marketing period, the processor had three alternatives: (1) overproducing, thereby reducing the market prices, (2) destroying the broilers, or (3) maintaining and continuing to feed the broilers until a demand developed, at which time they might be too old to be marketable. Processors ordinarily chose to overproduce and endure depressed prices. Processing costs depended primarily on the plant's hourly capacity. Soya, for instance, experienced significant economies of scale as the processing rate increased to six thousand birds per hour; however, rates of six thousand to ten thousand birds per hour resulted in no significant cost reductions.

Three salespersons, located in the central poultry marketing office in Atlanta, sold Soya's poultry products, primarily broilers. A fourth salesperson sold out of the Fort Wayne corporate office, but specialized in credit checks for new customers and in handling customer complaints. In overproduction situations, "plant salespersons" assisted the four regular salespersons in finding outlets. The four regular salespersons reported to the general manager of field operations. The plant salesperson's job was mainly to handle customer complaints, coordinate and process orders from the central office, and make processed broiler shipments.

Central office salespersons spent most of their time processing and following up customers' orders. They devoted little time to developing new prospects or contacting existing customers. About 90 percent of the orders came by telephone. Sales personnel consolidated orders weekly and transmitted them to processing plants.

Soya's marketing channel included large grocery chains, institutions, poultry distributors, and, on an "emergency overproduction" basis, smaller grocery stores and retail outlets near processing plants. The largest customer, Kroger, bought approximately 85 percent of Soya's production. Occasionally, Soya sold to A & P. Commercial buyers included such outlets as Colonel Sanders's Kentucky Fried Chicken. Soya also sold to distributors in Virginia, North Carolina, and Georgia, who in turn resold broilers to restaurants, independent grocery stores, hospitals, schools, and other outlets.

Soya fit its broiler-pricing strategies, to a large extent, to customers' purchasing policies. For example, Soya priced to Kroger on a mutually agreed price base, such as USDA's[1] daily *Dairy and Poultry Market News Report.* Soya also used the *Urner Barry Report,* another common price index, which summarized market conditions as to current production levels, market requirements, and wholesale and retail prices. It billed Kroger at the published price on the shipment date. The pricing procedure for sales to A & P differed, as processors submitted bids to A & P's corporate office and made shipments when notified that their bids had been accepted. Soya's prices usually included shipping, ranging from one to one and three-quarters cents per pound, from plant to destination.

Soya's average prices ranged from twenty-five to twenty-eight cents per pound. Kroger's retail prices varied from thirty-nine to forty-one cents per pound, a markup averaging about eleven cents per pound on whole broilers. Kroger secured an additional five- to thirty-cent premium by packaging select broiler pieces. Food distributors' resale prices ranged from twenty-eight to thirty-one cents per pound, giving them a three- to five-cent markup per pound. Retail outlets, supplied by poultry distributors, priced broilers at thirty-nine to forty-one cents per pound, thereby obtaining an eight- to eleven-cent markup per pound.

Primarily because of reduced earnings tracing to depressed broiler prices, Soya's management decided to centralize broiler marketing, with the goal of reducing pricing volatility. It also began using computers for controlling broiler production and distribution. Analyses were also made of the feasibility of freezing excess production in times of inadequate demand.

Studies showed that additional costs incurred in freezing and storing made frozen broilers less price competitive than fresh broilers. In addition, other problems existed: (1) consumers preferred fresh broilers, and (2) because it was difficult to know when to market frozen broilers, the usual result was to add to the oversupply, depressing prices further. Consequently, management sought to minimize shipping time from plant to retail outlet because of demand for fresh broilers.

Surveys identified six factors retailers regarded as important in choosing a supplier. These factors, in order of importance to buyers, were (1) product quality, (2) price, (3) supplier reputation, (4) supplier location, (5) supplier-provided merchandising and other services, and (6) established supplier relationships.

Up until five years ago the commercial broiler industry expanded output annually and sold all of it at profitable prices. After that time, rapid technological developments in broiler production and processing created an imbalance between broiler supply and demand. Noting this, Soya's management reevaluated its marketing program to determine the actions required to reduce price volatility inherent in broiler operations.

[1]U.S. Department of Agriculture.

Questions

1. What improvements, if any, should Soya's management have made in its pricing strategies?
2. Contrast the pricing of agricultural and other products.

8–1

ACE MANUFACTURING COMPANY

Decision to cultivate an additional market segment

Ace Manufacturing Company made baseball and softball bats in its Juniper, Alabama, plant and sold them throughout the United States and in Central and South America. The company used two marketing channels. (See figure following.) Ace's major line, Linedrive, was sold through wholesalers and direct to large retailers; bats made according to retailers' specifications and those carrying private labels were sold direct. Ace had never tried to secure orders from professional baseball teams but, believing that the top-grade Linedrive models were of high enough quality for professional use, top management was currently weighing the advisability of cultivating this market segment.

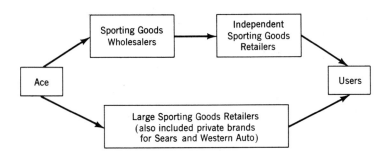

Ace ranked fourth in total industry sales, behind Hillerich and Bradsby (H and B), Hanna, and Adirondack, but ranked second in sales of softball bats. Regular brands accounted for 80 percent of its total sales of

$500,000, with the balance being made up of private-label business. Line-drive brands were bought and used primarily by semipro, school, and youth teams.

All industry members had difficulty in procuring raw wood for bat production. Smaller firms such as Ace had the most difficulty, as they had weaker bargaining positions. Ash grown in the northeastern United States was the best hardwood for bats. Used not only for making bats but for making skis, sleds, and furniture, ash wood was almost always in short supply, and fierce competition existed among buyers. This had led the larger bat makers to experiment with substitute materials, both other woods and some light metals. However, on laminated and aluminum models, product weight proved difficult to control in meeting required strength specifications. Players also balked at using the "new" bats, and industry executives concluded that the market wanted bats made of wood—preferably ash.

Ace offered twenty-eight models under the Linedrive name: four for semipro, college, and high school use; three approved for Pony and Babe Ruth leagues; six for Little League; and fifteen for playing softball. More expensive models were made of northern ash; less expensive models of hickory and other hardwoods. Bat models came in different finishes, colors (stains), lengths, weights, handle and barrel sizes,[1] and with or without handle wrappings (tape, foam rubber, or fiberglass).

Ace sold at competitive prices. The "top of the line" (used mainly by semipro, college, and high school teams) retailed at $9.80; comparable H and B and Hanna models retailed at $10.25. Little League models and softball bats carried lower prices. The "bottom of the line" retailed at $4.50. Retailers' markups averaged 40 percent.

Although some top-line Ace baseball bats carried the names of certain major league stars, none were either "signature" models or actually used by these players. All the stars had done was to "approve" certain styles as being similar to the bats they actually used. The rest of the baseball bat line and all softball bats carried names, such as Bomber, Swatter, and Slasher.

Ace employed thirty full-time people: twenty-four in manufacturing and six in sales. Sales personnel called on sporting goods wholesalers and large retailers, selling Linedrive models. The main office dealt directly with private-label accounts. Sales personnel received 15 percent commission on sales and paid their own expenses. In addition, each time a salesperson covered a trade show or a convention, he or she received a flat fee of $200.

Ace spent its entire $5,000 advertising budget last year on trade-journal advertising and product brochures. The ads, which appeared during the playing season, emphasized quality at reasonable prices. Product brochures stressed the modern manufacturing process, an aspect of the operation that had led to widespread industry emulation in the drying, curing, and finishing stages.

---

[1] The *barrel* is the bat's hitting portion.

Ace's main competitor was Hanna, a company also serving the non-professional market segment exclusively. H and B and Adirondack dominated the professional market, and Ace's top managers were considering the advisability of invading this segment of the market. The sales manager, a former H and B employee, assured other executives of Ace's ability to compete both on a price and on a quality basis.

Questions

1. Should Ace have continued its existing distribution strategy or should it have invaded the professional market segment?
2. What changes in marketing strategy would have had to be made to invade the professional market segment profitably?

8–2

FASHION FAIR COSMETICS

Problems with an ethnic product line

The merchandise manager of the Belk Department Store at Georgia Square Mall was wondering what to do about the fact that Fashion Fair, a Johnson Publishing Company cosmetic line, accounted for only 8 percent of the store's cosmetic sales, while Revlon, Estee Lauder, and Clinique each accounted for over 10 percent. The in-store Fashion Fair sales representative had voiced displeasure with both the location and space assigned to the Fashion Fair line and commented, "Bad location and not enough space as well as certain external factors explain the line's low share of sales."[1] The merchandise manager realized that the situation needed further analysis before taking any action, although he thought the simplest thing to do would be to drop the line and take on a faster selling brand.

COMPANY HISTORY OF THE BELK ORGANIZATION

Belk Department Store was founded in Monroe, North Carolina, in 1888 by William Henry Belk, who borrowed $500 and took $750 from his savings to open the first store. Three years later his brother, Dr. John M. Belk, a physician, joined him. Nearly a century later Belk had more than 400 stores, all owned and managed by the founders' descendants.

---

[1] As is common in cosmetics retailing, the Fashion Fair sales representative, although based in the store and handling retail sales of the line, actually was an employee of Johnson Publishing Company, parent company of Fashion Fair Cosmetics.

BELK AT GEORGIA SQUARE

The Georgia Square Belk store moved to the mall in early 1981. Previously it had been in downtown Athens, Georgia, for fifty-one years. The old store had approximately 50,000 square feet of space, while the new store had 120,000 square feet. The much greater space at the new location enabled the Belk store to broaden its merchandise offerings considerably, and the greater space given to cosmetics was used both to broaden existing lines sold and to add lines not previously carried.

The cosmetic department at the mall featured a variety of lines, including, among others, Revlon, Estee Lauder, Clinique, Ultimate, and Fashion Fair. All but Fashion Fair were targeted to the white female market. Fashion Fair was promoted and advertised to the black female market (see Exhibit 1). Fashion Fair developers believed that the skin characteristics of black females differed from the skin characteristics of white females, requiring special and different cosmetic products.

EXHIBIT 1 · Example of a Fashion Fair Magazine Advertisement

Advertisements such as these are used in *Ebony* and *Jet* magazines to capture the black female cosmetic consumer. This is a summer line of cosmetics featuring a collection called "Magenta Pink."

HISTORY OF FASHION FAIR COSMETICS

Fashion Fair cosmetics was organized in 1973 by Mrs. Eunice Johnson, wife of black entrepreneur John H. Johnson, president, Johnson Publishing Company. Mrs. Johnson, producer and director of *Ebony's* Fashion Show, realized her black models had difficulties in finding cosmetics to accentuate their features and give their skin a "natural" glow. The models resorted to blending and creating their own colors. Recognizing this opportunity, Mrs. Johnson developed a limited line of high-quality black cosmetics and sold over 100,000 cosmetic kits in the first six months. The Fashion Fair line later expanded to include specially formulated skin care treatments, makeup, nail polish, fragrances for men and women, and hair-care products. Fashion Fair's success traced in large part to its parent company, Johnson Publishing Company, publisher of *Ebony, Jet,* and *Ebony Jr.,* which provided the capital needed to give a strong start to Fashion Fair, named after the widely publicized Ebony Fashion Show.

THE BLACK COSMETIC INDUSTRY

Fashion Fair was not the only black cosmetic line; several cosmetic companies had launched products targeted to black females. In the late 1960s Flori Roberts, a white cosmetic company, began distributing a black cosmetic line nationally. Other early entries included: Avon with its "Shades of Beauty" line, Revlon with its "Polished Ambers" line, and New York Pencil Company's Nu-Musa cosmetic division with its "Honey and Spice" line. L'Oreal of Paris entered the black hair market with its "Radiance" line of seven hair colors and three hair relaxers.

Other black-owned businesses had been active in the black cosmetic market, but invasions by the major white companies forced many black firms out of business. Johnson Products (not related to Johnson Publishing Company) early developed Ultra Sheen and Afro Sheen but its sales declined as competition stiffened and after the 1975 signing of a consent decree with the Federal Trade Commission (FTC). In what the FTC called a crackdown on beauty care products targeted to black consumers, Johnson Products was required to place a warning on its hair straightening products, while Johnson's competitors were not forced to do this until twenty months later.[2]

Many black-owned cosmetic businesses contended that the major cosmetics firms had ignored the needs of black consumers until they recognized the size of this market segment—black consumers spent an estimated $850 million annually on toiletries, cosmetics, and hair care products. Furthermore, studies showed that 35.4 percent of black American females used perfume compared to 31.1 percent of white females; 56.3 percent of black females

[2]Complaints to the FTC had led to the finding that a chemical in the product, sodium hydroxide, weakened cells in hair shafts causing partial or total hair loss.

used bath oil compared to 49.6 percent of white females; and 66.4 percent of black females used cleansing creams compared to 57.6 percent of white females. The market for black cosmetics was growing at a 7 percent annual rate, while the total cosmetics market was growing at a 3 percent to 4 percent annual rate.

Fashion Fair was the early undisputed trailblazer of black cosmetics, and it became the first black-owned business listed on a major U.S. stock exchange. Through innovative promotional programs, Fashion Fair became the number one cosmetic line sold to black females (see Exhibit 2). But as the major cosmetic companies launched products for black females, Fashion Fair experienced sales declines.

FASHION FAIR AT BELK

Fashion Fair had been added to the Georgia Square Belk's cosmetic offerings at the time the store moved to the mall. Earlier Davison's, Belk's major competitor both previously downtown and now at the mall, added Fashion Fair to its cosmetic offerings. In fact, the Fashion Fair sales representative at Belk had worked previously as the Fashion Fair sales representative at

EXHIBIT 2 · A Fashion Fair Sales Promotion

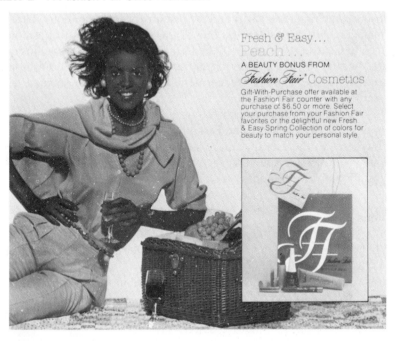

With any $6.50 purchase, customers would receive a free gift with their purchase.

Davison's. She had been instrumental in getting the product established at Davison's. Besides directing retail sales of the line in Davison's, she had held meetings for different black groups to show the Fashion Fair lines, announced Fashion Fair promotional events in churches and at other black social gatherings, and worked to stimulate word-of-mouth promotion. She left Davison's to join Belk's as Fashion Fair sales representative where she repeated her efforts to establish a customer base for Belk. This time the task was more difficult, because many of her former customers remained loyal to Davison's as the first Athens store in town to carry Fashion Fair. Davison's, in its new mall location, allotted four full counter slots to Fashion Fair, while Belk allotted one, although two counter slots had originally been promised. A competing Revlon brand, "Charlie," got the second slot.

The Belk–Davison competition was one of several reasons Belk's Fashion Fair sales were slow. February sales were down 23 percent from a year earlier. The sales decline partially traced to the new location, but additionally during the first part of the year, many people were pinched financially from filing income tax returns, renewing automobile insurance, and paying off leftover Christmas debts.

Still another reason for the decline in sales of Fashion Fair at Belk was the phenomenal sales success of Charlie, following heavy national advertising for the brand. Belk management had considered eliminating Charlie with the move to the mall, but right about that time Revlon launched a national advertising campaign for Charlie and the response was tremendous. This made Belk management reconsider and one of the slots promised to Fashion Fair was given to Charlie. Now much of the Fashion Fair line was stored in counter drawers, because of inadequate display space. Location of the Fashion Fair counter toward the rear of the cosmetic department also seemed a sales depressant.

Nevertheless March sales were up 6.4 percent and April sales up 5.5 percent over the year before. The Fashion Fair sales representative attributed these increases to the fact that more shoppers now knew where things were in the new store, were spending income tax refunds, and March and April were traditionally good months for the cosmetic business.

Questions

1. What factors should the merchandise manager consider before deciding whether to drop the line?
2. How could Belk have been encouraged to give more attention to Fashion Fair?
3. How might Fashion Fair have maintained its position given the increasing competition from the major cosmetic manufacturers?

8–3

BRUMFIELD PUMP WORKS

Market segmentation strategy

Herbert Brumfield founded the Brumfield Pump Works in Cleveland, Ohio, in the early 1920s. Gear pumps of that era operated on the principle of trapping a liquid between two meshing gears and forcing it out. Brumfield observed this operation, noted the excessive wear, and invented a simpler, more efficient product—the sliding-vane pump. His pump employed a single rotor with a set of sliding vanes arranged so as to slide against the cylinder wall when under centrifugal force, thereby decreasing friction and increasing pump life. This innovation gave his company an initial competitive advantage, led to rapid growth, and established Brumfield Pump as an industry leader. Competitors, however, soon followed with their own versions of the sliding-vane pump. Brumfield's major problem now was that its cast-iron pumps competed increasingly with stainless-steel pumps for business.

Stainless-steel pumps had made rapid inroads into the market, particularly in applications requiring certain specifications. For instance, the chemical industry wanted pumps capable of handling highly corrosive materials, and the food industry required pumps meeting high sanitary standards. Stainless-steel pumps could meet these specifications, whereas cast-iron pumps could not.

In deciding not only to follow the two main competitors but to participate in what appeared to be a growing market, Brumfield asked all departments to submit plans for entry into the stainless-steel pump field. The vice president of engineering submitted product parameter requirements, describing competitors' models from an engineering and pricing viewpoint and including estimates on Brumfield's probable development and production costs for the industry's biggest volume product—a three-inch truck pump for

165

liquid fertilizers. The vice president of sales, noting that his department lacked market information, recommended a thorough study of the market for stainless-steel pumps.

Although the Brumfield name was synonymous with high-quality rotary pumps, the company's prices on the cast-iron line were competitive. Management estimated that the industry priced stainless-steel pumps, on an average, 10 percent higher than cast-iron models. Brumfield enjoyed a high degree of brand loyalty among its customers, particularly those in the petroleum and chemical industries. Preference studies conducted by McGraw-Hill on behalf of *National Petroleum News* showed that 41 percent of the potential users of truck pumps preferred Brumfield over its two major competitors, Squirt and Slushwell.

Brumfield made and marketed four lines of cast-iron pumps:

1. *Power pumps:* motor- or engine-driven pumps mounted on stationary bases. They had numerous applications in nearly every major industry handling liquids, ranging from paint and peanut butter to gasoline and glue.
2. *Truck pumps:* pumps for mounting on tank trucks, such as gasoline and fuel delivery trucks and large highway transports. Brumfield was the world's largest supplier of rotary truck pumps.
3. *LPG pumps:* a Brumfield introduction, these pumps were for handling liquified gases such as butane, propane, and ammonia. This line included pumps for mounting on propane trucks used in residential delivery and for use as transfer pumps at bulk stations.
4. *Hand pumps:* hand-operated, barrel-mounted pumps used by industrial plants, building contractors, and farm operators for transferring small quantities of fuels, lubricants, and other fluids.

Power pumps accounted for 27 percent of total sales, truck pumps for 23 percent, hand pumps for 10 percent, LPG pumps for 9 percent, repair parts for 22 percent, and accessories and foundry castings for the remaining 9 percent. Sales by industry were:

	LATEST 12 MONTHS
Food processing	7.0%
Chemical processing	24.6
Petroleum	20.5
Nonmanufacturing	15.8
Machinery	16.4
Ships and boats	5.9
Miscellaneous manufacturing	9.8
	100%

A breakdown of *customers* revealed that 43 percent were in the petroleum industry, 25 percent were in general manufacturing, 16 percent were United States government agencies, 9 percent were in the LP gas industry, and 7 percent were foundry operators.

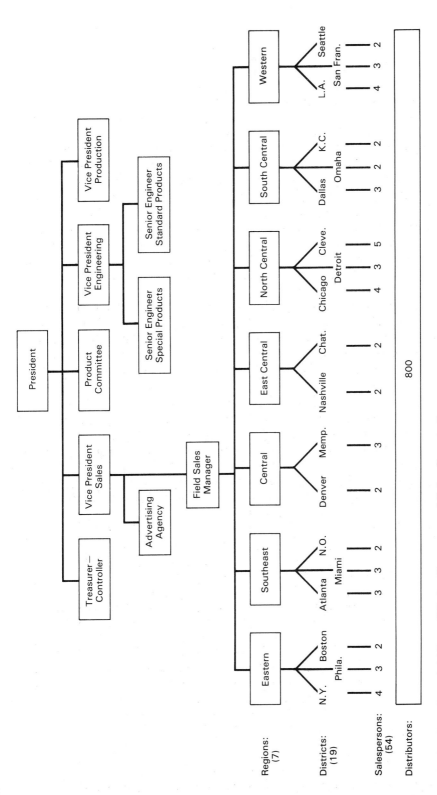

EXHIBIT 1 · Brumfield Pump Works: Company and Sales Organization

President

Treasurer—Controller

Vice President Sales

Product Committee

Vice President Engineering

Vice President Production

Advertising Agency

Senior Engineer Special Products

Senior Engineer Standard Products

Field Sales Manager

Regions: (7)

| Eastern | Southeast | Central | East Central | North Central | South Central | Western |

Districts: (19)

| N.Y. Boston Phila. | Atlanta Miami N.O. | Denver Memp. | Nashville Chat. | Chicago Detroit Cleve. | Dallas Omaha K.C. | L.A. San Fran. Seattle |

Salespersons: (54)

| 4 | 3 | 2 | 3 | 3 | 2 | 2 | 3 | 2 | 2 | 4 | 3 | 5 | 3 | 2 | 2 | 4 | 3 | 2 |

Distributors: 800

The sales organization, headed by Glen Martin, consisted of fifty-four salespersons who developed sales through more than eight hundred equipment distributors located throughout the country. Salespersons reported to nineteen district managers who, in turn, reported to seven regional sales managers. Martin was both vice president of sales and sales manager for the Central Region. He also coordinated and directed all aspects of Brumfield's overall marketing effort. The field sales force, under Bob Carter, operated in various ways to reach prospective buyers and to maximize sales coverage (see Exhibits 1–5).

Regional sales managers developed and supervised their respective territories, also performing engineering and field services. Regional and district managers received salaries and annual bonuses, which were based on sales over quota. Top management forecast sales, recommended quotas, and budgeted expense items. Controllable expenses became a base for further compensation; if a manager held such expenses under the budgeted amount, he or she received 50 percent of the savings. Conversely, if he or she exceeded the budget, 50 percent of the overage was deducted from his or her bonus.

Field sales personnel received salaries and commissions. Commissions averaged 8 percent of sales. Sales personnel paid their own expenses and submitted expense vouchers, and Brumfield reimbursed them monthly.

Sales personnel submitted weekly call and expense reports. Reports of contact, "pink sheets," were submitted when salespersons uncovered unusual sales opportunities. "Blue sheets" represented requests for pump types not in the Brumfield line, but which salespersons felt would be logical additions. Each blue sheet named the customer and the desired pump specifi-

EXHIBIT 2 · Brumfield Pump Works: Distribution System for Power Pumps

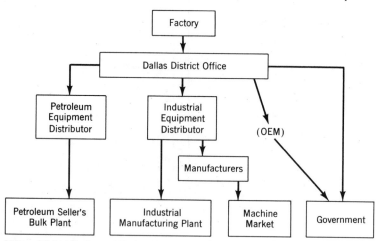

OEM = Original Equipment Market

EXHIBIT 3 · Brumfield Pump Works: Distribution System for Truck Pumps

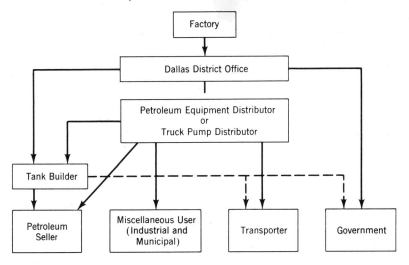

EXHIBIT 4 · Brumfield Pump Works: Distribution System for LPG Pumps

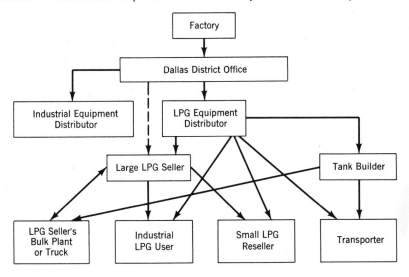

cations. Such specifications included size of pipes in the system, capacity of pumps (expressed in gallons per minute), differential pressure in the system, viscosities of the materials handled, and other properties of the liquid to be pumped. When blue sheets indicated a sufficient demand for a particular type

EXHIBIT 5 · Brumfield Pump Works: Distribution System for Hand Pumps

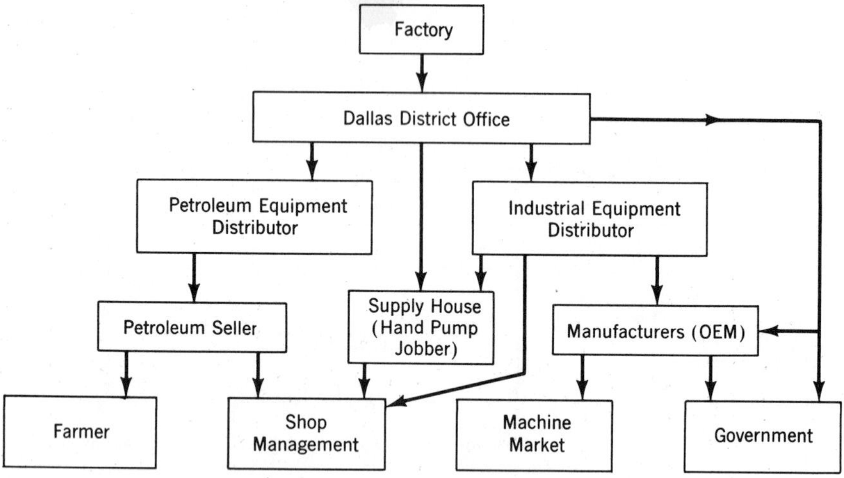

OEM = Original Equipment Market

of pump, Martin forwarded a report to the product committee and to Jacob Brumfield.

Authorized Brumfield distributors carried representative stocks and parts and employed crews trained in making pump installations. Distributors purchased the pumps for resale, not on consignment. Each distributor sold certain product types in an assigned area, usually specializing in one of the four pump lines.

A Cleveland advertising agency handled Brumfield's advertising and sales promotion. The company confined its advertising to trade publications and direct mail. Prime prospects for direct mail promotion were all contacts reported on pink sheets. The agency also performed some advertising research, but its efforts mainly reflected the results of published recognition and brand preference studies.

The number of blue sheets and product requests from customers arriving at the home office had multiplied greatly. More and more salespersons and factory-based engineers returned from the field with requests for items that the company did not make. The advertising agency reported that a study by McGraw-Hill for *Chemical Engineering* magazine indicated that over 50 percent of the rotary pumps being used in manufacturing plants were made of stainless steel. One chemical producer, with a pump maintenance budget of $.75 million, told Bob Carter, "Ten years ago, 85 percent of my pumps were cast iron, today 50 percent are stainless steel." Two more major competitors had introduced stainless-steel pumps during the year, and Jacob Brumfield appeared worried as he dictated a letter calling for a top management meeting to discuss market segmentation strategy.

Questions

1. Should Brumfield have introduced a line of stainless-steel pumps? Why? If so, as a part of which line(s)?
2. How might Brumfield have improved its marketing information system?
3. What recommendations would you have made to Brumfield concerning its market segmentation strategy?

8–4

GULFSTREAM AMERICAN

Segmentation and promotional strategy

Gulfstream American made both military and civilian aircraft. Its line of executive aircraft consisted of the Gulfstream I, II, and III. Through a subsidiary, General Aviation, the company produced the King Air line of executive aircraft.

Gulfstream executives were considering whether to expand production capacity for the Gulfsteam III. Orders to date exceeded expectations and order backlog extended well into the next year, so they were analyzing the prospects for continuing growth. As part of the analysis, they were reviewing past and present marketing strategies.

THE MARKET

Near-term growth prospects in the executive aviation market were believed excellent. Corporate buyers of executive jets found them desirable for several reasons. First, a fully loaded executive jet provided generally cheaper transportation than commercial airlines. Second, an executive jet conserved management time by leaving when needed and flying nonstop. Third, passenger compartments in executive jets were more comfortable and more suited to in-flight work than those in commercial aircraft. In addition, executive jet passengers were in constant communication with contacts on the ground, and they avoided luggage handling problems. Furthermore, executive jets could transport emergency shipments (an auto manufacturer had recently used one of its corporate jets to supply a critical component to an assembly plant, thus avoiding its shutdown).

Recent government deregulation of the commercial airlines also provided major impetus to growth of the executive jet market. Major commercial airlines were discontinuing service to more and more smaller airports, increasing traveling times for reaching the areas served. At the same time, on many routes the commercial airlines had put into effect higher fares for business travelers.

Additional growth in the market for executive jets traced to the post–1973 rise in aircraft fuel prices. Aircraft buyers were demanding more fuel-efficient planes, and manufacturers were trying to supply them. Initially, manufacturers refitted existing airframes with more efficient engines. But fuel costs continued to rise and ultimately forced airframe redesign. Manufacturers had delayed redesigning because of high retooling costs and their desire to prolong the lives of existing products.

Although the market outlook appeared favorable, industry observers avoided making definite long-term growth projections. However, one industry official forecast continuing 15 to 25 percent growth in unit sales accompanied by continuing increases in average prices. A second said that "if the airframe manufacturers could make more, they could sell more." Recent history indicated that when a major manufacturer introduced a new generation of aircraft, initial orders generated demand for up to three years of production.

THE GULFSTREAM AIRCRAFT

The Gulfstream III was the third executive aircraft added to the Gulfsteam series. Gulfstream I was introduced in the 1960s by Grumman Aerospace, at that time Gulfstream American's parent company. It was a propeller-driven aircraft with greater passenger capacity and range than competing products. Its large size, plush interior, and high price positioned it at the high end of the executive aircraft market. Gulfstream II was Gulfstream American's first entry into the jet market after Grumman Aerospace spun the company off. This product also was positioned toward the high end of the market. The Gulfstream II could carry seven to nine passengers, depending upon the interior design configuration, in comfort from New York to London or Paris without refueling. At capacity, it was the most fuel-efficient jet per passenger mile, combining unmatched quality and reliability. Only one Gulfstream II had ever crashed, and that crash was directly attributable to pilot error. Gulfstream avionics[1] were the industry's most advanced; the Gulfstream II was the "Rolls Royce" of jet aircraft.

Gulfstream III was a modified version of the Gulfstream II, redesigned for greater fuel efficiency. New engines were installed, wings redesigned, and a small on-board computer added to minimize fuel usage. The Gulfstream III had 18 percent better fuel economy than the Gulfstream II and greater

[1]Avionics refers to the electronic equipment used for determining altitude, speed, and location to provide virtually automatic flying.

range and speed. Gulfstream American expected the Gulfstream III design to be "state of the art" for at least ten years, although there would probably be minor engine and electronic changes.

MARKET STRUCTURE

Several companies competed in the executive aircraft market (see Exhibit 1). The market leader was Gates Learjet, which competed in all segments of the market and dominated most. Future competition was expected from aircraft industries based in developing countries and from the larger aerospace companies. A Brazilian manufacturer, for example, had been selling the commuter airlines small planes which could be downsized for the executive market. General Dynamics, a military aircraft manufacturer, also was expected to enter the executive market. Of the models currently on the market only those built by Gates Learjet and Lockheed Aircraft compared to the Gulfstream III in range and passenger capacity. Nevertheless, the majority of corporate buyers of executive aircraft were satisfied with performance specifications, so they found most manufacturers' products acceptable. A trend was developing among manufacturers to produce larger planes, similar to Gulfstream's.

MARKETING STRATEGY

Gulfstream American's marketing strategy relied on its planes being perceived as the Rolls Royces of executive aircraft. All three Gulfstream models were positioned at the high end of the market. The comparative advantages stressed were greater passenger capacity and range. The large size, plush interior, and superior technology, combined with the market's highest ticket price, supported the Rolls Royce image.

EXHIBIT 1 · Manufacturers, Models, and Prices of Executive Jets

COMPANY	MODEL	PRICE ($ MILLION)
Lockheed	Jetstar II	6.0
Canadair	Challenger	6.5
Dassault	Falcon III	7.0
British Aerospace	HS-125	4.505
Atlantic Aviation (marketer)	Westwind	3.375
Cessna	Citation III	6.295
Rockwell	Sabreliner	4.5
Gates Learjet	Learjet 25	1.497
Gates Learjet	Learjet 50	3.075
Gates Learjet	Learjet 55	5.75
Gulfstream American	Gulfstream III	7.4*

*Does not include interiors which cost approximately $1.5–2.5 million.

Gulfstream used a two-phase program to approach the market. The first was to appeal to noneconomic desires, such as those for luxury, comfort, prestige, and performance. Every advertisement for the aircraft included pictures of an elegant and comfortable interior. Prestige was projected through the product's word-of-mouth reputation and image, and its unparalleled performance characteristics. "A New Definition of the Ultimate," the advertising slogan, emphasized the prestigious image. The selling price, the market's highest, also contributed to this image.

Phase two focused on the economic justification for purchasing the aircraft, providing the rationale frequently required for approval of major capital expenditures by boards of directors. The points stressed were greater passenger capacity, resulting in economies in fuel consumption and other operating expenses, on a per-passenger basis.[2] Other economic advantages included the Gulfstream III's high resale value, attributed to the jet's reliability, and saving of executive time because of the jet's superior range and travel speed.

Gulfstream American blended these two major selling points, prestige and economies, into a total presentation. Economies were stressed to provide "rational" buyers with an economic justification for purchasing. However, prestige and comfort appeals provided prospects with the emotional support. Exemplifying the strength of Gulfstream American's approach was the Chrysler Corporation, which kept two Gulfstreams during its long period of great financial difficulty and, although the federal government forced the corporation to sell the aircraft, a leaseback arrangement was made immediately.

Gulfstream American aimed its marketing efforts toward three target markets. The first and largest market was made up of the chief executives of major U.S. and international corporations. The second market was made up of high-ranking officials and chiefs of state of foreign governments—jets were bought for use by cabinet officers in large countries and by chiefs of state in smaller countries.[3] The third and smallest target market consisted of wealthy private individuals—while Gulfstream's high price somewhat limited the size of this market, the number sold to Arab sheiks and other oil-rich individuals had been increasing rapidly.

Gulfstream American confined its media advertising to business publications such as *Fortune, Business Week,* and *Forbes.* Advertisements featured photographs of the aircraft's exterior and interior and copy describing the plane's performance and economic characteristics. Prospective customers desiring more information were encouraged to contact Gulfstream American's senior vice president of marketing.

High advertising frequency was used during the product development

[2]In reality, the jets seldom flew at full capacity.
[3]After a coup d'état, an executive jet was often the first purchase made by a chief of state, since ousted leaders typically used the existing executive jet to flee the country.

stage and flight trials of the Gulfstream III. After the product's market introduction, advertising was reduced to minimal levels. Gulfstream American had little data on the effectiveness of its advertising, but executives believed that company advertising generated three to four new customers per year.[4]

Most Gulfstream buyers were repeat customers either expanding their fleets or replacing their existing planes. Typically, the customer initiated contact with Gulfstream in order to assure delivery slots. Gulfstream kept in close contact with previous customers, not only to provide needed service and maintenance but to stay abreast of aircraft buying plans.

New customers were met by Gulfstream sales personnel for demonstration flights. Often prospective customers were flown to the Savannah, Georgia, plant to see the production facilities and to meet with Gulfstream American's executives. Over 50 percent of these demonstration flights resulted in sales.

The sales package included not only the plane but several auxiliary services. Typically, Gulfstream American arranged and paid for pilot training by Flight Safety, Inc., the leader in executive-jet pilot training. The company also had excellent contacts to use in recruiting pilots. Finally, Gulfstream American operated facilities for plane servicing and maintenance.

The typical sale was concluded by the purchase of a delivery slot for approximately $2 million. This amount guaranteed delivery and provided a tentative delivery date. The balance of the purchase price, except for costs of customizing the interior and painting, became due upon completion of the airframe. At the time of delivery, the customer paid for customizing the interior and painting. Once Gulfstream scheduled a plane for production, the sale was virtually assured because of the high price the customer had paid for the production slot. Customers were free to sell their delivery slots, but they rarely did. Delivery usually was made in from one to three years after order placement. Similar lead times were typical in the industry.

Recently, Gulfstream had undertaken a program to refit buyers' Gulfstream II's with new technologies, or take Gulfstream II's in trade as partial payments for Gulfstream IIIs.

Questions

1. How does the concept of market segmentation apply to Gulfstream American's situation?
2. What technique was Gulfstream American using to reach its target markets?
3. Appraise the likely effectiveness of Gulfstream's promotional strategy.

---

[4]Production capacity for the Gulfstream III was roughly two aircraft per month.

9–1

FOWLER PRODUCTS COMPANY, INC.

Export operations

Fowler Products Company, Inc., Athens, Georgia, after a long search for an executive to head up its export operations, ran across a young Colombian, Luis Saldarriaga, who had an M.B.A. from a U.S. university and wanted to return home to work and raise his family. Management believed the new export manager should be familiar with Central and South America because Fowler's export business was heavily concentrated there. Mr. Saldarriaga had been a successful businessman in Colombia and viewed the Fowler position as both challenging and providing sufficient room for both himself and the company to grow. He accepted the position and started work in September 1981.

Mr. Saldarriaga was in full charge of Fowler's export business, including all marketing activities, research, advertising, planning U.S. visits for prospects and customers, and handling customer complaints. Mr. Saldarriaga soon realized that he could not give all these areas the attention they deserved. Fowler seemed content with its small size and existing methods of operations, and Saldarriaga believed it would take time to get top management to make a strong commitment to export operations. He knew a larger staff was needed to handle day-to-day operations and to free up his own time for researching new export markets, traveling, and writing to prospective customers. He wondered if Fowler Products would invest more in its export business and cultivate new overseas markets.

COMPANY BACKGROUND

Fowler Products was established in 1957 with the main purpose of supplying parts for owners of bottling equipment. The company hoped to become a one-stop shopping center for bottlers looking for numerous assorted parts. Fowler Products quickly built up a large stock of high-quality parts supplied both by its own manufacturing operation and other manufacturers. Then Fowler developed the technology of rebuilding old, worn-out parts for resale at lower prices than conventional replacement parts, maintaining strict control during the rebuilding to assure quality and protect Fowler's reputation.

Established as a reliable high-quality-parts supplier, Fowler applied its parts-rebuilding expertise to remanufacturing entire bottling machinery units, reselling them at much lower prices than new machinery. Among the major expenses in fabricating new machinery were metal frames and stainless-steel parts, both easily salvagable at low cost. Rebuilt parts off old machinery units and new parts from Fowler's parts department went into remanufacturing the bottling machinery. Remanufactured equipment was particularly attractive to small bottlers, many of whom could not afford new equipment priced up to 40 percent higher than the Fowler offerings.

Bottlers could come to Fowler and not only obtain any part needed but select from among wide assortments of remanufactured and new bottling machinery. Fowler had become a one-stop shopping center for bottlers. Significantly, nearly 40 percent of Fowler's remanufactured machinery was sold in the export market.

Confident in the quality of its remanufactured machinery, Fowler extended the same guarantee as on new machinery, and gave bottlers the option of buying service contracts. In addition, bottlers setting up new bottling plants were encouraged to have Fowler's engineering department design efficient layouts for bottling lines at no charge. This service was especially attractive to bottlers without plant layout–planning capabilities. Fowler's extensive product line, large parts department, and customer services made it popular among small- and medium-sized bottling companies.

THE EXPORT MARKET

Fowler's first export order came from a small Caribbean bottler, who found the remanufactured machinery within an acceptable price range for him to start up his bottling company. Other orders from the Caribbean followed. There were few problems in exporting to the Caribbean, practically no language barriers, and no currency exchange problems. Fowler management began to see considerable benefits in exporting, as it smoothed out domestic sales downturns and broadened Fowler's reputation as a source for high-quality, low-priced machinery and parts.

Fowler next found that many bottlers in the Middle East were interested in purchasing remanufactured machinery. The Middle East soon became Fowler's largest foreign market and remained that way until the U.S. Congress passed the Foreign Corrupt Practices Act of 1977. This caused Fowler Products to abandon the Middle East market as too risky.

The Foreign Corrupt Practices Act prohibited the bribing of foreign officials and applied to both foreign and domestic business operations. Some of the act's most important provisions were applicable to the domestic operations of all companies under the jurisdiction of the Securities and Exchange Commission (SEC). One key provision stated that all reporting companies shall keep accurate books and accounts which reflect in detail all transactions and dispositions of assets. Just how accurately a company should keep books and accounts was determined arbitrarily by the SEC, which issued no specific guidelines.

Those sections of the act dealing with foreign corrupt practices were of limited scope. But a violation could cause a company to pay up to a $1 million fine. Specifically prohibited was the use of an interstate communications instrument, such as the telephone or mail, to make or offer payments or gifts to foreign officials or political parties, if the purpose was to promote actions that would assist a company in transacting its business.

Congress reportedly did not intend to outlaw "grease payments," that is, facilitating payments made to minor foreign officials to get them to perform customary services they might otherwise refuse to perform. In many Middle Eastern countries, grease payments to customs and other minor government officials were customary. Instead of placing an upper limit on the amount of a grease payment, the act defined grease payments in terms of the position of the recipient foreign official—the higher the official, the greater the risk of violating the act. Any executive who willfully violated the act could be held personally liable, imprisoned up to five years, and fined up to $10,000. With perceived ambiguity in the act, Fowler backed out of exporting to the Middle East.

Fowler's export attention turned to Central and South America. A Mexican bottler had visited Fowler looking for remanufactured machinery, and singlehandedly soon made Mexico Fowler's largest foreign market. This bottler was intrigued with Fowler's location and, when planning a trip to Athens, he always allocated several days for vacationing in Athens, enjoying its nightlife and surrounding recreational area. Fowler soon was transacting over a million dollars of business annually with this Mexican bottler. Fowler built a long list of Mexican customers, as its reputation spread to other bottling companies in that nation.

Then Fowler started to market itself in other Latin American markets. Advertisements were translated into Spanish and placed in Latin American beverage trade journals. Fowler's sales manager was made responsible for all of its export activities, and for working out details of sales contracts, arranging for shipments, setting payment terms, and deciding service contract provisions.

All sales were denominated in dollars, which reduced the risk of fluctuating exchange rates. However, whenever a Latin American country deflated its currency against the dollar, that country's bottlers had to come up with more local money to meet the same dollar-size payment. Many Fowler customers in Latin America were small and had difficulties in meeting payment schedules under these circumstances. Fowler limited accounts receivable to thirty days both domestically and in the export market.

THE MEXICAN MARKET

The Mexican economy had experienced rapid growth through the first half of 1981. There were strong private sector investments which resulted in a 7 to 8 percent increase in economic output. The accelerated pace of economic activity increased the demand for imports to supplement domestic production. Mexico's major export—crude oil—helped hold down trade deficits but an oil glut late in 1981 caused declines both in oil prices and exports. The glut combined with an increased demand for imports caused Mexico to have a $3.8 billion trade deficit that year.

The Mexican government responded with measures aimed to reduce imports. It reversed its policy of trade liberalization and imposed licensing requirements and tariffs on a number of import classifications. Imports subject to licensing rose to almost 85 percent of all imported goods. The government also put into effect an import substitution policy through stepped-up domestic industrial development and a wide variety of protectionist measures. Foreign firms launching Mexican operations were restricted to 49 percent equity positions, with 51 percent reserved for Mexican investors. Similar ownership restrictions were in effect in most other Latin American countries.

Other developments in the Mexican market impacted upon Fowler's business. Major competitors were becoming much more aggressive in their marketing and selling efforts. A Brazilian manufacturer backed by German technology announced plans to build a bottling equipment manufacturing facility in Mexico. Although Fowler did not expect the quality of the Brazilian bottling equipment to match its own, the new competitor would have a substantial pricing advantage. Through trade agreements between Mexico and other Latin American countries, bottling equipment made in Brazil and elsewhere could already be brought into Mexico with a 10 percent tariff while Fowler and other U.S.–made equipment was subject to an 80 percent tariff. Furthermore, the Brazilian government provided export subsidies to bottling equipment manufacturers enabling them to quote Latin American buyers even lower prices.

A former Fowler export sales manager commented:

> The people at Fowler, in my ten years with the company, were never enthusiastic or aggressive in their approach to exporting. They felt there was a monster behind every bush, a feeling of uncertainty, risk in doing business with foreign countries. Management had difficulty placing any trust in a foreign customer, which limited the growth of Fowler's export operations. Fowler could easily triple its export sales with a change in attitude and a more aggressive marketing and selling effort.

Questions

1. How should Mr. Saldarriaga have gone about persuading Fowler management to increase the company's emphasis on exporting?
2. What problems did Fowler encounter in its export operation?
3. Should Fowler have followed standardized policies in cultivating both domestic and foreign markets?

9–2

OMNI TRACTOR COMPANY, INC.

Examining an international opportunity

Bobby Wallace, president of Omni Tractor Company, Inc., was nervously rubbing his left arm. He had just received inoculation shots in preparation for a trip to Jakarta, Indonesia. His anxiety stemmed from what he hoped would be confirmation of a $40 million contract with the Indonesian government for the sale of his firm's tractors.

ORGANIZATION

Omni Tractor's plant and offices were located just outside a small town in northwest Georgia. Bobby Wallace, formerly a production shift manager at Lockheed Georgia, only recently had bought out his two partners. Other Omni Tractor employees included a general manager, a shop foreman, one full-time and one part-time bookkeeper, and twelve factory workers.

PRODUCT

The company manufactured a multipurpose tractor which could be used as a lawn mower, a farm tractor, and/or a garden tractor. Its design was unique since the different implements were for front-end attachment, unlike conventional tractors designed for rear-end implement attachment.

A wide range of optional implements, specifically designed for the tractor, were sold separately, but certain implements were often purchased at the same time as the tractor. For instance, 90 percent of Omni Tractor's buyers purchased the cultivator and 60 percent the disc harrow. Because the implements added versatility to the tractor, Mr. Wallace foresaw expanded sales of add-on implements.

MANUFACTURING

Omni Tractor manufactured all parts in its own plant, except the engine (costing $275 per unit), and the hydraulics (costing $272 per unit). The manufacturing process consisted of five stages: machining, metal fabricating, welding, assembly, and painting. Each factory worker was capable of performing as many as two or three of these tasks, and weekly plant output averaged ten tractors.

DOMESTIC DISTRIBUTION

Domestic distribution of tractors was handled by the over 200 Omni Tractor distributors, most of them in the Southeast, which accounted for almost 80 percent of Omni Tractor's sales. Omni Tractor had invested considerable time and money in recruiting and providing support to distributors. Promotional materials and various sales aids were continuously being made available to distributors. Mr. Wallace personally visited each prospective distributor, with a tractor, to demonstrate its use.

As Omni's reputation spread, almost all from word-of-mouth, the number of distributors increased rapidly. Materials of interest to prospective distributors were prepared and sent out regularly. A new approach to salesmanship had been undertaken in the form of a six-minute film, shot in Florida by a professional advertising firm, to be shown to prospective and present distributors to demonstrate the versatility and effectiveness of the Omni Tractor. Mr. Wallace believed that this sales tool would greatly stimulate domestic sales, and he planned to ask the distributors to share in the costs of making copies of the film if they wanted to use it.

Delivery of tractors to distributors was by Omni Tractor's own diesel truck and trailer. This "rig" could carry ten tractors at a time and rarely operated with less than a full load. Distributors had the option of accepting delivery by Omni Tractor and paying appropriate delivery charges or hauling the tractors themselves.

TARGET MARKET

Omni Tractor defined its target market as "professional weekend farmers," who cultivated from five to fifteen acres of land. The Omni fit a special niche in that market by providing all the features of a conventional tractor at a price much lower than comparable tractors. Omni Tractor's basic machine retailed at $3,600, compared with $5,000 to $6,000 for other makes. Further, the Omni was easier to use, more maneuverable, and more reliable than most competing tractors.

SALES AND PROFIT

Last year, its fifth year of operation, Omni Tractor sold 475 tractors and had gross sales of $1,175,000. This year Mr. Wallace expected Omni Tractor to do at least as well and he was forecasting a $300 profit to the company on each tractor sold. Distributor's markups on Omni tractors and implements were 25 percent on retail.

Omni Tractor had yet to show a profit. However, the general manager commented that the "bottom line" was highly illusory because Omni Tractor had made a considerable investment and had continued to expand. Even if the Indonesian contract fell through, Mr. Wallace predicted that Omni Tractor would move into the "black" this year.

INTERNATIONAL POSSIBILITY

Last March Omni Tractor ran a $1,000 "one-shot" promotion in *Farm Equipment* magazine. Although this publication had worldwide circulation, the ad was run primarily to stimulate domestic demand. Response, both domestic and international, was overwhelming in terms of both sales and requests for information. So many inquiries poured in that the August issue of *Farm Equipment* featured the Omni Tractor as one of its "hot products." By year's end interest of prospective buyers had yet to subside. *Farm Equipment* ran the ad again free of charge after choosing the Omni Tractor as one of the year's top ten products. This series of events continued to stimulate sales orders as well as information requests, especially from overseas prospects. To illustrate, a Mobile, Alabama, firm purchased two tractors for resale in India and one for resale in Australia. Mr. Wallace also had taken a verbal order from an official of the Nigerian government for two assembled and twenty unassembled tractors. (The tractors were requested unassembled due to Nigerian government requirements for domestically finished products.)

Bobby Wallace had given little thought to exports as a viable market alternative previously, but these orders caused him to reflect on possible opportunities. Then a Dutch company contacted Omni Tractor saying that after seeing the ad in *Farm Equipment* the Indonesian government was willing to negotiate a large order. The proposed Indonesian contract was as follows:

> 10,000 units to be provided over a 5½ year period at a total price of $40 million; 3,000 units, or 100 a month, to be shipped during the first 2½ years.
>
> 7,000 units or 200 a month to be shipped during the next 3 years.
>
> The Dutch company would purchase units as shipped from Omni Tractor, under terms of a 60-day irrevocable letter of credit, with terms of sale open to renegotiation every 90 days in case of inflation.

The Dutch company would provide Omni Tractor with a stipend of $240 per tractor to cover crating and transportation costs to Jakarta.

The Dutch company would be responsible for all shipping documentation, customs duties, and all necessary import/export licensing arrangements from the port of shipment to the final destination.

The possibility of firming up this contract encouraged Wallace to plan a trip to Indonesia.

There was a problem in financing increased production. Omni Tractor had long-term debt of $150,000 and had borrowed $100,000 in February to help offset inadequate cash flow. After several banks refused additional loans, Wallace obtained financing through the U.S. Small Business Administration.[1] SBA agreed to a $100,000 specific contract loan, 90 percent federally guaranteed, providing that the Indonesian contract be finalized. Mr. Wallace had learned that SBA had run credit checks on the Dutch firm.

Wallace did not expect to experience any difficulty other than financial in expanding tractor production. Labor was available for second-shift operation, and inventory on hand together with monthly production would be sufficient to meet the first Indonesian order of 100 tractors. If the contract were finalized in the next few weeks, something Wallace hoped the trip would accomplish, there would be two months' time to recruit and train the additional work force.

Wallace felt that the biggest problem now was how to package and ship the tractors. One possible solution would be to hire carpenters to crate the tractors in the plant, then use the company's diesel carrier to deliver the crates to dockside.

An alternative solution would be to ship twenty-five tractors per week to Indonesia. The tractors would be partially disassembled in order to make the best use of space and to meet Indonesia's restrictions on finished products (similar to the Nigerian restrictions encountered earlier). However, disassembly would be limited so unskilled workers in Indonesia could easily reassemble the tractors. But space, not weight, was the basis for shipping charges; the tractors needed to fit into a shipping container 40 feet long, 7 feet 9 inches wide, and 8 feet $10^1/_2$ inches high. Wallace doubted that the limited disassembly would leave sufficient room for twenty-five tractors in the container. Further, the container needed to be transported overland from the plant in northwest Georgia to the port of embarkation.

If Savannah, Georgia, was chosen as the port of embarkation, shipment could be via tramp steamer. One tramp steamer operator, Blue Sky Lines, had already offered to handle the shipment. This tramp line had no regularly established schedule, but it quoted a price within the $6,000 limit (25 tractors times $240).

---

[1]Due to the severe imbalance of trade payments, the U.S. government had set up a program under the auspices of the SBA to help encourage small businesses to export.

Wallace hoped that the Indonesian trip would not only answer these and other questions, but would pave the way for acceptance of the contract. He was looking forward to getting away as it was Omni Tractor's busiest season and he had been spending most of his time on intensified sales efforts and the linking of sales, tractor delivery, and production. He hoped that he could count on the long-run success and profitability of Omni Tractor for years to come. Meanwhile, additional foreign inquiries were arriving daily.

Questions

1. What problems should Omni Tractor have anticipated in entering the overseas market?
2. Assuming that the Indonesian contract was finalized, how should Wallace have solved the problem of crating and shipping the tractors?
3. Was Omni Tractor well advised to enter the international market?

9–3

METALLOTECHNICA ELEKTRA, S.A.*

Adjusting to changes in the competitive environment

Metallotechnica Elektra, S.A. (MESA), was a joint venture of Metallotechnica Incorporated of Athens, Greece, and the Westinghouse Electric Corporation, a multinational corporation based in Pittsburgh, Pennsylvania. During its first two years, MESA sold its entire output to a government controlled corporation which served as the exclusive marketing intermediary between MESA and its only competitor, on the one hand, and private industrial buyers of electrical equipment, on the other hand. This market setting changed in 1972 when the Greek government enacted a law permitting private industrial buyers to deal directly with electrical equipment manufacturers. However, MESA continued largely dependent on the government controlled corporation for sales, even though management planned to increase sales to private buyers, to diversify the product lines, and to strengthen export activities.

WESTINGHOUSE ELECTRIC CORPORATION

Westinghouse Electric Corporation was the oldest and the second largest U.S.–based manufacturer of electrical apparatus. It had over 100 plants throughout the world, sales offices in nearly every major industrial center, and more than 190,000 employees, of whom 40,000 worked overseas. Until 1963, Westinghouse had avoided direct investment overseas since World War I when its three European subsidiaries had been confiscated. In 1963, a new

*Professor Asterios G. Kefalas and Alexander Morndo, an International Business graduate of the University of Georgia, did the field work for this case during 1974 in Greece.

187

president launched an overseas expansion program with the aim of generating 30 percent of revenues from exports or manufacturing outside the United States. Westinghouse met this target in less than a decade, but overseas operations had been generally less profitable than domestic operations.[1]

Westinghouse's product lines included nearly all electrical and much related mechanical equipment required by electric power companies, railroads, city transit systems, and industrial plants, as well as propulsion and electrical equipment for the U.S. Navy and the marine industry, and certain electrical equipment for the aviation industry. Some products, such as motors and control devices, were sold to other manufacturers for application to their products. Electrical equipment was supplied for the mining, drilling, and recovery of coal, ores, oil, and other natural resources. Many Westinghouse products found important uses on farms and on farm implements. In addition, the company produced many consumer products.

The Westinghouse electrical apparatus lines were, in general, sold directly to industrial users, although the lighter lines were also marketed through distributors and dealer channels. U.S.–produced Westinghouse products were sold to overseas customers through more than 460 distributors and sales representatives situated throughout the free world. There were forty-one Westinghouse plants in sixteen countries outside the United States. In addition, Westinghouse had numerous licensees and sublicensees operating in countries around the world. In total, Westinghouse products were distributed in 195 countries.

Westinghouse had recently completed a major organizational change dictated by its emergence as a multinational corporation. Four new regional vice presidents were elected, with responsibility for representing Westinghouse overseas, and were combined with the seven domestic regional vice presidents and the Government Affairs office into a new World Regions organization. To support more effectively the manufacture and marketing of products and services worldwide, the Westinghouse Electric International Company was dissolved and its functions were assigned to those corporate staff departments responsible for corresponding functions within the United States. After this change, the customer in Paris or Sydney was served by the same organization that met the needs of the customer in New York or Atlanta. Westinghouse the same year entered into more than a dozen new business ventures overseas and export sales climbed to $279 million, up 20 percent over 1970. Meanwhile, the Westinghouse Research Laboratories realized a long-time objective of providing additional technical support for European operations and set up a research laboratory in Uccle, a Brussels suburb.

Two major Westinghouse European subsidiaries were those in France

[1]"The Luster Dims at Westinghouse," *Business Week,* July 20, 1974, p. 57.

and Belgium. The company acquired 96 percent ownership of the French subsidiary, Société Française de Ascenseurs Westinghouse (WELF), a manufacturer of elevators, in 1965. Control (68 percent ownership) of the Belgian subsidiary, Ateliers de Constructions Electriques de Charleral (ACEC), a producer of industrial, power generation, and consumer products, was obtained in 1970. ACEC had seven plants in Belgium and seven in other parts of the world and employed 23,000 people. Major labor problems soon developed in both subsidiaries. At WELF, after several changes in management personnel, Westinghouse dispatched an American general manager in 1973 to deal with not only labor but inflation problems. At both WELF and ACEC, inflation had been eating up profits because orders had not been filled rapidly enough and mounting costs were not accurately estimated in pricing the products. Moreover, as a source close to ACEC commented, "One of Westinghouse's mistakes was to take a back seat and leave the running of the company to the old management."[2]

THE GREEK COMPANY

Metallotechnica Elektra, S.A. (MESA), was organized in 1970 as a joint venture of Westinghouse Electric Corporation and Metallotechnica Incorporated, a subsidiary of Metallotechnica Nicolaidis & Son, a manufacturer of industrial goods. The Greek enterprise had concentrated on the manufacture of steel furniture, fencing, and metal supplies for the armed forces, such as helmets, dishes, and eating utensils.

When E. C. Nicolaidis became managing director in 1962, his first major move was to split the enterprise's operations into two parts. One part manufactured a widely diversified assortment of metal articles while the other part, Metallotechnica Incorporated, produced industrial electrical machinery and electrical apparatus such as transformers and switches.

Mr. Nicolaidis immediately began a long search for a partnership with an American firm willing to supply additional capital. The General Electric Company proposed a partnership but the terms were not attractive and Mr. Nicolaidis rejected the proposal. The next year he contacted certain executives of Westinghouse Electric Corporation, and in 1969 agreement was reached on establishing a joint venture. Under the terms of this agreement, Westinghouse had 75 percent ownership of the joint venture and Metallotechnica Incorporated 25 percent. In return for its 75 percent ownership, Westinghouse agreed to invest a total of $1,236,000 U.S. for use in expanding the existing Greek facilities and for adding new installations at the manufacturing plant. The newly formed company, Metallotechnica Elektra, S.A., had its main office in Athens, Greece, and its manufacturing plant at Oinofyta, Biotia.

---

[2]Ibid., p. 58.

The plant had a work force of 205 people, and the main office employed an additional 35.

MESA ORGANIZATION

MESA was organized along functional lines. The managers of marketing, finance, general services (procurement), and production reported to the managing director. The managing director, in turn, reported to the president of Power Systems Company at the Pittsburgh headquarters of Westinghouse Electric Corporation. The managing director of MESA and three of the functional managers were Greek nationals, while the financial manager was a United States citizen. (Exhibit 1 shows the organizational chart.)

Power Systems Company was one of the four main product groups at Westinghouse. Its products consisted of nuclear steam supply systems, nuclear fuel, capacitors and lighting arresters, electrical measuring instruments, high-voltage power circuit breakers, large generators, meters, relays, steam and gas turbines, steam condensers, switchgear, and transformers. Power Systems Company accounted for almost a third of Westinghouse's worldwide sales and for nearly 45 percent of its worldwide net profit.

EXHIBIT 1 · MESA Organizational Chart

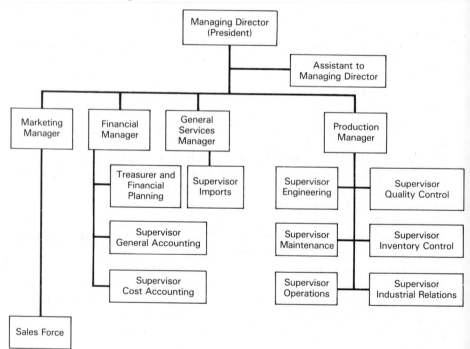

MAJOR PRODUCTS

According to the agreement, MESA was to manufacture industrial electrical machinery and parts. Five main categories of products were being produced:

1. Transformers with specifications of from 50 kilovolt-amperes to 1,000 kilovolt-amperes manufactured under a Westinghouse–owned patent and the name "Westco." This was an international patent and no other European manufacturer made comparable transformers, which were a revolutionary type and roughly half the size of conventional transformers carrying the same specifications.
2. Electrical equipment for transmission lines and protection of electrical energy, such as switchgears and low-, high-, and medium-tension distribution boards. The low- and medium-tension designs were produced under license from Westinghouse, while the high-tension designs were made under license from COG, a company based in Bordeaux, France.
3. Fuse cutout mechanisms. Currently, these mechanisms were being produced under license from an Argentine firm. Earlier, they had been made under a license from the Cravering Company, a West German firm, and before that had been produced under license from General Electric Company.
4. Parts of the above-mentioned equipment, as well as various types of nuts and bolts.
5. Electrical headboards. These were being made to fill an order received from OTE, the Telecommunications Organization of Greece.

These items were all manufactured at the plant in Oinofyta, fifty-five kilometers north of Athens. The plant worked three eight-hour shifts with most of the first-shift workers commuting on company-owned buses from Athens. Approximately 80 percent of the raw materials and fabricating parts were imported from abroad, chiefly from the United States, Western Europe, Japan, Bulgaria, and Romania.

MARKETING OPERATIONS TO 1972

Up to 1972, MESA management regarded marketing as being synonymous with order processing. Marketing began with the securing of an order through a public bidding and ended with the invoicing of the customer. This conception of marketing traced to the unique position occupied by MESA in the Greek market system which, in turn, resulted from a law regulating the selling activities of MESA and its only competitor, AEG, a subsidiary of Aktien-Energie-Gesellschaft, a West German company. This law prohibited the direct sale of electrical equipment by manufacturers to private industry. The Greek Public Power Corporation (PPC), a predominantly government-owned and -operated enterprise, acted as the marketing intermediary between the private industrial sector and the manufacturers selling equipment. Industrial users were obliged to submit requests detailing their requirements to the PPC which, in turn, after assembling all requests, announced a public bidding specifying the quantities and specifications of the needed equipment. The manufacturers, MESA and AEG, submitted bids and the lowest bidder received the order. The two manufacturers had an arrangement whereby they split the order beforehand and submitted bids that PPC could not refuse.

Given MESA's oligopolistic market position and its heavy dependence on a monopsonistic enterprise (PPC), management saw little need for marketing research and sales promotion. Approximately 90 percent of MESA's production was sold to PPC, and the rest was exported, mainly to countries in the Middle East.

THE NEW MARKET

In 1972, the Greek government enacted a law authorizing private industrial buyers of electrical equipment to buy directly from the manufacturers without the intermediation of PPC. This opened up new opportunities for competition in the industry. Shortly after the new law went into effect, a new company was set up, mainly to manufacture electrical generators and transformers— KHM, S.A., a joint venture of KHM Spiros Damidis, S.A., a Greek company, and Brown and Boveri Company of Switzerland.

CHANGES IN MESA'S MARKETING OPERATIONS

The selling techniques of MESA had been tailored to satisfy the idiosyncrasies of a single customer—the PPC. A MESA salesperson described them:

> All sales to private firms were handled by PPC. So the job of the sales department was quite simple. A bid was submitted to every PPC tender, and due to the fact that the company was in a very oligopolistic market position, it had success nearly every time. The only other company producing the same kind of transformers was the German company, AEG. The two companies would split the order beforehand and submit bids that PPC could not turn down. The pricing policy also was fairly simple: management would make certain that both fixed and variable costs were covered and then would add a percentage of "reasonable profit." The final decision, however, on bid prices submitted by the salespeople was made by the general manager.

The change in the competitive nature of the market and the new competition coming from the young and—in the opinion of some MESA managers—extremely well-organized and aggressive KHM, S.A., presented a substantial challenge. Even though the new law had been in effect since 1972, the private industrial sector had been an insignificant market for MESA, as the filling of previous contractual commitments to PPC required nearly all of the production capacity. In 1972, sales to the private industrial sector amounted to only 2½ percent of MESA's total annual sales.

MESA had three different types of contacts with buyers in the private industrial sector. The three-man MESA sales force contacted some customers directly. A company of manufacturers' representatives in Thessaloníki, Greece's second largest city, solicited some orders on a commission basis. And, on occasion, MESA had been contacted by private individuals, working on a commission basis, who served as agent middlemen between industrial buyers and sources of supply. All sales to private buyers were FOB factory. MESA provided no installation or repair services, but it had a small service force at the plant performing limited service work in the Athens area

MESA aimed minimal advertising to the private industrial market, mostly in three newspapers—*Financial Express, Vima,* and *Nautical News.* No advertising budget existed nor were there limitations on advertising expenditures. Advertising activities were among the marketing manager's responsibilities.

PLANNING FOR THE FUTURE

MESA's management in 1974 devised a strategy to reduce the dependence upon PPC. There were three objectives: (1) to increase sales to the private sector, (2) to diversify product lines, and (3) to strengthen export activities.

The marketing department was reorganized (see Exhibit 2). The marketing director was made responsible for coordinating three subordinates, each in charge of sales to one of the three market sectors—that is, two domestic (PPC and private sector) and the export sector. MESA executives knew little about either the private industrial or the export markets. Consequently, management had started to draft plans for training programs to acquaint selling personnel with marketing theory and research. Management planned to request the assistance of Power Systems Company in "beefing up" its marketing expertise.

MESA had accomplished little research and development on either its markets or technologies. One MESA employee described the situation:

> In 1972 a consulting team came from the U.S.A. to reorganize the inventory and production system at the plant. With the help of two Greek employees,

EXHIBIT 2 · Organization of the Marketing Department

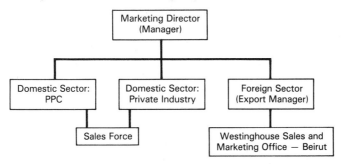

an improved system was conceived, reported to the management, and implemented in the operations. However, the system failed to produce favorable results. The failure might have been due to the lack of technical knowledge of such an elaborate scheme by the people doing the implementing. The plan might have worked had the parent company provided the experts to supervise the system for a certain period of time and had appropriate training seminars been organized for the Greek employees. In addition, a more general problem was the insufficient time that the home office people spent in the plant.

Management authorized the purchase in early 1974 of modern and efficient machines to make various sizes of nuts and bolts for industrial use. By mid-1974 the machines had been used only once—to fill an order from Greek National Railways. Since then they had remained idle, apparently because of the marketing department's inability to secure new orders. An aluminum casting machine had also been purchased but had not yet been used.

THE EXPORT MARKET

MESA's export sales had been limited and sporadic. The company had its best export year in 1972 when a sale of 300 transformers to a customer in Kuwait amounted to $2 million. The next year there were no export sales. During the first half of 1974 the company made one export sale—ten transformers to a buyer in an Arab state.

Recently, the position of export manager had been set up. MESA had been assigned markets in the Middle East and in some African countries, having first priority over other Westinghouse operations. Extended coordination existed between MESA and the main Westinghouse sales and marketing office for the Middle East and Africa, which was in Beirut, Lebanon. Working out of Beirut, Westinghouse sales personnel searched for customers and sent orders together with product specifications to MESA. The export manager at MESA's Athens office dispatched either an acceptance or rejection of each order to the Beirut office and issued necessary instructions to the production manager at Oinofyta.

The final price for each export sale was subject to approval by the managing director and was set as follows: The production manager estimated the costs of producing the order, added a "reasonable profit" percentage, and subtracted an amount equal to the amount MESA had paid in import duties for importing raw materials and fabricating parts—the Greek government permitted companies producing for export to apply for refunds of import duties on materials used to produce the exported goods. Finally, another percentage was subtracted to reflect the subsidy paid by the Greek government on goods exported (this percentage depended on the "value added by production" by MESA).

The export manager set a goal of increasing MESA's exports 15 percent annually. He had been in the Middle East twice during the first half of 1974. His appraisal was that competition for electrical equipment orders in the Middle East came mainly from European companies and their subsidiaries, and from state-owned enterprises in the Soviet Union and other COMEN-CON countries. The export manager believed that competition from behind the Iron Curtain used "political pricing."

The Westinghouse Beirut office handled marketing research and advertising for MESA's export sales. However, the MESA export manager placed some advertising in technical magazines circulating in Greece and abroad, such as *The Business Book of Greece, Trade with Greece,* and *Products from Greece.* MESA had no advertising budget for export sales. Most of Westinghouse's and MESA's advertising had been aimed toward prospective buyers in the "Petrodollar" market, primarily those in Saudi Arabia, Kuwait, Libya, Syria, Iraq, and Qatar.

Questions

1. Why was MESA so slow in developing export markets for its product lines?
2. What were the aftereffects to MESA of having regarded marketing as being synonymous with order processing?
3. How should MESA have gone about selling the private sector market in Greece?

9–4

OSAKA FIBER COMPANY

Use of trading companies as agents

Tokyo Textile Company, a large Japanese manufacturer, established Osaka Fiber Company to produce a new fiber which had been developed by the American Textile Company (U.S.A.). Under the licensing agreement, American Textile provided the required production and processing know-how and assisted in sales and marketing of Osaka's output to the Japanese market. Tom Yamada, with fifteen years sales experience at Tokyo Textile, was made sales manager of Osaka Fiber. American Textile sent George Williams, who had over twenty years of U.S. fiber sales experience, to Japan to serve Osaka Fiber as sales consultant. One of the initial marketing decisions that Yamada faced involved determining the advisability of using "trading companies" as sales agents.[1]

The new fiber, called Flexible, was a synthetic, unique in that it had high elasticity. When blended with other synthetic or natural fibers, the resulting fabric also became elastic. Thus, it was an ideal material to use in making swim wear, ski pants, socks, and underwear. Osaka varied its content between 10 and 20 percent of the total finished fabric, depending upon the fabric type and its end use. Mainly because of its limited number of uses, Flexible sold at a high price per pound. Since it was a new material concept

---

[1]Traditionally, Japanese manufacturers emphasized industrial technology, allowing wholesalers to dominate the marketing channels. When Japan was opened to Western trade, the largest wholesalers horizontally and vertically integrated into the Zaibatsu organizations, which have since dominated Japanese production and marketing. Zaibatsu descendants formed large, highly integrated general wholesale organizations known as *holding companies*. About twenty of these controlled basic distribution in Japan, acquiring some, if not all, of manufacturers' output in many industries.

to the textile industry, its use by a clothing maker required special technology in knitting, weaving, and other processing operations. Several other fiber manufacturers were known to be planning to produce a similar fiber, and considerable competition was expected at an early date.

Yamada and Williams recently discussed marketing channels for Osaka Fiber. Yamada believed the company should follow Japanese custom and sell through the trading companies, but Williams favored circumventing them and selling directly to textile manufacturers. The Japanese trading companies distributed the product of different manufacturers but refrained from handling competitive items (see Exhibit 1). Japanese manufacturers traditionally depended upon them for wholesale distribution. They provided most manufacturers with a much larger domestic and foreign sales force than they could otherwise individually afford. For example, one trading company had more than ten thousand salespersons covering the Japanese market and roughly two thousand working in areas outside Japan.

Yamada argued that Flexible fiber should be sold through the trading companies. His main argument was that the parent company, Tokyo Textile, sold its fibers, with which Flexible would be blended, through the trading companies, and if Osaka sold direct to users, then Tokyo would have trouble in getting the trading companies to continue handling the blended fibers. He also argued that the trading companies could be helpful in furnishing information on the market, ideas for new product uses, and suggestions as to new users. In addition, the trading companies assumed the risk of uncollectable accounts, helped finance their customers by extending credit, and helped customers plan advertising and sales promotion.

EXHIBIT 1 · Channels for Fiber Marketing in Japan

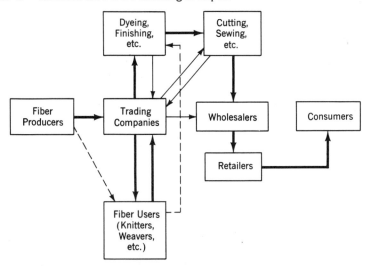

Manufacturers, in an effort to maintain stable prices, usually controlled both list prices to trading companies and resale prices to their customers, the actual users. Trading companies customarily maintained resale prices set by manufacturers, and instances of price-cutting were rare. Trading companies were paid commissions ranging from 2 to 5 percent.

Williams advanced arguments favoring direct sale to users: (1) Flexible fiber required special treatment in knitting, weaving, and other processing operations; therefore, sales and technical service were important. (2) Flexible's high quality strongly encouraged its use; consequently, users could easily sell their outputs with or without the trading companies' help. (3) Because of the limited number of uses for Flexible, there were only a small number of potential users, thus making it easy for Osaka to obtain market coverage. (4) Trading company sales personnel lacked technical know-how and therefore were not well equipped to help in the development of new end uses. (5) Leakage of secret know-how to competitors would be easier to control if trading companies were not used.

Trading companies were quick to detect any movement by any of their principals toward selling direct. Thus, Osaka management regarded a market test of direct selling as being clearly out of the question. Nevertheless, a decision on marketing channels had to be made soon.

Question

Should Flexible have been sold through the trading companies or direct to users? Explain.

9–5

CROMWELL MANUFACTURING COMPANY

*Planning and researching international
marketing operations*

Cromwell Manufacturing Company, located in upstate New York, made and
sold electrical construction materials, outdoor lighting equipment (including
airport lighting systems), and traffic signals. Its annual sales approximated
$60 million, the electrical construction materials accounting for 55 percent of
the total. In the United States the company sold its products through wholesale
distributors to industrial users, institutional buyers, and government units and
agencies. All customers were required to buy through the wholesalers, so
Cromwell sales personnel worked mainly with the distributors, rarely calling
on final buyers. For many years Cromwell had routinely turned all buying
inquiries from abroad over to the distributors for processing, and although
the company had an International Division, the distributors were still selling
to foreign accounts. This put them in direct competition with three Cromwell
foreign affiliates, a source of considerable annoyance to executives of the
International Division. As part of a long-range program to "make more sense
out of Cromwell's international marketing," the division's marketing manager, Charles Williams, began an investigation of world markets, hoping to
arrive at better answers to the question, Who should handle sales in what
markets?

Cromwell of Canada, the oldest affiliate, and wholly owned, had a
strong market position in the Dominion. However, it had only a limited
manufacturing operation, producing only those Cromwell products for which
substantial Canadian demand existed. Orders for other Cromwell products
were forwarded to the parent company where specialized personnel analyzed
each order, determined whether it was profitable to pay the Canadian import
duty, and, if so, saw to it that the order was shipped and billed to the Canadian

buyer. Since Cromwell of Canada had its own management and sales force, the sole administrative link between it and the parent company was between its president and the president of Cromwell Manufacturing Company.

An affiliate in Mexico operated along the same lines as Cromwell of Canada. With its headquarters and manufacturing plant in Mexico City, it started as a joint venture of the parent company and a small group of Mexican businessmen. Later, Cromwell acquired 100 percent ownership of the Mexican affiliate. This affiliate confined its selling activities to Mexico, making no effort to cultivate sales throughout Latin America or the West Indies.

The third affiliate was based in Milan, Italy. It was the newest member of the Cromwell family of companies, having been started as a joint venture with several Italian industrialists. Cromwell management had decided to enter into this joint venture after seeing a research report focusing on the sales potentials of its product lines in the European Common Market. Although manufacturing operations had yet to start up, the plan was that this affiliate make and sell all the Cromwell lines to buyers in Italy, France, West Germany, Belgium, Luxembourg, and the Netherlands.

Williams, the International Division's marketing manager, reported to the division head, C. C. Lucido, who was also the vice president of international operations. Williams's main responsibility was to research and develop new international markets. He was assisted by two area representatives who had rather comprehensive duties and responsibilities; in fact, more so than any other Cromwell marketing personnel. Not only did the area representatives plan and perform international market studies, but they were active in such projects as making credit arrangements for foreign buyers and staging sales meetings in cooperation with the managements of the affiliates. Both area representatives were knowledgeable concerning international marketing procedures, and both knew a great deal about different socioeconomic and cultural factors influencing marketing abroad.

Recently, Williams and the two area representatives began a systematic investigation of world markets. Their first step was to divide most of the world, except for the United States and Canada, into three major geographical areas: (1) Latin America (excluding Mexico) and the West Indies, (2) the Far East, India, Pakistan, Iran, the Persian Gulf countries, and Africa (excluding those parts of Africa and the Near East bordering on the Mediterranean), and (3) Europe and those non–European countries fronting on the Mediterranean. At this point, the decision was tentatively made to assign responsibility for marketing operations in the third area to the Italian affiliate.

Determining "who should have the responsibility" for marketing operations in the other two areas proved more difficult. With respect to the second geographical area, further analysis was postponed until surveys of markets in the first geographical area could be completed and analyzed, and until a decision could be made for that area. In the meantime, existing customers were to be served under present arrangements, most of them buying from U.S. wholesalers of Cromwell's product lines.

Thus, the research team's effort focused mainly on finding good answers to the question, Who should supply customers in Latin America (excluding Mexico) and in the West Indies? Because of its proximity to these markets and because Spanish was the main trading language throughout most of this area, the Mexican affiliate would have seemed to be the logical answer. However, investigation showed that shipping costs out of Mexican ports were high and shipping service was irregularly scheduled. Land carriers, both rail and truck, from Mexico City to Gulf and Pacific Coast ports did not appear capable of providing the special handling Cromwell products required. Coupled with these issues, of course, was the fact that the Mexican affiliate did not manufacture all the items in the three product lines. Thus, it was infeasible to service Latin America and the West Indies from the Mexican affiliate.

The procedures used in appraising the Venezuelan market were representative of those carried out in other Latin American and West Indian markets. The first step was the collection and analysis of statistical indicators and the compilation of a roster of Venezuelan business contacts. Three main information sources were tapped: (1) U.S. Department of Commerce publications and listings of Venezuelan firms, (2) previous buyers of Cromwell products with operations in Venezuela, and (3) the Venezuelan consulate in New York City, which proved the most fruitful source. The research team concluded, in fact, that the U.S. government information on Venezuela gave a somewhat distorted view. "To investigate any foreign market realistically and effectively," Williams said, "you've got to go to the particular country and draw your own conclusions, because you must see what the potential is in the country for your own particular product line."

The next step was an actual visit to Venezuela by the research team. They had two purposes: (1) to make an on-the-spot market survey and (2) to make preliminary arrangements for local distributors to handle Cromwell's lines when the decision was made as to how they would be supplied. The team made contacts with the U.S. and British embassies, the Venezuelan Ministry of Public Works, and utilities and construction companies; these contacts were to obtain data on sales potential and on marketing possibilities. In seeking candidates for distributorships, the research team looked for Venezuelan businessmen operating businesses covering all important areas of the country, but they were also careful to investigate each prospective distributor as to his relationships with other manufacturers, his government contacts, his financial resources, his technical capability to market the Cromwell lines, and his capabilities for stocking and servicing the lines.

At first the research team concluded that by selling through several Venezuelan distributors, perhaps four or five, Cromwell could attain a Venezuelan sales volume of roughly $200,000 annually. Further investigation, however, revealed that certain local firms could probably design and turn out competing items in two or three years. Locally based competitors, too, could get the government to erect trade barriers to imports, thereby hindering if not altogether stopping the flow of Cromwell products into the country. The team thus revised its earlier conclusion and decided to establish a joint venture with a Venezuelan manufacturer. Further study indicated that the market was large enough to support a joint venture, and Cromwell launched a search for a Venezuelan partner. Not finding a local manufacturer both equipped and interested in such a venture, Cromwell finally joined one of the firms it had previously investigated as a possible distributor, and a local manufacturing operation was thereby organized.

Questions

1. How might Cromwell have improved its approach to international marketing?
2. As Cromwell extended the scope of its international operations, what problems should it have anticipated in its relationships with its domestic distributors? How should these problems have been handled?

9–6

CONTINENTAL FOOTWEAR COMPANY

Foreign source of supply

Continental Footwear Company manufactured and marketed women's straw shoes and slippers throughout the United States. Sales to large chains such as National Shoe, Miles Shoe Company, and A. S. Beck accounted for more than 80 percent of the company's sales. The remainder went to independent jobbers who bought rejects and cancellations. Fourteen full-time salespersons, averaging eight years' service, sold to the chain store buyers. Continental also had sales representatives, in nine market areas, who sold primarily to "job lotters" of rejects and cancellations. Continental's sales declined last year by 15 percent compared with the year before, and management was alarmed because many chain store buyers were buying more and more foreign-made shoes.

Continental shoes, marketed under each chain's brand name, retailed from $15.98 to $25.98 per pair. Competitive foreign-made shoes retailed from $13.98 to $21.98 per pair. In addition to their price advantage, imported shoes, according to chain buyers, had more original styling, higher quality, and better craftsmanship.

Continental's top executives recently met to discuss the ever increasing competition from abroad. Charles Stone, the general manager, proposed the following solution:

> Our sales to the chains have dropped off due to the influx of foreign shoes. We must do something to counter the increased sales of Asiatic shoes, but because we cannot match the original styling and lower production costs which exist in foreign countries, we cannot make a competitive shoe in America. Marketing research shows the Asiatic-styled shoe is growing in popularity. I propose that Continental set up a subsidiary company, which we will call

Intercontinental Shoe, to import the vamps, patterns, and lasts from the Hamas Company of Hong Kong. They will make arrangements with us whereby they will export the desired product to our Intercontinental Company. The shoes can be finished in our present plant and made ready for sale. The facilities there are more than adequate and since the straw patterns have already been woven and designed, the finishing of the shoes at our plant will be relatively simple.

It will take about 40 days to ship the shoe components from Hong Kong to New York. Continental will be vulnerable to cancellatons if the shoes are late but, if we add a safety margin to our production and shipping schedules, we shouldn't run into trouble. We might have to face the problem of a rise in tariff rates, but these rates would apply to all imported shoes including our competitors.

Instead of distributing our foreign shoes to chain stores, why not market them to large department stores such as Sears? For years we have only sold to chain stores, never to department stores. With these foreign shoes, we have the right goods to break into the department stores. Someday we may be able to sell them our domestic shoes if we get a foothold through our foreign shoe sales. I would like to put our own brand name on the imports. Perhaps we could call them "Flickies." With our own brand name and a good advertising campaign, our sales will surely rise.

By selling these shoes to department stores we will be opening a new market, plus eliminating any intracompetition that would occur if the shoes were sold to the chains already buying Continental's domestic line.

Questions

1. Should the semifinished shoes have been imported by Continental?
2. If Continental had decided to market imported shoes, should it have sold them under its own brand name?

10–1

BUTTERICK FASHION MARKETING COMPANY

Growth from a new market segment

Butterick Fashion Marketing Company's sales of See & Sew, a new product, were higher than expected, but total company and industry sales continued to decrease. Mr. John Dodson, a Butterick sales manager, felt better understanding of product demand was needed to aid both corporate and sales planning.

COMPANY OPERATIONS, HISTORY, AND MARKETING DEVELOPMENT

The Butterick Fashion Marketing Company made and distributed home sewing patterns. Its product line consisted of Butterick patterns, Vogue patterns, and See & Sew patterns. Three companies dominated the industry—Butterick, Simplicity, and McCall's.

One evening in 1863 in Sterling, Massachusetts, Ellen Butterick remarked to Ebenezer, her husband, that her sewing projects would be easier if she had patterns to go by. Ebenezer, a tailor and inventor, soon began publishing practical and fashionable pattern designs, and by spring he was selling graded paper patterns in boxes of 100. The boxes sold at $10 wholesale and $25 retail. In 1864 he opened a New York City sales office. Pattern sales continued to increase, keeping pace with the then new acceptance of home sewing machines. By 1868 the pattern package consisted of the tissue pieces folded together in a neat rectangular package somewhat smaller than today's pattern envelope. The label carried the picture, some simple directions without diagrams, the price, and other pertinent data.

Butterick went into partnership with two other men in 1867 under the name Butterick & Company. The same year the first issue of *The Ladies'*

Quarterly Report of Broadway Fashions appeared, the earliest of many Butterick magazines aimed to serve specific markets.

Butterick expanded to 100 offices and 1,000 agencies throughout the United States and Canada and in 1876 opened offices in London, Vienna, and Paris. In 1905 Butterick erected a sixteen-story building in Manhattan, which is still the company's headquarters.

For years Butterick practiced selective distribution, offering its products in certain department and dry goods stores and refusing to sell in variety stores. This provided an opportunity for competitors, and other pattern companies entered the market (Simplicity was among them) offering good products at slightly lower prices. Simplicity and the others first offered their lines in variety stores, then entered department stores.

The Great Depression left its mark on Butterick. By the early 1940s the company was almost bankrupt. It owed the Paragon Press more money than it had in assets. A retired banker, Leonard Tingle, bought the company for about ten cents on the dollar.

The World War II years, 1941 through 1945, were good for the industry. Limited selections of fashion merchandise in the stores caused more and more women to turn to home sewing. But Butterick did not benefit as much as Simplicity. Simplicity was able to receive larger allotments of supplies due to its resources, and from then on Simplicity led the industry.

Butterick's strategy during the 1950s was to have a strong sales force to gain distribution in the many independent fabric shops emerging nationwide and to gain a foothold in the new suburban shopping center department stores. In 1958 Butterick tried to penetrate the variety store market, having developed a revolving rack with 112 styles, in all sizes. The rack gave variety stores the chance to sell patterns without maintaining a large pattern inventory and to receive the costly support publications (counter catalogs, *Fashion News*). For the first time in many years, Butterick's market share reached 12 percent. This was considered to be a turning point for the company. Meanwhile, Simplicity signed up the J. C. Penney and W. T. Grant accounts, two of the largest fabric retailers.

In the 1960s Butterick developed a small selection of styles for supermarkets, for sale through wholesalers with in-store maintenance programs. The fixture featured fashion and sewing notions. The program peaked with distribution in 10,000 stores and over $1.2 million in annual sales but rack fixtures in supermarkets were short-lived, and the program diminished in value each year.

Harry Howard, a Wharton M.B.A. and Leonard Tingle's son-in-law, became president in the mid-1950s. Recognizing a good opportunity, he approached Condé Nast, publisher of *Vogue* and other magazines, and suggested that Condé Nast's *Vogue* pattern be added to Butterick's product line. Condé Nast could not continue to make *Vogue* patterns, as production was too costly for the limited distribution, so it sold to Butterick.

In 1968 American Can Company bought Butterick and named the company Butterick Fashion Marketing Company. *Vogue, Glamour* and American Can's capital enhanced the Butterick image as never before.

Two important things happened in the 1970s—the development of polyester knits and the proliferation of national and regional fabric chains. Polyester knits were easy to sew, and the versatile fabric facilitated pattern design. Home sewing and the pattern industry boomed. Butterick fielded a larger sales force than the much larger Simplicity and McCall's, whose strengths were in the national chains (Sears, Penney, Ward's, Woolworth, Kresge, etc.). The proliferating independent fabric shops diluted the department store and national chain businesses, and Butterick became the strongest supplier to the stores doing most of the business—the fabric shops. Butterick doubled its sales force from seven to fourteen—seven district managers and seven salespersons. Managers were responsible for supervising and motivating the salespersons as well as for selling and servicing their own accounts.

The Butterick sales force made both personal and telephone sales. Usually, phone sales were contacts or renewals of existing accounts. Members of the sales force were paid salaries plus bonuses for sales over quotas. Typically, the sales effort included cold calls to potential customers and attempts to persuade existing customers to reorder or to increase current orders.

The peak year for home sewing was 1975. The tremendous success of polyester knits caused nationwide proliferation of not only thousands of fabric shops, but led to the creation of regional and national fabric chains. Butterick increased its market share because it had distribution in places where consumers were shopping (see Exhibit 1).

After 1975 technological advances brought down retail polyester knit prices from $6.98 to $1.00 per yard, and many independent stores closed their doors. The major regional and national fabric chains became very strong. During 1976 and 1977, Butterick held its unit sales constant due to improved pattern styling and catalog presentation, but Simplicity and McCall's began to record declining sales. The late seventies saw a new trend in fashion—blue jeans.

In 1977 Butterick launched a multimillion-dollar research program to determine consumer satisfaction/dissatisfaction with price points, styles, service, and out-of-stock situations. At the same time management analyzed the

EXHIBIT 1 · Distribution of Pattern Business, Butterick Company

TYPE OF OUTLET	1960 SALES %	TYPE OF OUTLET	1980 SALES %
Department stores	35	Department stores	15
National dry goods chains	45	National dry goods chains	20
Fabric shops, others	20	Regional and national fabric chains	45
		Independent fabric shops, other	20

number of styles retailers sold versus the number carried. A key finding was that pattern sales were highly unprofitable for the mass merchandise and dry goods chains, because of the large inventories required and high costs for support material and freight. The large inventory resulted in average annual inventory turnover of less than one-half. In addition, all the pattern companies had so increased their prices that pattern retailing did not fit the images of low-price stores.

Then Butterick developed a new product, the See & Sew pattern, to retail at $.99 per unit. It was first distributed in 96 styles made up of two home sewing categories—Misses and Children. Each style was available in two sizes: A (for size 8, 10, and 12) and B (for size 14, 16, and 18). A self-service fixture was designed for displaying the patterns. The total inventory for the retail store consisted of 576 units worth $570 at retail. Stores were memo-billed (account outstanding, no interest) and paid only for units sold between calls or reorders.

The Butterick sales force placed See & Sew racks in independent fabric shops and handled rack servicing. Each salesperson serviced up to 120 racks, for which they received flat bonuses, some of which amounted to $6,000. Later, an outside firm took over rack servicing. This firm's representatives dusted the racks, cleaned them, and took inventories. Inventories were sent to Butterick offices where they were computer-compared to a model, creating orders for the accounts represented. Each account was visited an average of four times a year, at an approximate cost of $30 per visit.

See & Sew patterns also became a part of the Butterick line providing automatic sales to 9,000 existing accounts. By the end of 1979, See & Sew accounted for less than 10 percent of the Butterick selection but over 22 percent of its sales. In January 1980 the company decided to take See & Sew out of the Butterick pattern book and develop it as an additional line, using self-service fixtures in the existing accounts. Most of the largest fabric chains accepted this concept wholeheartedly, as stocking costs for See & Sew were a pittance compared to total pattern inventory costs, averaging $6,000 to $7,000 per store. By February 1980, 1,850 accounts had been sold (see Exhibit 2); See & Sew inventory turnover was predicted at twice per year.

EXHIBIT 2 · Breakdown of See & Sew Sales (as of February 1980)

RETAILER	NO. OF ACCOUNTS
Cloth World	250*
House of Fabrics	500*
Fabric Center	500*
Hancock Fabrics	200*
Independent retailers	400

*Expected to sell 2,000 units/fixture/year.

FUTURE DIRECTIONS

Reflecting on the success of the See & Sew line within the overall fabric of Butterick's marketing program, Mr. Dodson recognized the need to position the company for further growth. He knew this would be difficult in the face of continuing socioeconomic changes. He hoped to rely on See & Sew without worrying about competitive retaliation, but he felt the need for better understanding of the demand for Butterick's products.

Questions

1. What were the major determinants of demand trends in the pattern industry?
2. How should Butterick have responded to these trends?
3. Was the See & Sew line likely to continue to grow? Why or why not?

10–2

FABRIK-ARTS, INC.

Development of a growth strategy

Mr. Brian Cross, general manager, Fabrik-Arts, Inc., and Ms. Linda Jensen, sales and marketing manager, met to discuss company goals and strategies for the coming year. Both realized that the company needed continuous strong growth to provide acceptable and improving profitability from scale economies. Both were concerned with procedures for reaching customers to acquaint them with Fabrik-Arts products and services. Several alternatives were discussed, including enlarging the sales force and expanding overseas.

COMPANY BACKGROUND

Four years before, Mr. Brian Cross had finished graduate work in product design. While in college he had helped his older brother develop a prosperous screen printing business. Upon graduating, he felt that his strong academic background and practical experience could be combined to develop a successful business. Recognizing the growth opportunities in screen printing,[1] he opened his own business in the heart of the North Carolina textile industry. Because of his limited capital ($5,000) Mr. Cross built his own processing equipment (an infrequent but not unheard of practice in this industry). The business started with one-part time and three full-time employees three and a half years ago and had first-year sales of $60,000, almost all representing

---

[1]Screen printing permits the reproduction of reasonably fine detail by forcing paint or ink through a stencil made of fabric (silk, polyester, or nylon, for example) onto the material to be printed. The procedure, materials, and equipment necessary are simple and inexpensive. Silk screen printing lends itself to short runs, such as for posters, wallpaper, and window cards; it is widely used for printing textured surfaces and curved objects such as fabrics and cans.

subcontracted printing work for Mr. Cross's brother on a "Wrangler" contract.

During the company's second year, Mr. Cross designed and built additional production equipment to meet the needs of anticipated increased demand. In order to achieve higher flexibility it was decided to maintain an inventory of 2,000 basic T-shirts; this inventory was gradually increased over the next three years to 30,000. Last year facilities were relocated to increase production space from 2,000 to 5,000 square feet.

A short time ago, Mr. Cross hired Ms. Linda Jensen, a recent college graduate, as marketing and sales manager. Mr. Cross retained responsibility for technical aspects, managed the personnel, and continued as the primary contact with established customers. Fabrik-Arts, Inc., employed eleven people at the plant and fielded two college sales representatives.

INDUSTRY STRUCTURE AND COMPETITION

There were many small companies in the screen printing industry. Two characteristics of the industry were responsible. First, local personal contact was needed to work out design solutions to customer problems. Second, entering the screen printing business was easy, as it was a low-overhead business requiring little equipment. Most of these small firms were technically competent and creative designers but had weak managements. According to Mr. Cross, "They come and go rather frequently."

There were also some large screen printing companies such as Velvashee, Champion Productions, and Collegiate Pacific. They concentrated on getting large orders from department stores and colleges and generally avoided soliciting small orders.

A third segment of the industry was conventional printing firms. Due to equipment and other limitations, however, this segment presented only a minor threat to Fabrik-Arts, Inc.'s, business. Still, Mr. Cross continuously monitored competitive activities of all types by reviewing catalogs and advertisements featuring products and services of competing firms.

Price was not critical in selling screen printing, especially where small- and medium-sized companies competed. Mr. Cross felt that his company had an effective closing rate of over 90 percent, once a contact was made. The important competitive factors were product quality, art and design work, and personal presentation of the product. Customers did not usually solicit multiple proposals to compare prices, but among larger accounts bidding was common.

PRODUCT LINE

The Fabrik-Arts product line included T-shirts, football and baseball jerseys, golf shirts, nylon jackets, sweatshirts, promotional totes, aprons, spirit scarves,

EXHIBIT 1 · Fabrik-Arts Product Line

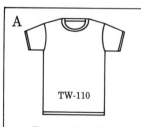

TW-110

Promotional T

100% Cotton medium weight T-shirt.
Sizes: Adult S,M,L,XL. Youth S,M,L.
Color: White.

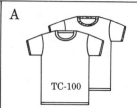

TC-100

Medium Weight T

100% Cotton medium weight T-shirt.
Sizes: Adult S,M,L,XL. Youth S,M,L.
Colors: Black, Gold, Lt. Blue, Navy, Orange,
Red, Tan, White with blue ringer, Yellow.

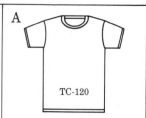

TC-120

Premium Weight T

50% Polyester 50% Cotton premium
weight T-shirt.
Sizes: Adult S,M,L,XL. Youth S,M,L.
Colors: Black, Gold, Kelly, Lt. Blue, Navy,
Orange, Red, Tan, Yellow.

TH-130

Heavy Weight T

100% Cotton heavy weight T-shirt.
Sizes: Adult S,M,L,XL.
Colors: Gold, Lt. Blue, Navy, Red, Tan,
White.

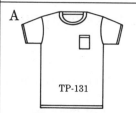

TP-131

Heavy Weight T

100% Cotton heavy weight T-shirt
with pocket.
Sizes: Adult S,M,L,XL.
Colors: Gold, Lt. Blue, Navy, Red, Tan,
White.

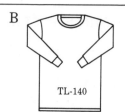

TL-140

Long Sleeve T

Heavy weight long sleeve T-shirt.
Sizes: Adult S,M,L,XL.
Colors: Lt. Blue, Tan, White, Yellow.

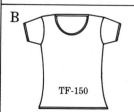

TF-150

Ladies Top

50% Polyester 50% Cotton medium
weight ladies top with scoop neck and
cap sleeves.
Sizes: Adult S,M,L,XL.
Colors: Lt. Blue, Navy, White, Yellow.

JF-200

Football Jersey

50% Polyester 50% Cotton top stitched
jersey with ribbed collar and cuff
Sizes: Adult S,M,L,XL.
Colors: Lt. Blue, Maroon, Navy, Red.

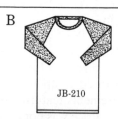

JB-210

Baseball Jersey

50% Polyester 50% Cotton premium
weight jersey. White body with solid
color, 3/4 length sleeves.
Sizes: Adult S,M,L,XL.
Colors: Lt. Blue, Maroon, Navy, Red.

EXHIBIT 1 · (continued)

C

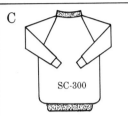

SC-300

Sweatshirt

50% Polyester 50% Cotton long sleeve crew neck sweatshirt.
Sizes: Adult S,M,L,XL.
Colors: Gold, Gray, Lt. Blue, Navy, Red, White.

C

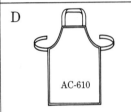

GW-400

Golf Shirt

50% Polyester 50% Cotton lacoste knit golf shirt with pocket.
Sizes: Adult S,M,L,XL.
Color: White.

C

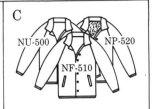

NU-500   NP-520
NF-510

Nylon Jacket

100% Nylon jacket. Snap front, elastic cuffs, draw string bottom, & 2 pockets.
Sizes: Adult S,M,L,XL.
Colors: Gold, Kelly, Lt. Blue, Maroon, Navy, Red.

B

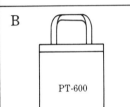

PT-600

Promotional Tote

50% Polyester 50% Cotton tote bag.
14″ x 14″ with two straps.
Color: Natural.

D

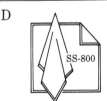

AC-610

Apron

65% Polyester 35% Cotton BBQ apron.
Colors: Brown, Gold, Kelly, Lt. Blue, Navy, Orange, Red, Tan, White.

D

SS-800

Spirit Scarf

65% Polyester 35% Cotton scarf.
Ideal for athletic events. 14″ x 14″.
Colors: Black, Brown, Gold, Kelly, Lt. Blue, Maroon, Navy, Orange, Peach, Red, Royal, Tan, White, Yellow.

B

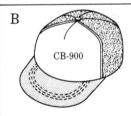

CB-900

Baseball Cap

100% Polyester seamless white front, with colored mesh and matching visor.
One size fits all.
Colors: Gold, Kelly Lt. Blue, Maroon, Navy, Red.

B

VW-950

Visor

100% Cotton visor with adjustable elastic strap.
Color: White.

D

FF-810

Flippy Flyer

100% Nylon disc with weighted rim & 100% Polyester binding.
The original pocket flying saucer.
Colors: Black, Gold, Green, Lime, Lt. Blue, Navy, Orange, Red, Royal, Silver, White, Yellow.

baseball caps, visors, and flippy flyers (see Exhibit 1). All items were sold either printed or unprinted. The A items in Exhibit 1 accounted for 75 percent of sales, B items for 20 percent, C items for nearly 5 percent, and D items for less than 1 percent.

Fabrik-Arts equipment could print up to four colors and a five-color printer was being designed. Its art department helped customers design artwork to meet their expressed needs. The company's facilities could screen-print large production runs of T-shirts, sweatshirts, and other sportswear (current daily production capability was 500 dozen). Fabrik-Arts, Inc., was printing a large volume of Wrangler goods for export to Europe.

MARKETS

Fabric-Arts started as a 100 percent subcontractor of the Wrangler contract obtained by Mr. Cross's brother, but gradually this percentage had been reduced to 50 percent. Mr. Cross and Ms. Jensen had decided that market segmentation should be used to identify target markets. It was decided to explore the following target segments:

1. Boy Scouts (including summer camps)
2. Summer camps
   a. Church
   b. YMCA
   c. Girl Scouts
   d. Sport camps
   e. Vacation campgrounds
3. Tourist areas, beaches (mainly North Carolina)
4. Schools
5. Student organizations
   a. Dormitories
   b. Student Union
   c. Fraternity and sorority
6. Volume retailers
7. Export
8. Textile mills
9. Civic organizations
   a. Churches
   b. Jaycees
10. Small retail stores
11. Events
    a. Concerts and festivals
    b. Road runs
12. Distributors of unprinted goods

Ms. Jensen had begun to analyze sales by product line and developed the information shown in Exhibit 2.

EXHIBIT 2 · Product Category Marketing Information

| | PRODUCT CATEGORY | | | |
INFORMATION	BUY, PRINT, RESELL	CONTRACT PRINT	PRINT ONLY	MISCELLANEOUS
Percent of gross sales	50%	47%	2%	1%
Number of customers	300+	5	6	2
Distribution of volume by customer	30/30% 255/69% 15+/1%	1/95% (Wrangler) 4/5%	6/100% (equally divided)	1/70% 1/30%

PROMOTION AND DISTRIBUTION

The Fabrik-Arts sales force consisted of the sales and marketing manager and the two college representatives. Mr. Cross handled the big Wrangler account and other customers acquired before Ms. Jensen's arrival.

Once a potential customer was identified, a presentation package was developed and contact followed. This was done either directly by a salesperson, a college representative, or a jobber. Sometimes, however, contacts were made through the mail or at trade shows.

Advertising was used sparingly because Mr. Cross doubted its usefulness. Some ads were run in the local football newspaper and calendar, the Yellow Pages, college newspapers, and *The Press* (a nationwide newspaper of the garment printing industry). The typical *Press* ad simply showed a product sample and listed prices and availability. The basic advertising strategy was to "keep a low profile" so as not to attract too many small customers. Mr. Cross wanted to do just enough advertising to maintain visibility, since he knew how difficult the big textile buyers were to reach.

Physical distribution was handled by United Parcel Service. Bus delivery was available and provided quicker service (customers could specify delivery by bus if they agreed to pay the higher charges).

PRICING PRACTICES AND POLICIES

Selling prices were arrived at through an experimental approach. The goal was to charge prices which allowed "good and fair" profits, but special prices were quoted in new markets. In general, a 20 percent margin was applied to unprinted T-shirts and a 100 percent markup on cost was applied to printed T-shirts to cover printing costs. Terms were "cash on delivery" (COD) or net 10 or net 30 days (depending on customer size). No discounts were granted.

FINANCIAL CONDITION

Fabrik-Arts' sales had steadily increased from $60,000 the first year to $145,000 the next year and $295,000 last year (see Exhibits 3, 4, and 5).

FUTURE DEVELOPMENTS

Mr. Cross was optimistic about the future. He felt that people would continue to buy Fabrik-Arts' products because they wanted to identify socially with names, products, and images, and printed T-shirts and other items were an

EXHIBIT 3 · Balance Sheet (previous year)

ASSETS		
CURRENT ASSETS:		
Cash		$ 4,564.36
Accounts receivable		35,864.50
Inventories		31,346.61
Total Current Assets		$71,775.47
FIXED ASSETS:		
Machinery and equipment	$14,276.03	
Automobile	5,206.25	
	$19,482.28	
Less: Accumulated depreciation	5,228.70	14,253.58
OTHER ASSETS:		
Organization expense	$ 300.00	
Deposits	225.00	525.00
		$86,554.05

LIABILITIES AND STOCKHOLDERS' EQUITY		
CURRENT LIABILITIES:		
Short-term borrowings		$13,000.00
Current portion of long-term debt		1,275.00
Accounts payable		10,628.64
Accrued expenses		13,520.93
Accrued income taxes		5,519.54
Total Current Liabilities		$43,944.11
LONG-TERM DEBT:		
Note payable—bank	$ 2,337.50	
Note payable—stockholder	12,207.76	14,545.26
Total Liabilities		$58,489.37
STOCKHOLDERS' EQUITY:		
Common stock—$1.00 par value; 100,000 shares authorized; 7,000 shares issued and outstanding	$ 7,000.00	
Retained earnings	21,064.68	$28,064.68
		$86,554.05

EXHIBIT 4 · Statement of Income and Retained Earnings (previous year)

Sales		$294,982.94
Cost of Sales:		
Inventory (beginning)	$ .00	
Material purchases	140,405.89	
Labor	56,895.60	
Payroll taxes	4,845.91	
Supplies	2,371.60	
	$204,519.00	
Less: Inventory (ending)	31,346.61	173,172.39
Gross Profit		$121,810.55
Selling, General, and Administrative Expenses:		
Advertising	416.61	
Amortization of organization expense	75.00	
Automobile expenses	622.91	
Commissions	3,716.23	
Casual labor	1,109.60	
Contributions	50.00	
Depreciation	5,229.00	
Dues and subscriptions	361.50	
Freight	3,668.33	
Insurance	3,360.91	
Medical expense reimbursement	118.83	
Miscellaneous	1,843.07	
Office supplies	4,519.69	
Officers' life insurance	1,385.74	
Payroll taxes	3,770.94	
Postage	242.95	
Professional fees	3,065.00	
Rent—building	3,810.00	
Rent—truck	343.93	
Repairs	536.92	
Salaries—office	21,274.43	
Salary—officer	23,000.00	
Taxes—general	639.79	
Telephone	3,792.53	
Travel	2,329.85	
Utilities	2,902.10	92,185.86
Operating Income (forwarded)		$29,624.69
Other Income—Interest		11.27
		$29,635.96
Other Deductions:		
Interest	$2,735.86	
Loss on disposals of fixed assets	315.88	3,051.74
Net Income Before Provision for Income Taxes		$26,584.22
Provision for Income Taxes		5,519.54
Net Income		$21,064.68
Retained Earnings (beginning)		.00
Retained Earnings (ending)		$21,064.68

EXHIBIT 5 · Statement of Changes in Financial Positions (previous year)

Sources of Working Capital:
Operations:

Net income		$21,064.68
Depreciation and amortization		5,371.74
Working Capital Provided by Operations		$26,436.42
Book value of fixed asset disposals		315.88
Increase in long-term debt		14,545.26
Issuance of common stock		7,000.00
Total Sources		$48,297.56

Uses of Working Capital:

Purchase of fixed assets	$19,866.20	
Increase in other assets	600.00	
Total Uses		20,466.20
Increase in Working Capital		$27,831.36

Changes in Components of Working Capital:
Current assets—increase:

Cash	$ 4,564.36	
Accounts receivable	35,864.50	
Inventory	31,346.61	
Net Increase		$71,775.47

Current liabilities—increase:

Short-term borrowings	$13,000.00	
Current portion of long-term debt	1,275.00	
Accounts payable	10,628.64	
Accrued expenses	13,520.93	
Accrued income taxes	5,519.54	
Net Increase		43,944.11
Increase in Working Capital		$27,831.36

inexpensive means to fulfill social identification needs. The products were also attractive to businesses for use as inexpensive promotional aids.

Ms. Jensen echoed these feelings and was anxious to get started on improvement of garment wash fastness; finer detail in prints; selling sleeve and pocket prints; and using more heat-resistant dye ink.

Questions

1. What problems were there in Fabrik-Arts' marketing program?
2. What target market(s) should have been pursued?
3. What marketing strategy should have been used to reach these market(s)?

10–3

ToLee Plantation, Inc.

A new segment strategy

ToLee Plantation in southwest Georgia was one of the Southeast's largest pecan growers; it also grew blueberries, peaches, corn, peanuts, soybeans, and wheat. The owners were considering a change in pecan marketing strategy. The proposal was to switch from selling to a sheller to shelling and packaging pecans under the ToLee name. The ToLee brand would be sold through mail order and through grocery stores, and bulk sales would be made to commercial buyers. The proposed strategy was attractive because:

1. The National Pecan Marketing Council had plans to educate consumers about pecans and hoped to create a larger demand.
2. Surveys showed consumers preferred pecans over almonds and walnuts.
3. ToLee would be one of the few pecan brands in retail stores.
4. ToLee already had retail distribution of its ToLee Plantation Blueberries.

The owners were convinced that it was important to move quickly. The first brand into the newly expanded market should achieve favored status. If the ToLee brand did not get into the stores first, a competitor might step in and take over the desired position.

THE PECAN INDUSTRY

Pecans went to market in one of two ways. Some growers sold their crops to shellers for processing and marketing. Other growers handled their own marketing and processing or contracted with shellers for the processing. Some growers kept pecans in cold storage to fill orders year round rather than just

219

after the harvest. Ninety-four percent of all pecans were marketed shelled for use as a cooking ingredient. Commercial bakers and confectioners bought about 47 percent of the production; retailers, 15 percent; ice cream makers, 5 percent; exporters, 5 percent; gift packers, 5 percent; and other small users, 23 percent.

Three problems confronted pecan growers. First, production varied from year to year, and prices fluctuated with supply. Second, the historically unstable crop size and price created a burden for commercial users, especially makers of pecan candy. If pecans were in short supply, users either could not buy enough or had to pay high prices. Third, pecan growers bore the brunt of highly aggressive marketing techniques used by their major competitors, the walnut and almond growers.

CONSUMER PERCEPTIONS

Marketing research showed consumers preferring pecans over other nuts for baking, but the market share for pecans had dropped steadily. The U.S. Department of Commerce reported annual per capita pecan consumption had fallen in the past fifteen years from .44 pounds to .28 pounds while annual per capita walnut consumption had gone up from .30 pounds to .52 pounds and per capita almond consumption had risen from .27 pounds to .43 pounds. Because of relatively high price and limited availability, pecans generally were used as a holiday item rather than an everyday cooking ingredient.

Also contributing to declining consumption was the fact that pecans were mainly sold commercially while walnuts were mainly retailed. Consumers looked upon pecans as seasonal luxuries, walnuts as everyday necessities. Supermarket managers said that pecans were usually carried only during the holidays because that was when consumers wanted them. Consumers said they bought pecans during the holidays because that was the only time they were on display.

Evidently, too, a substantial number of consumers believed that pecans were high in cholesterol. Actually, pecans are low in cholesterol, and the meat is nutritious as well as high in energy. Furthermore, nut aficionados say pecans have a richer flavor than most other nuts.

COMMERCIAL USERS

Commercial users benefited from consumers' beliefs that pecans were for special occasions. People considered candies and other sweets as treats instead of necessities, so treats deserved special ingredients; and because of this pecans were used in sweets more than other nuts. Any nut could supply the crunch, but the pecan offered superior quality and flavor. Some confectioners had found that sales of pecan items did not decline greatly when prices were raised to cover higher nut prices. The commercial user's main concern about pecans was the supply available each year.

EXHIBIT 1 · Proposed Advertising by National Pecan Marketing Association

THE NATIONAL PECAN MARKETING COUNCIL

The National Pecan Marketing Council offered membership to all pecan growers and shellers. Its main purpose was to build market demand for pecans. By educating consumers about pecans and their uses, the council hoped to increase the market share of pecans. The council used Atlanta and San Francisco advertising agencies to develop pecan marketing campaigns. (See Exhibit 1 for a sample advertisement.) Through television, magazine, and trade journal media, the council hoped to refute misconceptions of consumers and commercial users such as:

1. Pecan prices are higher than prices of other nuts.
2. Pecan supplies are unpredictable.
3. Pecans are used only for special dishes.
4. Pecans are not nutritious.

The council believed that once buyers were aware that pecans were always available and versatile in usage, additional demand would develop. With consumers demanding more pecans, retailers would carry them year round. The council planned, too, to create a second season for pecans. All varieties of nuts had peak sales during the winter holidays. The council decided to develop an advertising program aimed to develop a summer pecan season, starting the Fourth of July, during which pecans were "excellent for snacking or baking."

ToLEE PLANTATION

At one time ToLee Plantation had its own shelling plant and packaged pecans under the name Mr. Sam's Pecans for sale in bulk to bakeries and through mail order. Later, the shelling plant was sold and ToLee agreed not to buy or build a shelling plant for five years. Since that time ToLee had harvested, cleaned, sized, and graded the pecans, then sold them to shellers. ToLee also stored pecans for future price speculation, and had cold storage facilities to store 1 million pounds.[1]

MARKETING AND PROMOTION

ToLee had no specialized marketing personnel. The owners contacted buyers for ToLee's crops and negotiated for the best prices. Prices for pecans and the other crops, except peanuts (peanut prices were government regulated), were heavily influenced by market supplies. Often it seemed that pricing was determined by "playing the market" to generate the highest selling prices. The cold storage facilities were useful in this respect, since if ToLee could not get the price desired the crop could be stored in anticipation of higher future prices.[2]

NEW STRATEGY

ToLee Plantation's owners felt that the National Pecan Marketing Council was carving out a new market segment. The council's efforts were expected to increase year-round consumer demand for pecans and year-round stocking by the retailers. They wanted ToLee to be the first in designing a retail marketing strategy. Part of the strategy would be to develop packages and displays with strong retailer appeal. Another part was to formulate promotional strategy for ToLee Pecans.

Retailers surveyed by the National Pecan Marketing Council suggested certain changes that might increase pecan sales:

1. Packaging should be improved. The package should be strong and have less writing so the nuts could be seen.

[1]Pecans could be stored for two years.

[2]ToLee Blueberries, however, were sold direct to major grocery chains by an employee who contacted the stores and arranged the orders, delivery dates, and selling prices. Deliveries were by a farm van to customers' stores in Georgia, Florida, and Tennessee.

2. Packages should be available in several sizes.
3. Shelf life should be lengthened.
4. Suppliers should provide in-store merchandising aids as well as brand promotion. (Retailers said this improvement was the most important.)

ToLee management planned several packaging moves. The pecans would be packaged in several sizes. Also under consideration was an ultrasmall package to sell as a snack food and a large bag of in-shell nuts. All packages were to have see-through windows, and recipes on the package were under study. Plans, too, were to design a store display unit to make packages of ToLee Pecans a noticeable item in the store.

Promotional strategies were to aim at selling ToLee Pecans during the holidays when demand was high. Additionally, as the Marketing Council created more consumer demand for pecans, promotions would aim to satisfy these new consumer needs.

Starting up a mail-order operation would also require promotion. To reach mail-order buyers, different promotion techniques were under consideration including:

1. cable television advertisements for ToLee Pecans with a toll-free number for placing orders
2. local television ads
3. newspaper ads and supplements
4. magazine ads containing pecan recipes and order forms (this method was being used by almond and walnut growers)
5. direct mail brochures and order forms

The owners were optimistic about the chances for marketing success. They had sufficient storage facilities to assure a steady pecan supply for both retailers and mail-order buyers. They had some earlier experience in mail-order operations. They had good relations with major grocery store chains now carrying ToLee Blueberries and this should have favorable impact on the ToLee Pecans. Further, commercial pecan users could still be counted on to buy. Finally, since the five-year moratorium had expired, ToLee was free to buy or build a pecan shelling plant.

ADDITIONAL CONSIDERATIONS

Yet details needed working out before going ahead with the project. Most important was the packaging method. Packaging machinery, designed to package different sized bags with minimum nut breakage, ranged in price from $7,000 to $50,000. Outlays for packaging machinery could be avoided by hiring a contract packager, but this would mean hauling the pecans to Atlanta for packaging then back to ToLee for distribution; package shelf life would be reduced by the extra transport time.[3] Hand packaging was an alternative requiring very little investment but a heat sealing machine would be needed.

COMPETITION

There were three different sources of competition. One was from other local pecan growers and sellers. Plantation Pecans and Sunnyland Pecans were two area brands packaged locally and sold through mail order.

A second source of competition was the large nut grocery manufacturers that already were selling packaged pecans in supermarkets. Standard Brands (Planter's Peanuts), Goldkist, and Fisher were three of these manufacturers. If demand for pecans expanded, these manufacturers might decide to market packaged pecans more aggressively. The owners thought that ToLee Pecans could compete with these brands by offering several bag sizes and being first with attractive in-store promotions.

A third source of competition was from other types of nuts—almonds and walnuts, for example. Consumers preferred pecans but if they were not available or too expensive, consumers would substitute walnuts or almonds, both heavily advertised in women's magazines and in some business magazines. The almond growers' cooperative marketing association had recently begun some television advertising, and this might force ToLee to spend more for promotion to make consumers aware of its pecans.

Questions

1. Should ToLee have entered the retail pecan market?
2. What problems should ToLee have anticipated in introducing its pecans at retail?
3. How could ToLee have assured consumer demand for its brand while avoiding stimulating demand for all pecans?

---

[3]Shelf life was an important factor in making retail sales; customers buying rancid pecans likely would not buy them again. And retailers disliked carrying items that spoiled on the shelves.

10–4

CHORE-TIME CAGE SYSTEMS DIVISION

Strategy in a mature market

The management of Chore-Time Cage Systems Division (CCSD) had seen profits dwindle down to just slightly above the breakeven point. While this deteriorating performance was partly a function of intensifying competition in a mature market, management wanted to stem further erosion in profits.

COMPANY BACKGROUND

CCSD was a part of CTB, Inc., which designed, made, and sold equipment for poultry and livestock producers. CTB, Inc., was highly decentralized, each of its five divisions having its own sales force, product manager, and service organization. CTB, Inc., however, had several operations which had not yet been set up as separate divisions: one made plastic parts used in other CTB products; another handled equipment warehousing and sales in the western United States; another was a licensee in Australia making and selling CTB products for the Australian and New Zealand markets. CTB's five decentralized divisions were:[1]

> Brock Manufacturing Division—production and marketing of feed and grain bins
>
> Chore-Time Cage Systems Division—production and marketing of poultry cages, cage feeders, and collecting systems

---

[1]There was some product overlap in these divisions tracing to company acquisitions and brand-name loyalties. For example, Brock Division sold under both the Brock name and the Chore-Time name to take advantage of customer loyalties.

Chore-Time MB Division—production and marketing of Chore-Time equipment in Europe (located in Maldegem, Belgium)

Chore-Time Poultry and Livestock Feeding Division—production and marketing of poultry and livestock watering, feeding, and ventilation systems

Chore-Time Watering Systems Division—production and marketing of watering systems for poultry and livestock (also called the Swish Manufacturing Division

THE CHORE-TIME CAGE SYSTEMS DIVISION

CCSD, the newest division of CTB, had two plants: one in Decatur, Alabama, and one in Athens, Georgia. The Decatur plant was well known for making wire chicken cages. The Athens plant manufactured cage feeders and collecting systems.

PRODUCT

CCSD's biggest seller was the Pyramid Cage Layer System (see Exhibit 1). This system's advantages over competitors' included reduced egg breakage, higher egg production rate, and improved feed efficiency.

Egg breakage was reduced up to 50 percent relative to breakage in other cages. This reduction, from 7 percent to 3.5 percent of total egg breakage, was due to several factors. One factor was cage design (see Exhibit 2). With no birds at the rear of the cage, the eggs rolled a shorter distance causing less breakage. Cage slope was set at 5 degrees compared to 7 degrees or more for other cages, also reducing the breakage rate. Savings realizable over ten years through use of the Pyramid Cage Layer System are shown in Exhibit 3. With a flock of 60,000 birds, a reduction in cracked eggs to 3.5 percent meant $105,000 extra profit in ten years.

The Chore-Time pyramid system could also increase egg production. A flock of 60,000 birds, each laying five more eggs per year added $138,000 profit over ten years (see Exhibit 4).[2] Increased production resulted from each bird having enough space to eat but not enough to fight. This also softened the adverse effect of the pecking order as "boss birds" had no way to keep others from the feed.

But the system's greatest economies came from savings on feed cost. Research showed an average of .17 pounds of feed was saved per dozen eggs. With a flock of 60,000 birds, this was $150,000 saved over ten years from using the Chore-Time "Program Feeding" (see Exhibit 5). Birds were fed only at certain times of the day and were given just the amount of feed necessary to produce the optimum number of eggs. The feed remained in the trough until consumed, minimizing feed waste. Correct feeding helped the birds' digestion and ultimately their egg production.

[2]Average egg production of 252 eggs per bird per year; 1.9 percent of 252 equals five more eggs per year.

EXHIBIT 1 · Chore-Time Pyramid Cage Layer System

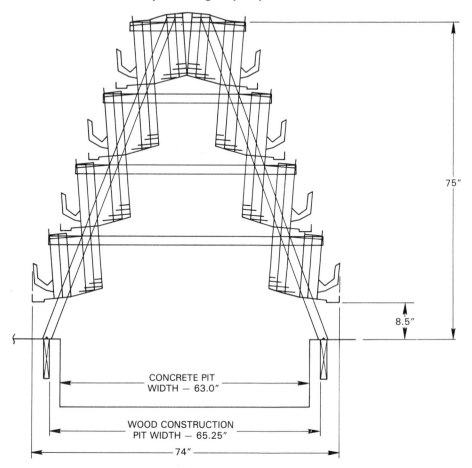

Another system, the "Mealmaster Feed Kar," had potential as a big seller. This product, designed to reduce labor and energy requirements, was introduced in 1980. Earlier feed systems required a separate motor for each trough, sometimes as many as eight in all. The Mealmaster Feed Kar needed only one motor. It increased control over the quantity of feed dispensed and would pay for itself in a comparatively short period.

COMPETITION

The U.S. market for cage systems was competitive. While several manufacturers had competing products, five U.S. companies accounted for over two-thirds of the market (see Table 1). Foreign cage-system producers were in the early stages of entering the U.S. market.

EXHIBIT 2 · Chore-Time Layer System Cage Design

|←———— 16″ ————→|

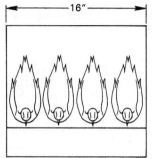

Chore-Time System locates 4
birds at the feeding trough.

4 Birds

|←——— 12″ ———→|

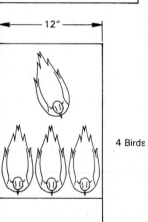

Competitors' 12″ cage has 25%
less feeder space per bird.

4 Birds

|←———————— 24″ ————————→|

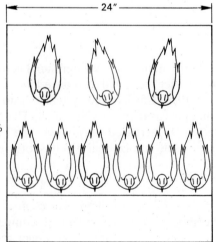

Competitors' 24″ cage has 33⅓%
less feeder space per bird.

9 Birds

EXHIBIT 3 · Cracked Egg Profit Loss (l0 year less breakage cost)

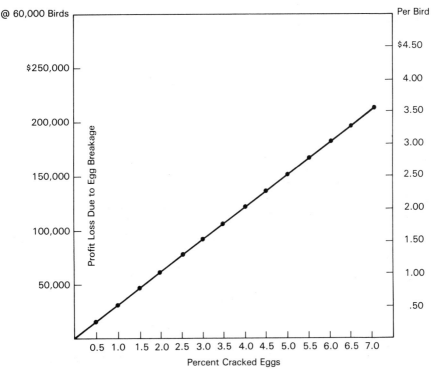

Chart based on 5.02 loss per cracked egg at 252 eggs/bird year (10-year period).

Big Dutchman and Favorite were the two largest U.S. manufacturers of cage systems. Big Dutchman was the best known but Favorite was the more aggressive and its market share had increased steadily. Industry analysts predicted that Favorite would surpass Big Dutchman in sales by 1990.

Cage systems producers based in West Germany, Italy, and Great Britain had begun to compete in the U.S. market as well as in Europe. A West German company manufactured an all-plastic system called the Farmer's Automatic System, which was displayed in the United States for the first time at the 1981 Southeastern International Poultry Show.

TABLE 1 · Competitive Structure of the Cage-Systems Market

COMPETITOR	SHARE
Big Dutchman	28%
Favorite	21
Diamond Automatic	9
Chore-Time Cage Systems Division	7
Northco–A. R. Wood	3
Others (no one accounting for over 1% of the market)	32

EXHIBIT 4 · Saleable Egg Profit Increase (10-year projection)

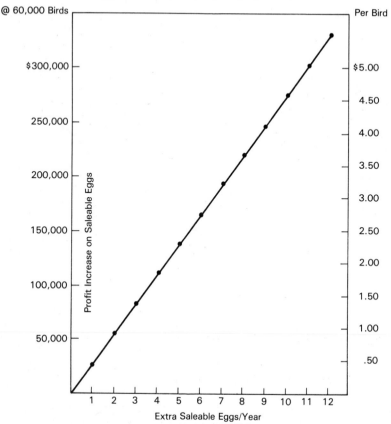

Values shown for 10-year period at $.55/doz.

PRICE

Prices of Chore-Time systems varied, as each system was put together to meet an individual farmer's needs. Major factors affecting a system's price were the size of the flock, location of the chicken house, and type and variety of equipment that the farmer both needed and could afford. Building and acquiring a chicken house for a flock of 40,000 chickens required an outlay of around $250,000 in the U.S. Southeast, considerably more in areas with cooler climates. Chore-Time constructed ten chicken houses in Florida at an average cost of $200,000 per house and built two large houses for a total of $1 million, or $500,000 per house.

Chore-Time targeted a 20 percent return on investment (ROI) before taxes on each construction project, but sometimes had to sacrifice margin to get the sale.

EXHIBIT 5 · Feed Conversion Profit Increase (10-year projection)

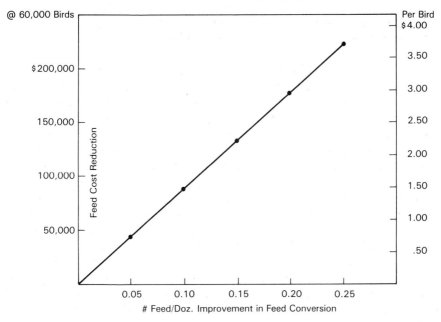

Chart based on 21 doz. eggs/bird-feed at $140/ton.

In 1980 Chore-Time first offered financing, largely because prospective customers were having a difficult time getting loans from banks and other financial institutions. High interest rates and the financial squeeze forced Chore-Time to work closely with lending institutions in providing buyer financing. In some cases involving very large accounts, Chore-Time did the financing on its own. CCSD had also begun to lease poultry houses to large operators not disposed toward outright purchases.

DISTRIBUTION

Distributors throughout the United States traditionally handled most Chore-Time cage system sales. At one time distributors sold not only the cage systems but unrelated products of other CTB divisions. Chore-Time now was recruiting a corps of distributors that would specialize in the unrelated products of other CTB divisions, leaving the established distributors as specialists in cage systems. It was hoped that the new distribution policy would increase sales of both product categories.

Distributors also played an important role in CCSD's overseas sales.

The largest distributor overseas was E. Holzer and Company, which, along with other distributors, sold and occasionally financed Chore-Time Systems for customers throughout Latin America, Africa, the Middle East, and the Far East. Customers in Canada were served by a network of distributors including Hearst Distributors and B. C. Farms. Chore-Time MB Division handled distribution in Europe and an Australian licensee made and distributed the cage systems "down under."

PROMOTION

Distributors still made most of CCSD's sales, but the division's own sales force had been stepping up its activities and now was directly negotiating an increasing proportion of the largest sales. Prospective large buyers were best approached through CCSD's own sales personnel, as cage systems were both large investments and built to customers' specifications. Prospective buyers compared the qualities and prices of systems offered by competing sellers. Personal rapport and professional expertise were important and Chore-Time made a strong effort to choose personable sales personnel and distributors and to keep them fully informed not only about Chore-Time's products but about those of competitors.

Advertising was through trade publications. Color advertisements appearing monthly or semiweekly in the large-circulation trade journals, such as in *The Poultry Times* and *Feed Stuffs,* were half page or full page and promoted Chore-Time's Pyramid system. All trade journal advertisements emphasized the special qualities and cost savings of Chore-Time products.

The two largest competitors, Big Dutchman and Favorite, were heavier advertisers than Chore-Time. Their advertisements featured the advantages of their products and emphasized the Big Dutchman and Favorite names as makers of quality poultry equipment. Competitors' advertisements were usually comparable in size and quality to those of Chore-Time but appeared more often and in more trade journals.

Trade shows were important vehicles for marketing cage systems. Both in the United States and abroad several large trade shows were held each year. The Pacific Egg and Poultry Trade Show was always a major event, as was the Southeastern International Poultry Show. At these and other shows Chore-Time, along with Big Dutchman and Favorite, contracted for substantial floor space to use for displaying their different systems. These displays usually generated considerable floor traffic and sales personnel "got lines on" many prospective buyers.

MARKET

CCSD's target market consisted of large poultrymen raising laying hens. The number of laying chickens in the United States totaled 420 million and was increasing at a 2 percent annual rate. CCSD estimated that 80 percent of all laying chickens were housed in cages. The average U.S. chicken farm housed 50,000 chickens, so the total U.S. market potential was roughly 8,400 farms. CCSD executives estimated that the rest of the free world had at least as many farms as the 8,400 in the United States.

With its 7 percent market share, CCSD had total sales of $8.5 million; while worldwide total sales of cage systems by the industry approximated $125 million. CCSD's sales were 51 percent domestic and 49 percent international. International sales were increasing faster than domestic sales.

Twenty percent of CCSD's sales were of replacement cage systems, for updating systems, or of repair parts. Consequently, customer service was an important factor in account retention.

Even though CCSD had distribution throughout the United States, the division was particularly strong in Indiana and Pennsylvania. California, Washington, and Oregon were growing rapidly as markets for Chore-Time products, as were Georgia and Florida. Elsewhere, CCSD met strong competition from Big Dutchman and Favorite.

International sales of CCSD had been growing steadily in South America and Mexico, despite high import tariffs. The division had investigated the feasibility of setting up a manufacturing and distributing operation in South America but rejected it mainly because of the area's political instability. CCSD also regarded the Middle East as a promising and growing market for the future, but hesitated to increase selling activity there because of continuing political unrest and tensions.

Both at home and abroad, demand for CCSD's products derived from demand for poultry products. When demand for poultry was depressed, farmers found investments in new equipment unattractive. In addition, farmers were reluctant to invest in periods of sluggish economic activity, high interest rates, or both. To deal with these business depressants, division management emphasized minimizing expenses and avoiding unnecessary risks. However, CCSD was moving ever more closely to the breakeven point, and management wondered if a plunge below breakeven was inevitable.

Questions

1. How would the cage systems marketed by Chore-Time have been classified in the Boston Consulting Group's business portfolio matrix?
2. How would the company's businesses have been classified according to the General Electric Nine-Cell Business Screen?
3. What should have been the marketing strategy of the Chore-Time Cage Systems Division?

10–5

HORMAS

Appraising the marketing function

Hormas, located in Bogotá, Colombia, produced wooden lasts used in shoe manufacturing. Although a small company, it was the industry's largest in Colombia, and management estimated its current market share at 27 percent.[1] Hormas sold its products nationally through distributors in the major cities to industrial and craftsman shoemakers. It sold direct from the factory to the large shoe manufacturers in Bogotá. Customers either sought out distributors or went direct to manufacturers, placed their orders, and deposited 50 percent of the invoice price.[2] Most last manufacturers promised one-month delivery, but orders from smaller shoemakers sometimes received lower priority and took longer. Market information was poor and the marketing process within Hormas was unwieldy, and the three owners sought improvements.

Last January Carlos Fernández, nephew of an owner, was hired as general manager. It was agreed that he could also continue his association with Bogotá, Ltd., a large Colombian company in which he was a partner. Because of Hormas' small size and lack of clerical problems, the owners believed that Fernández could handle the general manager's position on a part-time basis. Therefore, he reported daily at 5:00 P.M. and worked until about 6:30 P.M. Monday through Friday.

Two executives assisted Fernández—Juan Castillo, office manager, and Pedro Mosto, another partner in Bogotá, Ltd., who had earlier agreed to act as a part-time management consultant. Mosto recommended accounting procedures; performed studies in production planning, organization, and con-

---

[1]No industry data were available from either private or government sources.
[2]In effect, customers partially financed the manufacturers' operations.

234

trol; analyzed records; and prepared financial operating statements. His main responsibility, however, involved conducting market studies and recommending marketing policies. He studied company sales trends, estimated market potential, collected information about the industry's structure, and prepared the sales forecast. He recommended prices, product changes, and promotional policies to Fernández. One other key executive, J. D. Izaza, manufacturing supervisor, left in June to take a marketing manager's position with one of Hormas' competitors; his position had not yet been filled (see Exhibit 1).

Hormas had been founded in Cúcuta, a city of over one hundred thousand population about four hundred kilometers to the northeast of Bogotá; it retained its drying and cutting plant at Cúcuta but had moved the actual last-manufacturing operation to a larger plant in Bogotá, Colombia's shoe-manufacturing capital. Also in Bogotá were competitors: Luz and Dural, both long-established; El Mazo and Prohormas, both relative newcomers; and three very small shoe last makers, all of which had been recently organized. Thus the shoe last industry was concentrated in Bogotá, as was nearly all the shoemaking industry. Shoemakers ranged in size from factories ordering more than one thousand pairs of lasts annually down to what were essentially shoe repair shops that bought no more than ten pairs of lasts per year.

Shoe lasts made in Colombia were priced lower than those imported

EXHIBIT 1 · Hormas Organization Chart

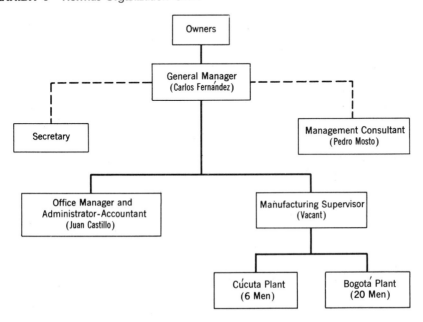

from Europe or elsewhere in Latin America. The Colombian government protected the last-making industy against foreign competition, setting import duties at two and one-half times the price of domestic lasts. Consequently, foreign competition was virtually nonexistent.

In shoe manufacturing, the lasts determine shoe length, width, and style. Therefore, each shoe size and style requires a different last. When a shoe style "went out," manufacturers generally discarded the lasts; but some smaller shoemakers cut down last tips and affixed other tips more nearly like the shoe style then in fashion.

Some Colombian shoe manufacturers had almost totally mechanized production lines, whereas others relied solely on hand craftsmanship. Shoe lasts made for industrial use came with two small additional accessories which enabled them to fit shoemaking machinery. Smaller shoe last manufacturers sold almost exclusively to craftsmen, but the largest firms—Hormas, Luz, and Prohormas—concentrated on the mechanized market segment. Hormas sold the greatest number of lasts to the largest mechanized manufacturers, but Luz and Prohormas both had increased in importance as competitors for the business of this segment (see Exhibit 2).

Hormas was the price leader, and the other last makers generally altered their prices in the direction of Hormas' changes. However, most sold their output at slightly lower prices; Prohormas was the only competitor charging higher prices. Hormas' management set prices for shoe lasts bought by mechanized customers at a level about 5 percent higher than for those paid by customers who were craftsmen. Prices varied according to last length and style; therefore, average price per pair of lasts changed from year to

EXHIBIT 2 · Colombian Makers of Shoe Lasts and Estimated Annual Unit Sales

SHOE LAST MAKER	LOCATION	MARKET COVERAGE	(PAIRS OF SHOE LASTS)			PERCENTAGE OF INDUSTRY SALES
			INDUSTRIAL	CRAFTS	TOTAL	
Hormas	Bogotá	National	17,500	12,500	30,000	27
El Mazo	Bogotá	Bogotá	—	17,500	17,500	16
Luz	Bogotá	Santander	2,000	13,000	15,000	13
Dural	Bogotá	Bogotá	—	12,500	12,500	11
Prohormas	Bogotá	Bogotá	2,000	4,250	6,250	6
Estuatua	Bogotá	Bogotá	—	5,000	5,000	4
La Patria	Bogotá	Bogotá	—	5,000	5,000	4
Concietro	Bogotá	Bogotá	—	1,250	1,250	1
Others (Bogotá)	Bogotá	Bogotá	—	7,500	7,500	7
Others (outside Bogotá)		?	—	12,500	12,500	11
Total			21,500	91,000	112,500	100%

Note: Estimates by Pedro Mosto for his market and sales forecast.

year, depending upon the particular mixture of last types ordered by the customers as a whole.

Hormas was the only company that had national distribution. All the competitors confined their distribution to areas near their factories. Hormas sold through "distributor-stores"; these carried not only shoe lasts but shoe findings such as leathers, tips, glue, and gum. Hormas granted its ten distributors exclusive distribution rights except in Bogotá where it sold direct to large "house accounts." Nevertheless, many old customers in outlying cities, most of them small accounts, also ordered direct from the factory. Distributors received a discount of 15 percent off list prices. At present Hormas had ten distributors and 135 direct accounts.

Shoemakers, large and small, ordered lasts for existing styles or provided last manufacturers with prototype lasts for new styles. The country's largest shoe manufacturer usually made its own prototype lasts, frequently copying popular European styles. Shoe last manufacturers merely built from the protoyped lasts provided by customers or from those already on hand. Some shoe styles retained popularity for several years, others for only a single season. Each last style was built in different lengths, with widths proportional to the width of the prototype. In Colombia, manufacturers did not "size" shoes by width. If a particular style did not fit a customer's foot because it was too wide or too narrow, he had to search for a proper fit in another style.

Fernández made two major marketing moves. First, he raised prices by 20 percent, increasing Hormas' average price per pair of lasts from 27.50 to 33.00 Colombian pesos. After this increase, which made the company's prices as high as those of Prohormas, Hormas suffered a sales loss estimated at three thousand pairs. Second, he and Mosto undertook a comprehensive study of the Colombian market for shoe lasts, seeking to learn more about customers' needs, market and sales potentials, and competitors' operations. They also analyzed company records, finding a high turnover rate for customers buying direct. However, the records were not in sufficient detail as to specific customers buying through particular distributors.

In December Fernández and Mosto met to discuss Hormas' performance for the year and to outline plans for next year and beyond. Fernández asked Mosto to submit major recommendations for improving future marketing operations. Mosto put forth eight recommendations:

1. That we hold the price line next year, since we have been able to lower production costs and obtain a satisfactory margin. We do not want to price ourselves out of the craftsman market segment.
2. That we reduce minimum order size from 30 to 15 pairs. Many of our craftsmen customers do not need 30 pairs in one order, and we can break even on 10-pair orders; therefore, a 15-pair order is profitable.
3. That we offer different widths in each style. This will give us a clear advantage over competitors.

4. That we launch an advertising campaign, particularly promoting our modern drying process which has eliminated shrinking problems.

5. That we identify all shoemakers, establish a direct contact with them, explaining the advantages offered by us.

6. That we establish personal contact with all distributors. Company officials have not personally met any distributor except the one here in Bogotá. We have no control and know nothing of their inventory situation.

7. That we hire another executive to take charge of all marketing activities.

8. That we get a replacement for Izaza as soon as possible.

Questions

1. What action, if any, should Fernández have taken on each of Mosto's recommendations?

2. What other factors should have been considered in improving this company's marketing performance?

10-6

SPRINGBOK VOLUNTARY WHOLESALERS, LTD.

Securing increased cooperation from members

Springbok Voluntary Wholesalers, Ltd., with central offices in Cape Town, South Africa, was the only voluntary grocery chain in an area one-sixth the size of the United States (five hundred thousand square miles). Its six hundred members had retail sales of approximately 84 million rand (about 15 percent of the total market).[1] However, members bought only about 16 million rand through Springbok's nine wholesale locations; they secured their remaining merchandise requirements from Springbok's wholesale competitors and direct from manufacturers.

Springbok's keenest competition at the wholesale level came from large manufacturers who sold direct, even to the smallest retailers, and at the identical prices they charged to Springbok. Furthermore, manufacturers' merchandising teams built store displays and assisted retailers in stock control and ordering. They also advertised extensively; consequently, their brands were well known throughout the country.

Springbok's retail members met intense competition from three large chains. Two were department store groups, the third operated both department stores and supermarkets. In South Africa most department stores had grocery departments. These three competitors transacted approximately 19 percent of the retail grocery business in the country. Springbok retailers also met local competition from nonaffiliated independent stores which accounted for 66 percent of the country's retail grocery sales. Springbok members, therefore, had a 15 percent share of the market.

Springbok retail outlets varied in size from forty to two thousand square

[1] A South African rand was the equivalent of 0.89 U.S. dollars.

meters; it was estimated that 75 percent had under two hundred square meters. Management had considered promoting standardization in store size because it was difficult for consumers to build up a "proper Springbok image" if they compared a large modern supermarket with a smaller traditional type store of forty square meters a few kilometers away. Although store size standardization was considered important in building a more favorable consumer image, Springbok had thus far failed to emphasize this aspect.

Springbok retailers handled diverse merchandise lines. Sales of "grocery-store" products accounted for most of their volume. However, most of the retailers, many situated more than eighty kilometers from the nearest large city, carried numerous other types of merchandise, including even such lines as fishing tackle and light farming equipment. The customary practice was to purchase nonfood lines not from Springbok (which did not handle most such lines) but from independent wholesalers.

Springbok's house brands (private brands) included food items and such household products as tissues and wax paper. Springbok imposed stringent specification control over the manufacture of its house brands. Periodically, management had each house brand chemically analyzed and compared with company specifications. Most relationships with suppliers of house brands had been satisfactory and long term.

Springbok's headquarters staff included an executive director, a marketing manager, a development manager, and a publications editor. The executive director, Dick Jones, a dynamic individual with an extensive sales background, managed the overall operation. The marketing manager, P. T. Wendt, negotiated with manufacturers for special offers to use as month-end promotions, developed new house brands, did quality checks on existing brands, and coordinated all promotional activities with the advertising agency. The development manager, J. D. Eakin, was responsible for training Springbok's members; he had studied operating methods of U.S. voluntary chains prior to joining Springbok, had considerable sales experience, and spent much of his time traveling the market area and leading training seminars for wholesale and member personnel. At times he served as a management consultant for the retailer–members. The publications editor, J. E. Leverette, edited two magazines: one, a house organ for the six hundred retailer–members; the other, a small monthly, distributed free to store customers.

Central office management dealt mainly through Springbok's nine wholesale branches. Each branch sold to retail members through a force of three field sales personnel who reported to a local sales manager. Field sales personnel acted as general consultants to the retailers, helped retailers present a good image, made recommendations for recruitment of new members, and sold and promoted Springbok's products, especially the house brands.

Few field sales personnel had university training and few had formal company training, but most had experience in food retailing. They were paid straight salaries but were eligible for annual bonuses. Generally, they were

poor planners, and the sales manager had little control over their activities.
Springbok's prices to its members were competitive except on lines
where the manufacturers sold direct to retailers at wholesale prices. Retailer
committees, meeting monthly, set members' resale prices on house brands
and month-end specials. Nine such committees, one for each wholesale branch,
set resale prices for all members in their respective zones. Management regarded decentralized pricing as necessary because of the large differentials in
transportation costs existing among the various zones. These committees had
the power to admit new stores and to request members' resignation. Prices
charged by Springbok retailers in the different zones on nonhouse brands
varied with the local competition.

Retail members paid an entrance fee of 40 rand plus weekly dues
ranging from 4.5 to 7 rand, depending upon the number of month-end leaflets
and point-of-purchase posters requested. In addition, retailers were asked
from time to time to contribute to zonal promotion funds, but the amounts
involved were inconsequential. Members received from Springbok: (1) the
right to use the chain's name, (2) uniform store signs, (3) house brands, (4)
centralized buying, and (5) promotional assistance and materials.

Early last year the executive director wrote each retail member, listing
"acceptable" manufacturers with whom they should cooperate. He further
asked that the products of nonlisted manufacturers be displayed only on the
retailers' bottom shelves and that the sales personnel involved be refused
permission to do in-store merchandising. With this tactic he hoped to force
manufacturers selling direct to Springbok retailers to change their policies
and to negotiate through Springbok's central office. The *letter,* as it was
subsequently called, was not altogether successful because many retailers
refused to act as had been requested. Furthermore, member retailers were
generally lethargic about trying to increase sales of house brands (on which
they averaged a markup of about 21 percent). Many times, too, they failed
to support month-end promotions (leaflets went undistributed and point-of-
purchase materials were not utilized).

Questions

1. What else, if anything, might have been done by Springbok to increase
   the cooperation of its members?
2. Should additional house brands have been introduced by Springbok?

11–1

COMMUNITY SYMPHONY ORCHESTRA

Marketing in an arts setting

The Community Symphony Orchestra was facing a problem; its expenses were exceeding revenues and were increasing at a faster rate than revenues. The Symphony General Manager, William Dobson, had done all that he could to reduce expenses without sacrificing the Symphony's quality. He now was interested in increasing revenues and thought that the best way to do so was to sell more season tickets. Dobson hoped that the result would be a breakeven season, something never accomplished by the Community Symphony Orchestra.

SYMPHONY BACKGROUND

The Community Symphony Orchestra had been organized in 1964 by a group of local musicians with the assistance of two civic organizations. The organizers felt that the city had grown large enough (280,000 people) to support such an endeavor. The first decade or so had been difficult due to a lack of both resources and community interest, but over the years the growth of several divisions of major corporations operating in the area had brought an influx of new employees with more cosmopolitan tastes. Also, increasing migration to the community's attractive sun belt location had caused the metropolitan area to grow to over 500,000 people. These factors and support gained from additional civic groups and other philanthropic organizations had enabled the Symphony to hire a full-time administrator and professional musicians. The administrator had been able to attract a full-time, internationally known conductor whose presence had served to attract even more accomplished musicians. With these changes, as well as greater community interest, the Symphony had come closest to breaking even three years ago when 68 percent of season tickets had been sold prior to the opening performance.

Since that time, season ticket purchases had averaged 65 percent of available seats, with the balance of sales going to nonseason ticket holders. Generally, however, during a typical performance only about 75 percent of available seats were occupied because some season ticket holders did not attend and "walk-ins" (nonseason ticket holders) did not fill the remaining general admission seats.

A review of Symphony statistics over the past four years showed that at least 10 percent of season ticket holders did not renew their subscriptions in the following year. Dobson felt that this was in line with the experiences of other small metropolitan area symphonies (based on phone calls to other general managers), and that new subscribers generally replaced those lost in the previous year. However, since budget projections were based on known season ticket sales, a reduction in turnover would make possible larger budgets and more ambitious programming. Also, in the face of increases in costs of operation (salaries, rent, printing, royalties, etc.), the goal of breaking even seemed more and more unreachable. With the "cut the deficit and balance the budget" movement gaining momentum, the future looked even more uncertain as the prospect of reductions in government support for the arts loomed.

It was about this time that Dobson's daughter, Melissa, a junior business major at the University of Arkansas, arrived home for the Thanksgiving holiday. She was just finishing a basic course in marketing and had heard her professor tout the universality of marketing concepts. Melissa suggested that her father consider retaining a marketing consultant to work on the problem. Dobson, thinking this a good idea, resolved to suggest it to his Board of Directors at their next meeting.

THE MEETING

After the normal business of the Board had been covered, Dobson broached the idea of retaining a marketing consultant to help the Symphony improve concert attendance. Was he surprised at the reaction! It was overwhelmingly negative. The conductor, an *ex officio* member of the Board with a well-known "artistic" temperament, thought that using marketing would be undignified. The Symphony, he felt, had an intrinsic value that didn't require "artificial" stimulation. Other members of the Board, a prominent physician and several socially prominent wives of area professionals, echoed these sentiments and also reminded Dobson of the Symphony's severe budget limitations.

There were, however, two members of the Board, in addition to Dobson, who thought that marketing did have a place in stimulating demand for Symphony performances. One of these people, George Manus, was the president of the local electric utility company, a long-time and successful user of marketing (and demarketing). The other, the provost of a nearby branch of the State University, had seen marketing used successfully to stabilize enrollments on his campus. Together they managed to get the other members of the Board to agree on a minor foray into the marketing area.

They were able to do this, to some extent, by reminding the Board members that the Symphony was already doing some marketing. Program announcements, discounts for season ticket holders, the season opening gala, and mailings to Symphony patrons were all marketing tactics. They now wanted to take another step frequently employed by marketers, a survey.

Their plan was to survey the walk-in audience at the next performance of the Symphony. They hoped to determine why these patrons weren't season ticket holders, what they liked and/or disliked about the Symphony, and something about their demographics. They believed that this would provide some basic information for use in further planning. They were optimistic that those surveyed would be knowledgeable and enthusiastic; after all, these people were interested enough to attend the Symphony even without season tickets.

By the time the meeting had adjourned, Dobson had agreed to prepare the audience survey questionnaire. Although he had no formal training in questionnaire design, he felt that he knew "what he wanted to find out," and that he could do the job for a lot less than a consultant would charge. The questionnaire which he developed is shown in Exhibit 1.

Questions

1. If you had been at the meeting of the Board of Directors, what would you have said to support the application of marketing concepts in this situation?
2. Critique the questionnaire developed by Mr. Dobson.
3. What other groups might have been surveyed by Mr. Dobson? Why?

EXHIBIT 1 · Community Symphony Orchestra Questionnaire

1. What was the last grade of school you completed? (Please circle)
   A. Some high school or less
   B. Completed high school
   C. Some college
   D. Completed college
   E. Graduate school
   F. Other education beyond high school (business, nursing, etc.)
2. Please circle the letter which indicates the age group you are in.
   A. Under 18 years
   B. 18–24 years
   C. 25–34 years
   D. 35–49 years
   E. 50–64 years
   F. 65 years or over
3. Please circle the letter which best represents your family's total yearly income
   A. Under $5,000
   B. $5,000 to $7,999
   C. $8,000 to $9,999
   D. $10,000 to $14,999
   E. $15,000 to $19,999
   F. $20,000 to $24,999
   G. $25,000 and over
4. How did you become aware of the Community Symphony Orchestra?_____

5. How many Community Symphony concerts do you attend a season?_____
6. If the price of walk-in tickets increased, and the subscriptions stayed the same, would you be interested in subscribing?
   (Please circle)   Yes   No
   Why?_____
7. Do the concert hall acoustics affect your preference as to the location of the concert? (Please circle)   Yes   No
8. Have you ever subscribed for season tickets to the Community Symphony Orchestra? (Please circle)   Yes   No
9. What kind of concerts do you prefer?   (Please check)
   Classical
   Pops
   Other (specify) _____
Thank you very much for your cooperation.
                          William Dobson
                          General Manager

11-2

WEST COAST SEROLOGY FOUNDATION

Marketing to stimulate supply

Ms. Betty Stokes, general manager of West Coast Serology Foundation (WCSF), was working on developing a strategy to assure the resumption of the growth of her organization. She knew that she would need to develop a plan that would carry her through the slow summer months, as well as be effective for the rest of the year. She hoped that the result of her efforts would be a program that would guarantee a long-run supply of low cost blood products to the hospital relying on the Foundation.

WCSF, a privately operated nonprofit plasmapheresis[1] center, was in the business of extracting blood (plasma) from donors. It was opened in May three years ago, by a group of doctors, pathologists, and administrators on the staff of a large county hospital who were concerned about the continuing availability of blood products for their hospital. The local "voluntary" suppliers could not keep up with the hospital's demand since much of their supply was shipped to military installations overseas. The plasma collected by WCSF was sold under an exclusive contract to that county hospital. WCSF sold blood products at cost,[2] in contrast to the for-profit centers in the area which included approximately 15 percent profit in their prices. The existence of WCSF served as a restraint on the pricing policies of the for-profit centers; otherwise, according to Ms. Stokes, their prices would probably have been even higher.

---

[1]Plasmapheresis is a procedure used to obtain plasma from whole blood. The blood is removed from a donor, the plasma separated by centrifuge, and the remaining red blood cells are then returned to the donor.

[2]Costs were those associated with collection, processing, storage, and distribution of blood products.

Ms. Stokes, a registered nurse, was hired to operate WCSF. During the first few months, WCSF averaged about 75 donors per week. By the end of the second year of operation, however, a peak of 530 donors had been reached in one week, the typical week brought in 450–500 donors (see Exhibit 1), close to the level of full capacity for the center.[3] Donors received $7 per visit, or $8 for the second visit if they donated twice in one week. FDA regulations set limits on how often donors could be bled, how much blood could be taken at each sitting, and who might or might not give blood, and allowed a maximum of two donations per week.

Ms. Stokes resigned briefly as manager of the center at the end of its second year of operation. She then served in an advisory capacity, but had no voice in management. There was a drastic reduction in the number of donors during this period, as the new manager proved his incompetence. Ms. Stokes then returned as manager and began the task of rebuilding the center. She knew from previous experience that the organization needed not only a highly professional and friendly staff, but also an effective marketing program.

The market for potential donors consisted of all healthy adults living

EXHIBIT 1

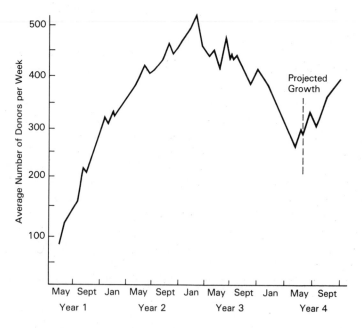

[3]Capacity was limited to about 525 donors per week due to the limited number of beds for donors, the size of the staff, the hours of operation, and the number of centrifuges available.

in the surrounding area. The common characteristic among all donors seemed to be the need for extra money. A regular donor could earn about $75 per month for five hours per week.

A full-time donor was one who donated twice per week. Ms. Stokes estimated that WCSF received about 100 full-time donors per week. She described a "good" or regular donor as one who donated at least five or six times per month. During an average week about 25 new donors visited the center. Ms. Stokes felt that one key element necessary for growth was to increase the number of new donors signing up for the program.

As of June there were 4,400 donors registered with the center. It was not known, however, how many of these had since left the area. This number could be assumed to be relatively large, however, due to the high proportion of university students on the donor rolls. Ms. Stokes estimated that almost 75 percent of the donors were students at a large public university located near WCSF; the university had an enrollment in excess of 20,000 students. The remaining 25 percent of the donors consisted of people living in the area who needed extra money for various reasons. Although there were no accurate statistics on the employment status of these individuals, Ms. Stokes felt that most were either unemployed or retired. Approximately 75 percent of WCSF's donors were male.

To begin participating in the program, all an individual needed to do was undergo a general physical examination, given by the resident physician at the center. WCSF provided this service at no charge to the donor. Continuing donors were required to have a physical once a year. Every three months a small blood sample was taken from each donor to insure continued good health. The only other requirement for participating was to sign a consent form, which familiarized all donors with the rules and regulations of the center.

Ms. Stokes felt that the key to success and growth for WCSF was "getting new people to walk in the front door." Due to a limited budget, it was important that she utilize only the most efficient means of advertising. For this reason, she felt that the high cost of television was prohibitive. Although radio advertising was possible financially, Ms. Stokes thought that this method was not as effective as newspaper advertising. Thus, WCSF's two main sources of advertising were local newspapers and a sign in front of the building.

Depending on which segment of the population (students or nonstudents) she wished to reach, Ms. Stokes used either the local neighborhood paper or the university paper. Advertisements in these issues came not only from purchased space but also from various articles which had been written concerning the center and its association with the nearby hospital. Advertisements placed in the newspapers attempted to include some current event which would be of interest to those reading the paper.

The center was located on a busy thoroughfare about one mile from the university and was close to the downtown area. Therefore, the sign in front of the building served as a very important means of attracting attention. Below the main sign was a panel used for writing short messages in an attempt to arouse the interest of passersby; a typical message might stress the money to be earned ($75 a month), the hours of operation, or the availability of a special incentive.

Ms. Stokes felt that promotional efforts were effective in both attracting new donors and encouraging full-time participation in the program. One promotional activity that also served as a means of advertising was the T-shirt program. On their third visit to the center, donors received a free T-shirt that displayed the WCSF logo and thus served as another source of exposure.

In an attempt to attract new donors to the program, a recruiting contest was run periodically. By recruiting a new donor, a current donor could earn an extra $2, and the new donor would also get a $2 bonus.

Last fall WCSF ran a prize drawing contest that proved very successful. Donors were allowed to enter each time they donated. Ms. Stokes felt that this encouraged repeat donations. Some of the prizes were purchased by WCSF and others had been donated by the hospital. The grand prize was an Adidas jogging suit, valued at about $90.

The monthly bonus plan was another attempt to encourage individuals to participate as full-time donors. On the seventh visit each month, the donor would receive an additional $10 bonus.

In an effort to maintain a steady flow of donors throughout the day, Ms. Stokes began offering a bonus of $1 per visit if the donor made an appointment during the morning hours. Since many donors were students, it was often possible for them to come in during the morning, and the extra $2 per week provided the incentive. The main benefit from this program came from the ability to schedule the staff more efficiently.

Ms. Stokes felt that all of these advertising and promotional activities were successful, and she planned on combining these with new ideas in the future. The effectiveness of these programs was determined by asking each new donor how they had become aware of WCSF. A very common response to this question was "word of mouth."

As long as the center's growth could be maintained, Ms. Stokes felt that the future looked bright for WCSF. The rapidly approaching summer, however, presented quite a problem. A large portion of the student population, on which the center depended heavily, would be leaving for three months. Ms. Stokes realized that she would have to rely on the neighborhood population to pick up some of this slack. Her goal for the summer months was 300 donors per week. She hoped this would increase to about 525 per week during the fall. With these goals firmly established, she now had to devise a strategy that would make them possible.

Questions

1. What were some environmental factors that needed to be considered in the development of WCSF's marketing plan?
2. What is your opinion of the marketing program being practiced by WCSF?
3. How should WCSF alter its marketing approach to deal with fluctuating supply?

11–3

SAINT CATHERINE'S HOSPITAL

Marketing issues in a hospital

Mary O'Connor, the new Director of Marketing for Saint Catherine's Hospital, was worried. After six months on the job Ms. O'Connor seemed to be identifying still more problems, in addition to the most pressing ones of occupancy, image, and market share. She had hoped that by this time the necessary solutions would be identified and well on their way to being implemented. Although she felt well-acquainted with hospital operations due to her more than ten years in nursing, she wondered if her newly acquired MBA had prepared her adequately for the challenges she was facing. It didn't seem that her texts had indicated that it would be this complicated. . . .

HOSPITAL HISTORY

Saint Catherine's Hospital opened in 1916, with thirty-five beds in an old wood-frame, two-story parish hall. The hospital was founded by the Sisters of Charity at a time when the community had a serious shortage of hospital beds. The hospital remained at its early site until 1926 when overcrowding, threat of fire, and lack of modern facilities required building a new hospital. This hospital opened in 1929 with ninety beds.

Since the 1930s, there had been a series of changes at Saint Catherine's:

1936 — 30 additional beds increased capacity to 120
1946 — 90 additional beds increased capacity to 210
1955 — Radiology Technology School was opened
1962 — Intensive Care unit was opened
1971 — Coronary Care Unit was established

1977 — Remodeling and expansion increased size to 355 beds
1982 — $1.2 million CAT Scanner was installed

Throughout this period the hospital was managed by the Catholic Sisters of Charity. Although the Sisters provided able and compassionate administration, the image of a Catholic facility in a predominately Protestant metropolitan area had often proven disadvantageous.

PROBLEM IDENTIFICATION

Ms. O'Connor, Saint Catherine's first Director of Marketing, had spent her first six months on the job gathering information. She identified many problems through selective interviews with both medical professionals and citizens in the community. For example, both physicians and consumers indicated some reservations about the Catholic operation[1] of the hospital. Non-Catholics, who comprised over 95 percent of the metropolitan population of over 400,000, were reluctant to use the facility. Ms. O'Connor felt that this had a bearing on the occupancy problem.[2]

Another problem of significance was the image that many nonmedical people had of Saint Catherine's. Many thought of the hospital as it was when it had a deteriorating facility and a largely general practice medical staff. Further, its nuns were viewed as "kindly and benevolent" rather than efficient.

Ms. O'Connor was surprised at these findings since the hospital had one of the newest and most modern facilities in the area. It had over 350 physicians on its staff, with specialties in fourteen medical areas. Also, only two Catholic Sisters had positions of responsibility in the daily operation of the hospital.

Interviews and surveys of the medical community also identified significant misconceptions of Saint Catherine's on the part of physicians. They often viewed Saint Catherine's as a surgeon's hospital, lacking balance in family practice and internal medicine. This view was directly opposite that of nonphysician citizens in the community who viewed the hospital as composed of a largely general practice medical staff. Just as the citizens' views were largely misconceptions, the physicians' views were also ill-founded. There were over 90 family practice and general medicine physicians on the staff of over 350. These physicians admitted about one-third of the hospital's total patients.

Saint Catherine's also had problems with regard to market share. It had an occupancy rate of 88 percent, the lowest of any of the four major

[1]Actually the hospital received no operating funds from the Catholic Church nor was it owned by the Church; it was owned and operated on a nonprofit basis solely by the Sisters of Charity.
[2]Although the occupancy rate was just under 90 percent, the mix of patients was 40 percent private pay/60 percent public support. In order to break even, the typical hospital seeks a minimum mix of 50 percent private/50 percent public and prefers an even higher percent private.

hospitals in the metropolitan area (see Table 1). Also, Saint Catherine's drew a larger proportion of its patients (45 percent) from outside the county, whereas the other three hospitals averaged only 35 percent out-of-county admissions. Ms. O'Connor was acutely aware of plans for a new 300 bed hospital just across the county line (the proposal was under study by the state medical board) which, if approved, would greatly exacerbate her occupancy problems.

Through a study of patient zip codes (gathered from admissions records), Ms. O'Connor also found that her hospital was attracting few patients (14 percent) from the most rapidly growing and affluent sections of the area. Fully 30 percent came from inner-city and less affluent neighborhoods—some of which were in proximity to Saint Catherine's.

COMPETITIVE STRENGTHS

Despite the problems facing Saint Catherine's, the hospital had some real strengths. It had the staff and facilities to perform both heart catheterization and open heart surgery (not available at Methodist Hospital). The hospital had a CAT Scanner, equipment which was not generally available in hospitals of its size. Saint Catherine's offered outpatient surgery and neurosurgery. It had the ability to provide gynecological laser beam treatment (not available at General Hospital). Additionally, it had special stroke, oncology, and AIDS units. Saint Catherine's was also the first hospital in the area to employ a full-time Director of Marketing, although Ms. O'Connor had heard that General Hospital was seeking to add such a person to its staff in the next six months. Also, Saint Catherine's modernization and expansion program was complete; General Hospital was just beginning an overall face lifting.

Ms. O'Connor was aware, from reading trade literature and from talking with Marketing Directors in other cities, that the situation at Saint Catherine's was not unique. She also was aware that the general public had grown suspicious of hospitals (particularly in the area of costs) and that these attitudes had fostered a growing bureaucracy to review, audit, and regulate the health care industry. As a result, the traditional responses of individual community hospitals were being increasingly questioned, especially as these responses related to the addition or expansion of inpatient programs. She thought that this environment would perhaps have a negative effect on the

TABLE 1 · Hospital Capacities and Occupancy Rates

HOSPITAL	CAPACITY (BEDS)	OCCUPIED BEDS
Babies' and Children's	80	75
General	1105	1061
Methodist	750	713
Saint Catherine's	355	312

proposal for the new county hospital (it was taking an inordinate amount of time for a decision), but the rapid population growth in the area required additional health services.

Ms. O'Connor felt that Saint Catherine's and the other community general hospitals stood on the threshold of a new medical era. The answers of the past were no longer adequate, but future responses were not clearly indicated. Hospitals needed to live within constraints imposed by regulatory bodies, yet also had to be responsive in order to protect their markets.

Questions

1. Propose a series of questions that Ms. O'Connor should consider in determining an appropriate course of action for Saint Catherine's.
2. How could Saint Catherine's correct its confusing and inconsistent image in the community?
3. In what ways could Saint Catherine's respond to the changing environment for health care services?

ff
17
082 J

US80